CUSTOM AND CONTRACT

Custom and Contract

HOUSEHOLD, GOVERNMENT, AND THE ECONOMY IN COLONIAL PENNSYLVANIA

Mary M. Schweitzer

1987

COLUMBIA UNIVERSITY PRESS

New York

Columbia University Press
New York   Guildford, Surrey
Copyright © 1987 Columbia University Press

Clothbound editions of Columbia University Press are Smyth-
sewn and printed on permanent and durable acid-free paper

Library of Congress Cataloging-in-Publication Data

Schweitzer, Mary M.
   Custom and contract.

Bibliography: p.
   Includes index.
   1. Pennsylvania—Economic policy.   2. Pennsylvania—
Politics and government—Colonial period, ca. 1600–1775.
3. Pennsylvania—Social conditions.   4. Money—
Pennsylvania—History—18th century.   5. Land use—
Pennsylvania—History—18th century.   6. Finance, Public
—Pennsylvania—History—18th century.   7. Households—
Pennsylvania—History—18th century.   I. Title.
✓HC107.P4S417   1987   338.9748   87-8003
   ISBN 0-231-06288-5

The Allen Nevins Fund of Columbia University and the Philadelphia Center for Early American Studies, through special grants,
have assisted in publishing this volume.

FOR
BOB, ERIC, AND CAROLYN

Contents

Tables and Illustrations

Illustrations

Acknowledgments

The research for this study was funded in part by dissertation grants from the Department of History, Johns Hopkins University; the Regional Economic History Research Center, Eleutherian Mills-Hagley Foundation, Greenville, Wilmington, Delaware; and the Philadelphia Center for Early American Studies. The seminar of the Center for Early American Studies as well as the Economic History Workshop at the University of Pennsylvania served for me as invaluable forums for the exchange of ideas in colonial and economic history. I wish to thank Tom Blantz and Don Kelley, and my colleagues at the University of Notre Dame and Villanova University for their support. My research at the Historical Society of Pennsylvania was aided by Peter Parker, Linda Stanley, Amy Hardin, and Bruce Laverty; Laurie A. Rofini, Jack McCarthy, and Barbara Weir at the Chester County Archives were also extremely helpful. In particular, I would like to thank Lucy Simler for taking the time to explain many of the sources at the Chester County Archives.

I am grateful to a number of scholars for their contribution to the ideas in this study, including Joyce Appleby, Robert Gallman, Lois Green Carr, Kenneth Waterman, Tonnes Stave, Bill Mulligan, Larry Herbst, Jack Michel, Joan Jensen, Glenn Porter, Bert Levin, Richard Dunn, Marianne Wokeck, Jean Soderlund, Billy Smith, John McCusker, Claudia Goldin, Bob Margo, Marc Trachtenberg, Steve Happle, and Ed Perkins. Richard Beeman, Richard Ryerson, and Gary Nash were particularly helpful in the early stages of this project. My father, George W. McKinney, Jr., read and offered comments on an earlier draft.

David Dauer and Lucy Simler graciously provided access to work in progress. Harold Woodward and Joel Mokyr provided useful comments on an early version at the Dissertation Session of the Economic History Association meetings in 1984. Stuart Bruchey read the entire manuscript and contributed many useful suggestions. Kate Wittenberg, my editor at Columbia University Press, was very patient and helpful. This project (and my graduate career at Hopkins) was guided by Louis Galambos and Jack P. Greene, whose patience, assistance, and judicious editing I gratefully acknowledge. My mother, Lucy McKinney, and my mother-in-law, Regina Schweitzer, came to the rescue more than once at deadline time. My children, Eric and Carolyn, put up with the disruptions this study caused in their lives and served as a constant reminder that there are more important things in life. Finally, I wish to thank my husband, Robert Schweitzer, for his unlimited emotional and intellectual support, without which I could neither have conceived nor written this manuscript.

CUSTOM AND CONTRACT

Introduction

> All trading Nations . . . have made Laws,
> to regulate . . . Trades and Manufactures, and more
> especially, their Staple Commodities, to prevent Frauds
> and Deceits in them.
> Anonymous Maryland Planter, 1753[1]

Economic policy was a matter of no small import to the colonists of British North America in the eighteenth century. The colonies owed their very existence, after all, to the economic policies of Great Britain. It was not British economic policy that concerned colonial legislatures, however, but their own. Britain provided a useful model for imitation, being "a Nation that very well understands their true interest."[2] But the true interest of the various North American "nations" lay on the other side of the Atlantic from London.

In recent years, a variety of studies have suggested that once the British North American colonies had passed the initial stages of dependency upon the British economy during their first decades of settlement, the colonies enjoyed considerable autonomy until the last two intercolonial wars. Some colonies remained more dependent on Britain than others, and all of them were aware of the protection they received from the larger, more powerful nation on the high seas and at home on their borders. They also would not challenge the home government in matters London considered important. By and large, however, they were able to behave as other "trading nations," not as tightly controlled satellites to a metropolitan economy across the ocean.

These relationships have attracted considerable

scholarly attention. Starting with the basic premises of the imperial school of American colonial history, Jack Greene persua-
sively argued in *Quest for Power* that the legislatures of the southern colonies were able over the course of the eighteenth century
to wrest effective powers of government from the governors, the
only representatives of Britain on American soil. Bernard Bailyn
and others have maintained that in the northern colonies (and
probably the southern as well) the restrictions imposed by the
Navigation Acts were disregarded rather than obeyed. A series
of economic studies of the Navigation Acts concluded that the
scope of their burden was limited to only a few colonies. When
looked upon as a tax for belonging to the British Empire, the
burden appeared insignificant compared to the benefits derived
from the British protection of American ships on the seas, access
to British ports in an age of mercantilism, and defense of the
American frontier against the French.[3]

Two pathbreaking studies of seventeenth-century
England also help us to understand eighteenth-century America.
Joan Thirsk argued in *Economic Policy and Projects* that the un-
derpinnings of future British manufacturing development could
be found in the production of supposedly insignificant items, such
as pins and stockings, in the outlands of the British Islands, far
away from the mercantilist restrictions of London. Much farther
away from London than Liverpool, the American colonies were
by this same logic a likely place for such early manufacturing
industries to take root. Joyce Appleby's study of mercantilist and
free trade ideology in seventeenth-century England has some
relevance to America as well. As Appleby argued in "The Social
Origins of American Revolutionary Ideology," the free trade
philosophies temporarily suppressed in England after 1700 continued to develop in the American colonies.[4]

If some of these colonies were neither economically
nor politically dependent upon England to the extent previously
assumed, then studies using 1800 as a starting point for American development might have to be pushed back farther, to a
period before the Revolution—indeed, to the period before the
Seven Years War. Louis Hartz assumed that the conflicts he found

between protectionism and free trade in early nineteenth-century Pennsylvania were part of a linear progression from a period in time when mercantilism was dominant before the Revolutionary War to the triumph of free trade after the Civil War. But he did not consider an alternative possibility: namely, that the colonists' own economic policies developed a century earlier were not mercantilist, and that the protectionist side of the Pennsylvania debate in the early 1800s developed concurrently with, perhaps even after, the development of free trade theory in the colony.[5]

Many of the trends economic historians believe began in the early 1800s in America may also have been present in the colonial period. The rapid industrial development of England in the late 1700s and early 1800s was preshadowed by financial and manufacturing growth over a period of centuries, and it is equally likely that the foundation of the first industrial revolution in the United States rested on similar developments in the American colonies generations before the Revolution. The types of intraregional trade discovered in early nineteenth-century Pennsylvania by Diane Lindstrom seem likely to have already existed, only to be temporarily disrupted by war and the problems of setting up a new nation.[6] Another recent concern of economic history has implications for this study. In Douglass North's recent work, *Structure and Change in Economic History,* he emphasized the relationship between institutional structure and economic development. North's stress on "the costs of acquiring information, uncertainty, and transaction costs" precisely targeted the economic concerns that sent colonial Pennsylvanians to their legislature for redress during the colonial period.[7]

On the assumption that these and similar possibilities can best be illuminated through the careful analysis of specific aspects of the economic developments in one colony, I have chosen Pennsylvania and the development of economic policy as a focus for this study. Several considerations dictated this choice. First, Pennsylvania's geography and climate closely resembled the most prosperous regions of those sections of Britain and Germany from which many of its first settlers had emigrated and

it seemed a likely candidate for the continuation of trends well
under way in Europe. First systematically settled in 1683, relatively late in the colonial period, Pennsylvania avoided many of
the costs associated with the establishment of the other colonies
by adopting the already settled trade patterns of its neighbors,
New York, New Jersey, and Maryland. Second, the type of fam-
ily-run agriculture mixed with manufacturing that developed in
Pennsylvania would become the prototype of the settlement of
the entire Middle West. Finally, the historian of colonial Pennsylvania can rely on a variety of useful studies, in particular those
of Gary Nash, Joseph Illick, Alan Tully, Frederick Tolles, James
Lemon, and the above-mentioned studies by Lindstrom and
Hartz.[8]

        In addition to these several historical studies, I have
drawn upon five different lines of work in the recent economic
literature: the studies of rent-seeking; information and signall-
ing; externalities and public goods; the economics of regulation;
and the theory of the household production function. All of these
theories have in common a foundation in the microeconomic
side of the discipline, as opposed to the macroeconomic—that
is, they focus more on individual behavior than on the movements of aggregates in the economy. In this and other regards I
have attempted to blend economic analysis with detailed historical research on the sources and nature of the economic policies
of Pennsylvania.[9]

THE GOVERNMENT OF COLONIAL PENNSYLVANIA

In order to understand the main components of Pennsylvania
economic policy in the 1700s, it is necessary to have some
knowledge of the structure of government in colonial Pennsylvania and the changes in administration which took place during the period before 1755. Formal governmental structure and
actual practice were quite different from one another, however.

Many of the agencies with nominal authority over Pennsylvania had very little real power; an examination of the daily operation of the Pennsylvania government reveals that during the period before 1755 Pennsylvanians chose to use their government very little, and got their way in most of their disputes with the theoretically more powerful metropolitan government.

Government power in Pennsylvania stemmed first of all from the King-in-Parliament. All Pennsylvanians were British subjects. This fact did not mean, however, that they were automatically subject to all laws passed in Britain. Only legislation in which the colonies were specifically named applied to them. When a law came before Parliament that might affect Pennsylvania, the colonists hired a lobbyist to see that their interests were also considered. Word reached the colonists in the 1730s that West Indian interests had introduced a bill in Parliament to tax colonial importation of foreign molasses. The Pennsylvania legislature immediately hired a lobbyist to prevent the passage of the bill, to no avail. While the lobbyist proved unsuccessful, the colonists never cooperated with the collection of the tax on molasses and continued with impunity to import foreign molasses; thus they avoided the bill's intent if they could not prevent its passage. The Navigation Acts, passed by Parliament between 1660 and 1696, also applied to Pennsylvania, of course. Like the Molasses Act of 1733, however, these laws were honored only if they did not interfere with local interests. Smuggling to and from forbidden ports was open and rampant; laws forbidding iron and woolen production were ignored. These laws proved important to the colonists only in a negative sense: because they were not supposed to be participating in these activities, they could scarcely enact protective legislation to "encourage" them. The King-in-Parliament did affect the outcome of the ongoing dispute between the Penns and Lord Baltimore over the Pennsylvania-Maryland border. Until the Seven Years War, however, the metropolitan government seemed a very distant entity with little interest in Pennsylvania.[10]

Potentially far more troublesome for Pennsylvanians was the Board of Trade, an executive agency set up by the Nav-

igation Act of 1696 to oversee the British Empire. All laws passed
by Pennsylvania could be repealed within six years by King-in-
Council upon the Board's recommendation if found "offensive"
to the needs of the Empire. In practice, the threat was not very
serious. The Board had more important colonies to consider than
Pennsylvania and generally took its time getting around to re-
viewing Pennsylvania's laws. The colony carried on a few running battles with the Board over the course of the century: over
the issues of Quaker affirmation (affirming one's honesty rather
than taking an oath in proceedings of law); establishment of
courts of judicature; printing paper money; and granting support for British troops. The court dispute was potentially dam-
aging to Pennsylvania, as the Board rejected virtually all the laws
enacted to create a judicial system between 1701 and 1722. From
London, it might have seemed that Pennsylvania had no working judicial system at all. Each time a law was disallowed, however, the legislature simply repassed the law with a few minor
changes, and the courts continued to act on that basis until the
newest version was repealed. In the end, patience won the dispute. The law of 1722 was apparently misplaced or neglected by
the Board. Never formally accepted, it was never formally repealed either.[11]

    This practice of repassing a disallowed law and con-
tinuing to behave as if nothing had changed worked with other
laws as well. Another method of getting around the Board was
to put a time limit on a law. Tariffs on imports were usually
passed for one year only; by the time the Board found time to
review the law, it had long expired. Finally, the legislature tried
to avoid negative action by the Board by keeping the laws out
of England until the last minute, then sending a large package
at once. Some laws never made it across the Atlantic at all. The
Board's response to this sort of misbehavior was to put pressure
on the proprietors to make the Pennsylvania legislature conduct
itself more in accordance with the charter requirements. In the
case of paper money, the Board took the problem to Parliament,
with only mildly satisfactory results; Parliament banned legal

tender paper issues in New England in 1751, but allowed them to continue elsewhere until 1764.[12]

Pennsylvania was unusual among the colonies in that it remained a proprietorship throughout the colonial period. As such, Pennsylvania had a third master residing in Great Britain: the family of founder William Penn. In 1681, Penn set up his massive landed estate in the wilderness to provide a haven for Quakers, experiment with ideal government, and secure a steady income for himself and his heirs. By his death, only the last goal remained of the three. As an investment, however, Pennsylvania proved less than profitable. Penn put much of his life into the colony and received little in return except for having his name affixed to a large geographical area.[13]

As proprietor, Penn was entitled not only to sell the land in Pennsylvania but to collect "quitrents" on it. Quitrents were a late feudal payment "quitting" the manorial subject's obligations to his lord, Penn's technical classification in his colony. Penn and his family, legally entitled to the quitrents, were deeply concerned through most of the colonial period with their collection. In Pennsylvania, however, sentiment regarding quitrents ran heavily against the Penn family's entitlements. As far as most Pennsylvanians were concerned, the Penns received enough money from selling land. Besides, they paid no taxes on the lands they still held and performed no services worthy of a further payment. The Penn family's agents in Pennsylvania, notably James Logan, complained constantly that they received little local cooperation collecting the quitrents. In fact, the Penns had no mechanism to force payment, and it was unrealistic to expect the colonists to do so voluntarily. Clear title to land could not be acquired without first disposing of back payments, but most land transactions in the first two generations apparently occurred without benefit of final registration. It was not until the opening of the General Loan Office, which required clear title to land before an applicant could receive a mortgage, that land transactions were registered with any regularity and quitrents actually paid. Before a loan recipient received his money from the government, back quitrent payments were deducted and sent to the Penns. Neither William Penn nor his descendants, however, understood the hostility to quitrents in Pennsylvania or appreciated the value of the General Loan Office in finally having them collected.[14]

In fact, so long as the Penns remained in England they had very little power in Pennsylvania. Their agents constantly reminded them of this. The relationship between proprietor and government ran the smoothest in the few years Penn actually resided in North America; later, his son would find it much easier to prevent the passage of unfavorable laws when he was in the colony than to scold the legislature or veto laws once they had gone into effect. Until Thomas Penn arrived for a prolonged stay in 1733, therefore, the proprietors were no more a factor in Pennsylvania policymaking than other government actors in London. Moreover, even when the younger Penn was in residence, his obsession with quitrents apparently kept him out of much of the other activities of the government. Not until the end of the period, when he began actively to resist new paper money issues, does he appear to have significantly influenced policy.[15]

King-in-Parliament, King-in-Council, the Board of Trade, and the proprietary family thus found their power over Pennsylvania far more limited in practice than in theory. Enforcement across an ocean proved extremely expensive although not impossible, and no one really cared enough about Pennsylvania to do what was necessary to bring the colony into line. Parliament could not or would not enforce the Navigation Acts; the Board of Trade could do little to prevent the passage of laws directed against the spirit, if not the letter, of earlier Board objections; and the only way the proprietors could successfully collect their quitrents was to move to Pennsylvania themselves, a solution they personally found far less than satisfactory. During the first half of the 1700s, enforcement of British plans in Pennsylvania depended in the main on the sole British representative on Pennsylvania soil: the governor.[16]

The governor of Pennsylvania was appointed by the proprietors to represent their interests and those of the Crown. He had to sign all laws before they went even temporarily into effect; thus, on paper, he could be an effective block against a disobedient legislature. Practice again, however, proved to be something less than prescription. For while the proprietors *appointed* the governor, the legislature *paid* him. Only the legislature in Pennsylvania had the power to vote taxes. Unless the proprietors were to pay them directly, which they were hardly willing to do, governors were dependent on the Pennsylvania legislature not only for their own salaries but also for the funds with which to pay their deputies. Displeasing the proprietors entailed long-run risk: eventually the governor would be removed. But this risk proved no match for the far more immediate threat the legislature offered to the governor's current income.[17]

The first two governors of Pennsylvania quarreled frequently with the legislature. Both John Evans, governor from 1704 to 1709, and Charles Gookin, governor from 1709 to 1717, used force rather than persuasion to coerce the legislature into cooperating. Neither proved successful. The legislature simply ignored both governors, refusing to pass laws at all rather than acquiescing to the governor's veto. Penn himself was of no help to the governors. Mismanagement of his estate had landed Penn in debtors' prison during Evans' term as governor. Released from prison, Penn had just begun to clear up his personal finances when he suffered an incapacitating stroke which left him unable to run his own affairs from 1712 until his death in 1718. From the onset of his stroke through the rest of the colonial period, the proprietorship would be in the hands of Penn's widow or his quarreling children, none of whom proved quite up to the task.[18]

The relationship between the legislature and the governor changed considerably when Gookin was replaced by Sir William Keith. Keith was governor during the key period 1717 to 1726, when much of the legislation concerned with economic policy in Pennsylvania was originally passed. It did not take Sir

William long after his arrival to discern that the legislature, not the proprietary family, held the keys to the safe.[19] According to one contemporary,

> however [Sir William Keith] was instructed here at home, either by his Principal or the Lords of Trade, [he] resolv'd to govern himself when he came upon the Spot, by the governing interest there. . . .
>
> With as particular an Eye to his own particular Emolument he did indeed make his first Address to the Assembly. . . . He did not so much as name the Proprietary: And his Hints were such as could not be misunderstood, that in case they would pay him well, he would serve them well.[20]

As a result, Keith received double the usual first-year salary for a governor. James Logan, who was responsible for the Penns' land holdings, the fur trade, and quitrent collections, found Keith's openly mercenary behavior appalling. But despite Logan's complaints, the Penns allowed Keith to remain governor for a decade.[21]

Keith was replaced in 1726 by Patrick Gordon, who was equally cooperative with the Assembly, but far more tactful toward proprietary interests. Gordon assured the Assembly he would not obstruct its desires, and it in turn responded that "inasmuch as the Governor is pleased . . . to concur with [the Province's] Representatives . . . we can do no less than assure him; that nothing shall be wanting on our Part to make suitable Provisions for his Support . . ." Under Gordon, the Assembly continued the practice of formally handing him the money order for his annual salary at the same time he handed them the signed bills from the session. The Assembly complained that Gordon catered too much to the proprietary family, but he seems in retrospect to have gone along with the legislature's plans without much protest. Gordon ignored explicit instructions from the Penns and the Board of Trade not to pass any more paper money bills; in fact, he offered suggestions as to how to sneak money bills past the Board without raising its ire. Gordon's administration ended in 1736 with his death. For the twenty years prior to that date, the legislature in Pennsylvania, through the cooperation of Governors Keith and Gordon, had behaved as if it governed a separate state, not a dependent colony.[22]

Gordon was replaced by George Thomas (1738–1747), who could not be ruled by the legislature's powers of salary control: Thomas was independently wealthy.[23] Moreover, Thomas Penn began taking a more active interest in government affairs, particularly where he thought judiciously applied pressure in an issue important to the colonists would win him a quitrent victory elsewhere. The legislature frequently ignored Thomas' requests, specifically when it came to mounting a military expedition, an understandable action given that most of the legislators at this time were Quakers. Thomas proved adept at compromise. In the case of the legislatures' desires for a new paper money bill and his explicit orders against it, he had the legislature include a clause effectively paying the proprietors a bribe of £1,200 current money for permission to pass the bill and to make future quitrents payable in paper. Thus altered, the bill was signed into law.[24]

The last two governors during the period, James Hamilton and Robert Hunter Morris, fought with the legislature over money in general and military expenditures in particular. Hamilton, a native Pennsylvanian, quit in frustration in 1754, only to return later as Morris' successor. By this point war loomed larger than economic policy.[25]

Through most of the colonial period, then, true governmental power on the provincial level lay in the House of Representatives. The legislature of Pennsylvania was unique among colonial governments in that only the lower house possessed the right to enact legislation. The Charter of Privileges of 1701, perhaps reflecting Quaker distaste of inherited privilege in general and the nobility in particular, allowed the Council only a weak role as advisor to the governor. The bulk of the power to make laws, to raise and disburse funds, and to make most administrative appointments belonged to the Assembly.[26]

The legislature was split by political factions in the early years of the colony's history. A small group of wealthy

Council members, led by Penn family agent James Logan, defended proprietary interests against the more popular faction led by Speaker of the House David Lloyd. After Logan's effective withdrawal from politics in the late 1720s, however, the legislature evidenced remarkable political stability until the Seven Years War.[27] Elected annually with a minimum of turnover, the Assembly tended to overrepresent Quaker, English, and Eastern interests. The Assembly was late to admit new western counties consisting of immigrants and stingy with representation once they were admitted. But the Assembly most likely represented the provincial interests better than would have the Governor, the Proprietors, the Board of Trade, King and Council, or Parliament. Furthermore, the Assembly knew far better than those in England just what could be enforced in Pennsylvania, and what could not.

Government functioned most efficiently below the provincial level—in the counties and city of Philadelphia. The three original counties (Bucks, Chester, and Philadelphia) were joined by Lancaster in 1729. By 1755, Berks, Northampton, and York were added. Much of the day-to-day operation of the government occurred at the county level and had to do with civil and criminal justice, road-building, poor relief, licensing of innhouses, and market days. Taxes were assigned by county and collected by township. The assessors and the justices of the peace, who made most of the decisions regarding county administration, were elected for periods of from one to three years by all "freemen" in the county, as were the legislators, who were elected for one-year terms.[28]

The townships governed a variety of activities and had several officers, from the keeper of the pound, who collected and returned (or sold) all stray animals, to the supervisor of the roads, who was responsible for cutting new roads and keeping old ones clear, and the overseer of the poor, whose duty was to feed and house those designated as "poor" by the justices of the peace. While the county court settled many disputes and enforced most laws, members of the community frequently brought their problems to a justice of the peace for arbitration out of court. Finally, local Quaker Meetings functioned to discipline members of the community of Friends, who saw courts as an unfortunate final resort.[29]

The City of Philadelphia had most of the powers of a county vested in the mayor, aldermen, and common council of the city corporation. Modeled on English town corporations, the Philadelphia city corporation was not elected, unlike virtually all other Pennsylvania governing bodies. Original members were named in the Charter of 1701; membership was for life; and new members were elected into the body by old. The aldermen with the mayor also served as justices of the peace for the city. The city corporation functioned originally much as the county governments. In addition to tax collection and road maintenance, the city also ran the public wharfs and the public market and regulated the importation of firewood and the (mis)behavior of teamsters. The closed nature of the corporation, however, left it far less responsive to its constituents than the county governments. Furthermore, the corporation exhibited a remarkable carelessness with its duties and with the handling of funds. By the 1720s complaints had reached such a level that the Assembly created a board of assessors as an elected body to make many of the decisions regarding taxation and public works that originally had fallen to the city. By the mid-eighteenth century, the only functions retained by the corporation were those similar to those of justices of the peace in the counties.[30]

The course of local and provincial government ran relatively smoothly during this period. There were several potential sources of political faction in eighteenth-century Pennsylvania. The first split formed between the proprietors and their agents and virtually everyone else. The largest schism occurred in the depression of the early 1720s, when the faction led by Governor William Keith and Speaker David Lloyd allied itself with the countryside in favor of paper money and against the Penn family's representatives in Pennsylvania, James Logan and Isaac Norris. Once the paper money had been printed and the economy revived, factionism died down. Keith tried to maintain power by running for the Assembly after his removal as governor by the Penns, but he and his running partners lost at the polls as Lloyd switched allegiances. Anti-proprietary sentiment flared up again in 1739 over the issue of servant enlistment in the defense army, but was resolved without the serious quarreling of the 1720s. In general, the period between 1727 and 1747 passed relatively peacefully in the legislature.[31]

Proprietors and colonists fought again, severely, from 1748 to 1755. The first area of contention was the attempt by Thomas Penn to regain some of the proprietary powers lost during the period before 1720 when his father lay disabled by a stroke. Penn intended to regain the ability to tax and disburse funds, a right the legislature had absolutely no intention of giving back. Small skirmishes were fought over the nomination of ferrykeepers and supervisors of the public hospital in Philadelphia, but the major issue at stake was the disposition of government money.

The rapid expansion of the colony had outpaced early money issues, and demand for new issues increased in the legislature every year after 1748. The Penns, however, refused to permit Governor Hamilton to sign a new paper money bill without including a clause assigning the interest money to the governor in partnership with the legislature. This dispute was compounded by the impending war with France. The Penns were forced to ask for money for defense spending at the same time as they were trying to regain more control over government spending in general. The discord ended with some of the most dedicated Quakers walking out of the government. New issues of paper money were authorized, but they were no longer backed by loans. The issue of the disposition of interest money, which had caused the deadlock between the legislature and the Penns, was thereby avoided. After the war, the continuation of efforts by the Penns to regain control over the government would eventually lead to lobbying efforts in London by Benjamin Franklin and others in an attempt to have the colony taken away from the Penns altogether and designated a royal colony.[32]

Other potential areas of conflict remained relatively calm during this period, only to flare up later. Factions formed and reformed out of a variety of religious and national groups. Quakers generally opposed Anglicans, but they both found themselves allied against the fundamentalist revivalists who overran the countryside in mid-century. A natural split existed between the English-speaking colonists and the large number of Germans, but the Quakers soon found they had more in common with the sect Germans, who like the Quakers prospered in trade and preferred a relatively inactive government. Potential for a severe split between the city and the countryside did not become reality until later in the century. Far more serious was the division between the settled areas and the newly opening regions to the west. Because of a reluctance on the part of the settled colonists to share political power, western counties were formed very late when compared with their settlement dates. The newer counties, whose populations were predominantly new arrivals, non-English, and susceptible to evangelical religion, were denied the same numerical representation as the old, even when finally given political boundaries. More likely to settle in the west, Ulster Scots found themselves allied against politically powerful Quakers in virtually every case.[33]

Another area of potential conflict never developed into a political struggle because only one of the contending groups had political power. The very large groups of young adults and adolescents, apprentices, servants, and hired labor, preferred a life-style quite different from the more settled, older, family heads. The differences between these two groups resulted in conflict from time to time. Laws against open revelry and many of the tavern regulations were aimed at the potentially boisterous behavior of this segment of the population. A major uproar occurred in 1735 and 1736 when fishing with weirs was prohibited by law to protect the spawning of fish in the rivers.[34] The governor's explanation of the need for such legislation focused as much on the undesirable social aspects of that style of fishing as on the need to protect the provincial fishing industry:

this Practice is, for great Numbers of People mostly on Horseback, for a mile or two, or more, with large Bushes, Stakes, or

other Instruments, that may best answer the End, to beat the
Water with Great Noise, rake the Bottom of the River above the
Racks, and to take all the Methods in their Power to force the
Fish down into the Racks . . . And further, there have such Accounts been yearly given, when any Racks have either publickly
or otherwise been erected, of the tumultuous Meetings, riotous
Behavior, Quarrels, Contentions, and even Outrages, amongst the
young People and Others, who assemble as to a Merry-making,
or a publick Diversion, at the Time of Fishing by Racks.[35]

While potential thus existed for internal strife, most
of the major political issues of the period pitted the Penn family
against the colonists. When Pennsylvania faced encroachment
from outside, the Penns supported the colony, but many internal
disputes were either sparked by Penn policy or the by the Penns'
support of the unpopular side. The Penns expended quite large
sums of money defending Pennsylvania against attempts by Lord
Baltimore to acquire some of the colony for Maryland. They believed that their lobbying on behalf of the colony, as well as
their position as proprietors, should have earned them the re-
spect and obedience of its legislature. But such was not the case.
Throughout the period, the Penns and the legislature quarreled
over paper money, the payment of quitrents, and the Penns' legal protection against the payment of taxes on their manorlands.[36]

The final major issue during these years was the ap-
propriation of money for defense spending. The Quakers in the
legislature proved reluctant to appropriate any money for defense, in part because of their pacifist sentiments, but in the main
because they did not wish to have to tax the populace. They
were not the only colony to resist paying defense money—
Maryland was infamous in this regard—but they were the only
colony with such an exposed flank consistently to refuse to grant
money for defense. The problem of defense spending not only
set the Quakers and their German allies against the British government, which in turn put pressure on the Penns, but it also
widened the split between the settled and frontier areas. West-
erners wanted protection against Indians; easterners responded

that the settlers should stay away from the edges of the frontier, which technically belonged to the Indians anyway. It was a battle the legislature could not win. The result was the above-noted departure of Quakers as a group from government under British and proprietorial pressure to vote defense money.[37]

From 1681 to 1755, power in Pennsylvania essentially was situated in the countryside. Economic policy was formulated either explicitly, through the passage of laws in the legislature desired by the countryside, or implicitly, through selective enforcement in the countryside, by appeal to custom, of the policies they wished to see enforced. Practice in the countryside negated the effects of unpopular policies emanating from England or Philadelphia.

Land policy in Pennsylvania was an example of a policy planned in England but ignored in practice by the settlers. The policies developed through custom in Pennsylvania rewarded the settling and improving of land rather than the holding of land until it rose in value. The family-oriented goal of buying up land to settle future households was encouraged, as long as the land was soon settled. Large tracts of vacant land were abhored, and it did not take the colonists long to learn how to overturn the technicalities which might keep land out of cultivation.

While the land policies of the colonists could be regarded as somewhat passive, other economic policies were distinctly active in nature. The colonists actively sought laws to increase the money supply, for example, and to reduce information costs of trade within the colony. In the case of the money supply, pressure from the legislature's constituents led to the enactment of all of the laws authorizing paper money despite explicit restrictions against this practice on the part of the British government. The trade regulations combined lawmaking and the power of localities. Only the legislature could pass export inspection laws, but no laws could be enforced without the cooperation of localities and the households involved.

The purpose of this study will be to analyze the effects of both the explicit and implicit economic policies pursued in Pennsylvania before the Seven Years War. Colonists in Pennsylvania used the courts and the power of the colonial legislature to control matters involving land use, the money stock, capital development, and trade. The government itself produced public goods and services for the colony. While they freely used the government for specific purposes, colonists in Pennsylvania demonstrated a distrust of the power that government could provide individuals and kept a guard up to prevent the acquisition of power by those who sought to gain materially from its use. Before discussing the relationship between the economy and the government in colonial Pennsylvania, however, it will be necessary to describe the economy itself. To the extent that the government of Pennsylvania was controlled by the colonists themselves, economic policy began in the economic goals of the Pennsylvania household. These goals will be discussed in chapter 1.

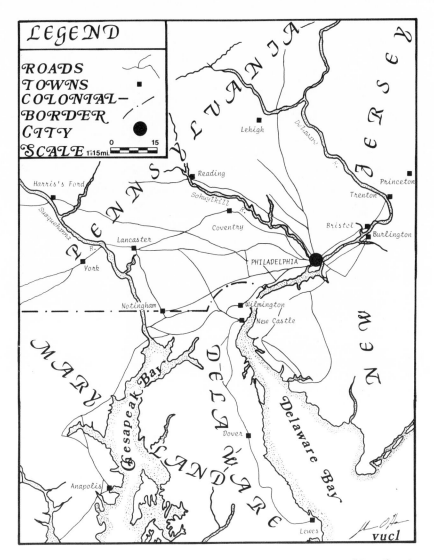

Map of Delaware Valley Road Network, 1749. From "A Map of Pensilvania, New Jersey, New York and the Three Delaware Counties," by Lewis Evans, 1749, in the map collection of the Historical Society of Pennsylvania, Philadelphia. Drawn by John O'Hara under the direction of Elaine Bosowski at the Cartography Laboratory of Villanova University.

CHAPTER ONE

The Household Economy of Colonial Pennsylvania

The economy of Pennsylvania centered on the household as the decision-making unit of production as well as of consumption. Production of all goods and services in Pennsylvania took place not within the confines of a profit-maximizing firm but within the context of a family household: an older adult couple, several young adults, adolescents, and children. Farms, merchant houses, and artisan workshops were organized to function within the household. In almost all cases non-family workers, whether indentured servants, slaves, apprentices, or temporary wage earners, were brought into the household during the period of their employment. Not only did they physically live with other family members, but they participated in many family activities, with a specific role assigned as member of the household.

While production *within* the household was structured along traditional lines, trading *between* households took place through the use of a highly developed market economy. The average householder in Pennsylvania not only participated in an active domestic market for goods and services, but also found himself tied to the international market through a sequence of events by which the wheat he sold to his local miller was consumed as flour in Boston, South Carolina, the West Indies, Portugal, or France. Through the century, and indeed to the present time, households turned increasingly to the production of goods for market in exchange for other goods once produced at home.

This process occurred as a response to innovations in production (both internal to the household and external) and declining costs of trading. One of these innovations would be the substitution of the firm for the household as unit of production, but this would not occur until the next century.

The most noticeable difference between the economy of Pennsylvania during the colonial period and in the present time would thus be the organization of all production within the framework of the household.[1] The basis of this household organization of production was a division of labor within the household based upon social role. The head of the household, ideally a middle-aged man but sometimes his widow or eldest son, made final decisions as to what was produced and how, with or without the advice of other family members. Labor was then divided between male and female members, generally by custom, which reflected differences in skill, physical strength, and the childbearing function of women. While households proved flexible to a degree in assigning work, decisions as to division of labor were strongly influenced by traditional assumptions about the roles different family members could play in production. Male members typically worked the fields, practiced the family trade, and added to or repaired the stock of physical capital belonging to the family. Women might work in the fields, particularly during harvest, but most typically they performed household work. Women tended the physical needs of children; provided day-to-day food; made, to varying degrees, and repaired clothing; cared for farm animals; and sometimes kept or shared in the keeping of the kitchen garden. Women also produced dairy and textile products for the market.

The household consumed as a unit. That is, the primary decision as to what products would either be made for the household or purchased in the market was made on the level of the household as a whole, not by each individual. The household first had to decide on a level of consumption and investment; investment is used here in the economic sense as the purchase or manufacture of goods which could in turn be used to produce more goods and services in the future. The presence of an active market for loanable funds, even in the countryside, enabled households to avoid having to match exactly their desired investment with their actual savings. If their consumption level was lower than their income, they could choose either to add to their own capital stock or to loan their savings to another in exchange for interest. Conversely, a household wishing to add to its capital stock without curtailing its consumption could borrow another's savings.

On a farm, much of the savings and investment occurred directly. Investment consisted of taking time away from income-producing activity to clear land and remove stones, plant meadow and orchards, build fences and outbuildings, erect a family home and barn. Tools had to be either made or purchased and kept in repair. The tools of the household had to be considered investments as well. Scissors, needles, thread, iron kettles, and spinning wheels were not luxuries, but investment items that enabled women to produce goods used by the family. A farm family might choose to borrow during the period of capital accumulation rather than use its own savings. Borrowing for investment could be separated as an activity from buying goods for consumption. Because of the active capital market, the family was not dependent on the local trader, shopkeeper, or merchant for borrowed funds.

There was room for households to differ greatly in regard to what was consumed, and they did. Not only goods such as clothing, food, and, for wealthier households, clocks and looking glasses, but time could be consumed as well. The family could choose to spend time away from income-producing activity. They could consume religious sentiment on Sundays by not working on the Sabbath, or visit friends, or sit on the porch watching the rain. But even the decision to consume leisure time was a household decision: normally a young adult seems to have had no more option than a servant in deciding to consume more leisure rather than produce more goods. The head of the household made these decisions.

Beyond the constraints of a 24-hour day, the major determinants of what was produced and what was consumed,

The Household Economy

how much was saved or how much was borrowed, were the
capital endowment available to a household and the stage of the
household life cycle. Household estates can be divided into five
categories, each easily reconstructed from information available
in wills and accounts giving the number of children in the family and their ages.[2] A "household" in the first stage consisted
only of the householder himself, presumably a young man, as
he began to acquire capital with which to set up an independent
farm. Such single member households were rare. Stage two included a spouse. Stage three consisted of a family with only minor children at home. Stage four included the mixed family, with
both minor and married children and, presumably, a large number of adolescents and young adults. Finally, in stage five, the
household reverted to the beginning, with the family of married
and grown children in the process of dispersing, or having already left to form their own households. The stages can be con-
veniently labeled the single youth, married youth, young household, mature household, and dispersal phases.

At different stages of the life cycle, households were
more likely to borrow or to save. The types of assets they chose
to hold differed throughout the household life cycle, as did the
goods they produced and those they purchased in the market.
The ability of a household to receive or pass on an endowment
affected the decision-making process as well. A young household equipped with a sizable endowment could skip the more
difficult stages of production and consumption; a mature household's economic decisions were frequently made on the basis of
a desire to pass on some sort of endowment to all the family
members.

By comparing information compiled from wills with
assets listed in inventories in the Chester County Archives, it is
possible to identify differences in the type of assets held by
householders in different stages of the life cycle. The inventories
are biased both in favor of those with greater assets than average
and toward older households, but the information they provide
is enlightening. Unfortunately, real estate was not valued in the
inventories. The average personal estate rose through the stages

of the life cycle, as expected, during the first two periods studied (see table 1.1). The distribution of personal estate among different life cycle stages in 1748–51, however, did not follow the same pattern. In part the change can be attributed to an age distribution quite different from the one found in their first two samples, as a result of an unusually large number of deaths in Chester County in the winter of 1748. The decedents in stage two stand out in the third sample as well. Apparently, a number of youths died in 1748 in the possession of large endowments from their families.

In all three periods studied (1717–1722, 1732–1737, and 1747–1751), single and married youths held very little real estate or livestock and proportionately a much greater amount of financial assets (see tables 1.2–1.4). Single artisans also apparently had a preference for expensive horses and comparatively expensive clothes. Book debts were generally found only in those inventories where the householder practiced a trade, a method by which many young householders were able to establish their independence. As a result, the average value of book debts as a proportion of total financial assets was greater in the personal estates of types 1 and 2 households than in other types. These households also contained a greater than expected share of bonds or other long-term debts, with young householders perhaps saving up in expectation of purchasing land.[3]

The amount of financial assets dropped sharply for households with young children in the first two samples. Young householders were also more likely to employ hired labor, as the children would still be a burden to the family and not yet able to provide help either in the fields or in the house. As a result, young households also held more bound labor, specifically, indentured servants of both sexes (see table 1.5). All of the energies of the family seemed at this point to be devoted to producing current income for the household; not only were savings lower than in other households, but the tendency was also greater for these young householders to have been trapped with fairly high levels of debt at the time of death. By 1748–51, however, the young households appear to have caught up with the

The Household Economy

Table 1.1. Stages of the Life Cycle and Value of the Personal Estate
in Chester County Inventories

	Average Value of Personal Estate[a]	Number of Inventories	Percent of All Valid Cases
1717–1721			
Stage 1	102.50	9	15.8
Stage 2	115.31	4	7.0
Stage 3	181.89	17	29.8
Stage 4	194.08	14	24.6
Stage 5	259.72	13	22.8
All applicable cases	185.42	57	68.7[b]
All inventories	159.60	83	
1732–1737			
Stage 1	124.71	7	6.4
Stage 2	218.00	2	1.8
Stage 3	171.63	46	41.8
Stage 4	203.71	21	19.1
Stage 5	316.03	34	32.4
All applicable cases	220.25	110	59.5[b]
All inventories	179.57	185	
1748–1751			
Stage 1	83.64	24	14.2
Stage 2	390.71	11	6.5
Stage 3	292.78	48	28.4
Stage 4	249.65	24	14.2
Stage 5	219.06	62	36.7
All applicable cases	236.22	169	55.6[b]
All inventories	189.58	304	

SOURCE: Chester County Wills and Inventories, Chester County Archives, West Chester, Pennsylvania. There were 83 valid cases, 1717–1721; 185 valid cases, 1732–1737; and 304 valid cases, 1748–1751. The values given are in pounds Pennsylvania current money, recalculated to control for changes in the price level using the Pennsylvania pounds to British pounds sterling exchange rates in John J. McCusker, *Money and Exchange in Europe and America, 1600–1775*, table 3.7, pp. 183–185.

Note: The household life cycle stages are: Stage 1, single householder; Stage 2, married householder with no children; Stage 3, young household with children all under 21; Stage 4, mature household with adult children and adolescents; Stage 5, householder after disbursal, with married children and grandchildren. Information from wills and accounts were used to classify decedents according to the appropriate stage of the life cycle.

[a] Converted to pounds British sterling.
[b] Percent of all inventories.

Table 1.2. Stages of the Life Cycle and Value of Financial Assets (excluding cash) in Chester County Inventories

	All Inventories		Inventories with Financial Assets			
	Average of Financial Assets[a]	% of Personal Estate	Average of Financial Assets[a]	% of Personal Estate	Number of Inventories	Percent of All Applicable Inventories
1717–1721						
Stage 1	35.13	34.27	35.51	38.54	8	22.9
Stage 2	23.99	20.80	31.98	27.77	3	8.6
Stage 3	7.16	3.94	17.40	9.57	7	20.0
Stage 4	23.11	11.91	53.91	27.78	6	17.1
Stage 5	135.39	52.13	160.02	61.61	11	31.4
All applicable cases	45.92	24.77	74.78	40.33	35	42.2[b]
All inventories	43.70	27.38	72.55	45.46	83	
1732–1737						
Stage 1	50.00	40.09	58.33	46.77	6	7.9
Stage 2	14.00	6.42	28.00	12.84	1	2.4
Stage 3	41.11	23.95	61.67	35.93	30	29.5
Stage 4	33.14	16.27	53.54	26.28	13	17.1
Stage 5	174.82	55.32	228.62	72.34	26	34.2
All applicable cases	81.36	36.94	116.68	52.98	76	41.1[b]
All inventories	64.05	35.67	96.46	53.72	185	
1748–1751						
Stage 1	35.35	42.26	50.81	60.75	16	12.3
Stage 2	106.45	27.25	167.28	42.81	7	5.4
Stage 3	106.16	36.26	124.29	42.45	41	31.5
Stage 4	84.80	33.97	106.00	42.46	20	15.4
Stage 5	97.87	44.68	129.79	59.25	46	35.4
All applicable cases	90.28	38.64	116.67	49.39	130	42.8[b]
All inventories	67.46	35.58	90.75	47.87	304	

SOURCE: See table 1.1.

Note: For household life cycles, see table 1.1.

[a] Converted to pounds British sterling.

[b] Percent of all inventories.

Table 1.3. Stages of the Life Cycle and Value of Various Categories of Financial Assets in Chester County Inventories

	Bonds, Bills, Notes[a]	% of Personal Estate	Book Debts[a]	% of Personal Estate	Number of Inventories	Percent of All Applicable Inventories
1717–1721						
Stage 1	26.91	26.25	8.76	8.55	8	17.8
Stage 2	20.50	17.78	4.10	3.56	3	6.7
Stage 3	4.48	2.46	2.11	1.16	14	31.1
Stage 4	7.59	3.91	2.25	1.16	12	26.7
Stage 5	93.17	35.87	1.54	0.59	8	17.8
All applicable cases	26.13	6.40	3.36	1.81	45	54.2[b]
All inventories	22.00	13.78	6.55	4.10	83	
1732–1737						
Stage 1	1.20	0.96	50.00	40.09	5	6.0
Stage 2	14.00	6.42	0.00	—	2	2.4
Stage 3	27.31	15.91	11.92	6.95	36	42.9
Stage 4	12.81	6.29	7.25	3.56	16	19.0
Stage 5	81.96	25.90	15.80	5.00	25	29.8
All applicable cases	38.02	17.26	14.17	6.43	84	45.4[b]
All inventories	29.19	16.26	17.34	9.66	185	
1748–1751						
Stage 1	22.29	26.65	11.12	13.30	22	16.3
Stage 2	116.13	29.72	4.11	1.05	9	6.7
Stage 3	37.40	12.77	46.35	15.83	39	28.9
Stage 4	31.69	12.69	39.16	15.69	18	13.3
Stage 5	75.80	34.60	13.51	6.17	47	34.8
All applicable cases	52.79	22.35	25.31	10.71	135	44.4[b]
All inventories	40.35	21.28	19.13	10.09	304	

SOURCE: See table 1.1.
Note: For household life cycles, see table 1.1.
[a] Converted to pounds British sterling.
[b] Percent of all inventories.

population average in terms of the amount of credit they were able to extend, which probably reflects the effects of endowments. Older generations were able to assist younger ones in the setting up of separate plantations.

Table 1.4. Stages of the Life Cycle and Value of Livestock as Percent of Personal Estate in Chester County Inventories

	Livestock	Horses	Cattle	Sheep	Swine	Number of Inventories
1717–1721						
Stage 1	22.00	15.73	5.06	0.40	0.80	9
Stage 2	26.40	10.40	10.67	2.67	0.53	4
Stage 3	32.18	12.21	14.44	3.54	1.16	17
Stage 4	33.46	16.32	14.37	2.85	1.43	14
Stage 5	11.58	5.32	5.36	0.80	0.22	13
All applicable cases	24.79	11.08	10.37	2.15	0.84	57
1732–1737						
Stage 1	19.70	13.06	5.27	1.37	0.34	7
Stage 2	14.68	7.11	6.19	1.38	0.00	2
Stage 3	22.60	9.64	9.63	1.95	1.14	46
Stage 4	29.43	13.25	14.00	2.60	0.93	21
Stage 5	14.23	6.82	5.21	1.29	0.31	34
All applicable cases	19.83	9.13	8.24	1.74	0.68	110
1748–1751						
Stage 1	15.01	9.50	3.53	1.01	0.60	23
Stage 2	11.46	4.63	5.53	0.93	0.36	11
Stage 3	20.23	10.58	7.23	1.36	0.83	48
Stage 4	26.96	12.09	8.87	1.80	1.05	24
Stage 5	15.52	8.26	5.79	0.81	0.58	62
All applicable cases	18.51	9.35	6.64	1.81	0.72	168

SOURCE: See table 1.1.

Note: For household life cycles, see table 1.1.

The mature household appears to have been operating at the peak of efficiency. If we visualize the household as the "firm," then the "optimal size of the firm" could be said to correspond to the stage of the life cycle where adolescents and young adults were available to provide labor for the household. At this stage the attention of the household appears to have turned from higher levels of consumption to the business of providing enough capital to enable each child to skip some of the more difficult stages in starting up a household of his or her own. It was the responsibility of the children to remain with the household not

Table 1.5. Stages of the Life Cycle And Labor in Chester County Inventories, 1717–1751

Stage of Life Cycle	Percent of Applicable Cases with Bound Labor					Number of Inventories
	Male Servants	Female Servants	Male Slaves	Female Slaves	Apprentices	
Stage 1	.05	.05	.00	.00	.025	40
Stage 2	11.76	5.88	5.88	11.76	.000	17
Stage 3	26.78	12.50	4.46	4.46	.917	112
Stage 4	16.85	8.47	8.47	5.08	.000	59
Stage 5	16.36	10.00	2.72	.91	1.818	110
All applicable cases	18.34	9.76	4.14	3.25	1.479	338

SOURCE: See table 1.1.

Note: Apprentices are probably seriously underrepresented because of the personal nature of the indenture. Servants may also be underrepresented in cases where a servant had only a few months left to serve, where a verbal rather than a written contract held, or where a "servant" was actually a young child bound out by the Overseers of the Poor. As property, on the other hand, slaves are probably listed in the inventories fairly accurately.

For household life cycles, see table 1.1.

only until they had built up enough capital to start their own families, but until they had assisted younger brothers and sisters in the process of capital accumulation. The special role of older children in relation to younger siblings is reflected in the efforts by dying householders through wills to direct the manner in which the family would divide into new households.

A mature family first began buying real estate in the expectation of being able to settle the family's sons, and sometimes the daughters. Legally, Pennsylvania practiced a combination of partible inheritance and modified primogeniture. If no other provisions were made at the time of death, the widow received one-third of the estate. The rest was then divided into shares, with each child receiving one share and the eldest receiving a double share. In a family with three children, for example, the widow would receive one-third of the estate, the eldest son two-sixths, and the other two children one-sixth each. If the widow did not remarry, her third would eventually devolve upon the children; remarriage complicated the matter.[4]

Householders could settle the question of inheritance otherwise, however, either through a will or through gifts of land and personal goods before death. Most of the wills dictated that the land be divided among all the male children, if possible. Daughters received livestock, personal items, and cash. Usually the eldest son received the developed part of the land, but sometimes elaborate plans were made to even out the division by having some recipients of land pay their siblings in cash. For example, Nicholas Pyle's eldest son Nicholas was to receive the family's 450 acres in Concord at 21, paying £10 annually to the widow and continuing an annuity owed by his father to his grandmother Sarah Bushel. Nicholas was to pay for his sister and brother's schooling until they were twelve, and he was also to get the use of his father's portion of a corn mill until his younger brother Samuel turned 21. When Samuel turned 21, the corn mill was to be divided among the three brothers, Samuel, Nicholas, and Joseph, with Nicholas receiving half and the other two a quarter each. Samuel would then receive 205 acres in Kennet and £27, and Joseph would get 210 acres in Kennet and £27, all paid by Nicholas.[5]

Many similar arrangements can be found in the Chester County wills between 1715 and 1755. Sometimes the family plantation was sold, with money divided among the children and the sons moving on to another township, as Joseph Baker did in ordering his home plantation in Edgmont sold. Each son received land in Thornbury, and provision was made for the widow to move in with the eldest. John Vaughan of Uwchland apparently did not trust his children to wait until the estate could be formally divided, so he ordered in his will "that my children do not deal nor sell their share or portion to each other, nor to any other person, untill my [youngest] son Isaac do or may arrive to the Age of Twenty-one Years."[6]

Authors of wills in Chester County also made an effort to ensure that younger siblings would receive assistance when it came time to set up their households. James Brown ordered in 1714 that his sons assist each other in building fences and houses and sowing crops. John Hendricks willed his son Andrew "his share where I now dwell together with the Buildings and orchard and In Consideration thereof He shall assist his Brother John to Build a House and that they both Andrew and John do assist their younger brother when he comes of to age [sic] and is disposed to settle his part to build him a House and a Barn." James Gibbons in 1732 gave one son the developed portion of the plantation, but allowed the other £150 toward building on the unimproved land. David Thomas of Newtown left a complicated schedule by which his sons were to assist each other and a cousin in clearing land and planting crops. Alexander Fraizer of Kennett dictated in 1751 that his eldest, Moses, was to receive half of a 200-acre plantation in Kennet, but he was to pay his brother John £30 "toward building him a House" on the other half. Younger sons Aaron, James, and Alexander all received acreage in Lancaster County, Alexander paying his sister Mary £15 and Moses and John giving her a home until marriage.[7]

Wills also made provisions for the care of the widow. Frequently the elder son, who received the improved portion of the real estate, was also charged with the care of his mother. The widow was typically promised a specific room, sometimes with separate entrance, apple trees, sheep, a patch of flax, and sufficient firewood. "My wife shall have the stone end of my house with the Seller during her widowhood," Nicholas Pyle, Junior, wrote, "with Libertie to keep one horse and one cow in the fields in the Summer also have Libertie to cart her necessary fire wood off my sd Plantation but not to let the same to any Person or to take any Inmates in to the same." Philip Yarnall gave his wife a room and access, part of the cellar, a cow, two "Duch children," cider, and instructions that her son was to provide firewood and she was to have access to the other fire when hers was out. In lieu of specific gifts, a widow might receive an annual payment during her widowhood (unless she remarried) of from £5 to £8 Pennsylvania currency. If the children were minors, the widow was frequently left the proceeds of the plantation until the children reached the age where the estate could be divided. As the century progressed, a few widows appear to have already signed premarital agreements guaranteeing the portion of the estate they would receive upon the death of their spouse.[8]

In the final stage, the householder was in the process of completing the dispersal of the family into new households. Livestock had been distributed among the children, real estate had been disbursed as well, although not always formally. Several wills indicate that sons were already living on land provided by their fathers. Sometimes the son bought or was given the land before the father's death; sometimes the land was still owned by the parent. When Thomas Withers of Marcus Hook died in 1720, his son Robert was in the process of beginning to develop land owned by Thomas in Nottingham. Found on the Nottingham land by the assessors were two steers, two cows, one horse, one mare, a bed, blankets, an old pot and kettle, and various tools. Assessors for the estate of Joseph Roades of Marple were instructed in 1732 to value land he held further west; not "taking aney notes of what Improvements John Roads his son have don on parte of the Land his father Allowing him to setle there since hee came to Age." Several fathers provided for the conveyance of land to a son who had already settled there: John Yearsley of Concord, for example, gave his son Isaac "the land he lives on" in Thornbury; Jacob and Thomas the lots they lived on in West Town; and Nathan and John the homestead in Concord. Finally, some householders had already given away land to their children. Several testators gave little but a token to a son, having, as Samuel Sellers phrased it, "already done well for him."[9]

As a result, the householders in the final stage of the life cycle frequently had already passed on their land and much of their livestock to their children. In the estates where the children were all married or there were grandchildren present, at least half of the value of the personal estate was represented by financial assets. These were not book debts, as in the case of the young praticing artisans, but bonds—personal obligations held for interest by the decedent. Some of these debts were owed by children, and some represented mortgages for land recently sold, but most represented money owed with interest by neighbors.[10]

Not all families were successful in passing through the various stages leading to the settling of all their children in adult households on their own farms. The most common block to completing the cycle during this period was death or illness. Furthermore, a householder marrying too early or otherwise forced to begin stage 3 without sufficient capital could have difficulty reaching stage 4; some households had to bind children out as servants after the age of twelve, even with both parents living. These discontinuities in the family life cycle provided the basis for the labor market in Pennsylvania.

LABOR IN THE PENNSYLVANIA ECONOMY

The labor market in Pennsylvania relied in the main on teenagers and young single adults. Most of those who sold their labor in colonial Pennsylvania were young people old enough to be productive, but too young to set up an independent household. There were, of course, exceptions to that rule. Some householders owned slaves, and married householders did sell their labor either in trade for room and board, as "inmates," or for wages, as "day labourers." But most households which turned to nonfamily labor to augment their work force made use of the large group of bound minors and independent youths available through the market.

Children had an accepted role as producers in the colonial Pennsylvania household. The relationships between a child's chronological age and his presumed ability to contribute to family output can be seen in the standards used by the judges of the Orphan's Court to determine an orphan's contributions and costs to an estate. If children were twelve or younger, the guardians were generally permitted the cost of "maintenance" for the children, including clothing, food, and some sort of rudimentary education. Between the ages of 12 and 21 (or sometimes 18, particularly for girls), income earned by the chores performed by an adolescent was considered about equal to the cost of maintenance and the education in husbandry or housework received from the adults. After 21 (or 18), an adult child remaining with the guardians could charge the estate wages in compensation for his or her work in the household.[11]

Many households never reached the high-income stage where a middle-aged set of parents directed a crew of adult and adolescent children. Death or illness of the head of the household could break up the family unit before enough capital could be accumulated to allow the children to set up independent households.[12] Young adults quarrelled with their guardians and went off on their own.[13] Many households could not overcome costs incurred during the early stages when young children were a burden rather than a benefit to the household income. Even among those families that could afford to keep their adolescents at home, some preferred to send them off to learn a valuable trade that would be of use both to the extended family and to the child himself.

The supply of youthful native-born labor to the Pennsylvania labor market thus came from a variety of sources: children over the age of 6 were bound out as orphans or members of indigent families; children 12 and over were bound out for a payment to the family; apprentices were bound out with a payment to their new master. Young adults who for one reason or another found themselves outside the household system sold their labor by the day, month, or year, through written or verbal contracts. This last group included previously bound adolescents set free from their servitude, adults who no longer chose to live with their families, adults whose families had dissolved, or adults who felt they could make a greater contribution to the family income by selling their labor.

Demand came from the reverse needs of the household: a young household that contained minor children unable to contribute to family income, could take on a bound youth, a girl to help with the housework, a boy to help in the fields. The servant would be expected to perform the same chores as a family member of that age. Similarly, an elderly householder with no children left to help with the plantation, and not yet wishing to move in with his children, might take on a bound servant. The evidence from the Chester County inventories supports this conjecture: both of these age groups averaged higher numbers of bound servants than the other groups.[14] Even when operating within the household as a substitute for children, however, servants were seldom accorded the same treatment. To the extent that there were class distinctions in colonial America, perhaps the sharpest was between the youth living in his family's household and the adolescent who was bound out.

Often when an adolescent was bound to serve an adult, not his guardian, for a given period of time, a formal contract was drawn up to protect both parties. All contracts at the time, whether mortgages, deeds, debt obligations, premarital agreements, administrative bonds, or labor contracts, began with the phrase "This indenture." The term "indentured servant" thus referred to a servant who had signed a binding written contract with his employer and did not necessarily carry all the connotations later generations have added to it, specifically the assumption that the servant was an immigrant. Verbal agreements between servants and masters were apparently as common as written ones, however, particularly when an adolescent or child was being bound to a relative, or when an independent adult bound himself for one year's servitude.[15]

The binding of immigrants as servants, therefore, cannot be understood except within the context of the total Pennsylvania labor market. Immigrants were generally of an age when a native-born child or adult outside the control of his family would have been bound; their experience of a period of time as bound labor placed them within the mainstream of others their own age, or perhaps a bit younger, in colonial society. Once they had become familiar with the agricultural methods of the New World and perhaps had developed a reputation as good workers, they could move on to informal binding agreements on an annual basis; with a small amount of accumulated capital they might begin to make the first steps toward setting up an independent household. But generally upon their first arrival as immigrants they were in no position to do either, and at that age most natives were equally incapable of setting up on their own.

A bound servant was considered a member of the employer's household. The master was expected to provide "meat, drink, apparel, washing, and lodging" during the period of indenture. He was responsible for any debts incurred by his servant and expected to govern his servant's behavior as a father would his children's misdeeds. James Steel, for example, chided an acquaintance for his servant's part in the incident with the fishing weirs in 1736.

> I should not have given myself and the Propr[ietor] so much Trouble to serve a person and his family that by his behavior has so little deserved and what is more provoking a Servant just taken into thy house must be for such an unlawfull action Dub'd and called a Captn to lead and head a lawless Company of Rioters to fly in the face of the Governmt and Insult the Magistrate for putting the Laws thereof.[16]

In a similar vein, the Philadelphia Meeting included servants in the responsibilities of members of the meeting regarding noise and disruptions in meetings:

> all Parents, Masters, and Mistresses ought at all times to have a godly care over their Children and Servants in that respect [falling asleep or otherwise disturbing the Meeting] and caution them accordingly.[17]

Depending upon the agreement, the master might also be responsible for teaching the servant to read and write, and perhaps to cipher; the master of a bound apprentice had also agreed to teach the "mysteries" of his trade. On the servant's part, he was expected to obey his master, his family, or assigns; to do no harm nor permit it to be done to his master; to warn his master of impending harm if he knew of any; not to sell any of his master's goods or allow anyone else to do so; not to gamble, as gambling usually resulted in debts his master would have to pay; and not to marry or commit fornication.[18]

Long-term indentures contained an interesting combination of certainty and uncertainty for both parties. From the standpoint of the servant, once a child or adolescent had been bound, his master was required to support him. The servant could not be turned out. Courts and poorhouses returned the few who appeared back to their masters with orders to either take care of them or sell them to someone who would. On the other hand, virtually all indentures were assignable. If the court and estate records are any indication, servants changed hands with stunning frequency. Of course, court records are skewed toward unstable ownership. A servant does not usually appear in the records unless there was some problem, and the likelihood of a problem would increase with the number of owners. It was perhaps the fear of assignability that kept many agreements verbal rather than written. When ordering that their children be bound out, writers of wills sometimes inserted clauses restricting the degree to which the children could be assigned; in a few cases, sympathetic masters freed servants or assigned them before death to prevent their being sold with the estate.[19]

As far as the masters were concerned, the certainty of the length of contract allowed them the freedom to take time to train a servant to perform at a skill level desired by the master without worrying that the servant would disappear before the master reaped the rewards of his training. But there were uncertainties in a long-term contract for the employer as well: a servant could prove to be untrainable, lazy, troublesome. And a female servant could become pregnant. Masters, however, had greater recourse than servants when difficulties arose during the term of the indenture. A servant could be sold with greater ease than a master removed.

The relative lack of power on the part of the servants was inseparable from their chronological age in a society where age was awarded its deference. It is a mark of the traditional nature of the household economy of colonial Pennsylvania that the social role of bound adolescent labor could not be separated from the economic role. Binding was an experience as common to adolescents in the eighteenth century as public schooling would be to those in the twentieth. As an institution, binding out was supported by the community, and all participants were expected to behave according to the given set of rules.

In contrast to the frequency with which adolescents were bound, children under the age of 12 were bound out only when their parents had died or could not financially provide for them. Occasionally a childless couple would persuade a relative to bind over a child to them, presumably to be raised as a substitute heir. More commonly, however, an orphan with no estate would be bound out by the courts. Fatherless children (called "orphans" even when their mothers were living) were bound out if it was believed the widow either could not financially support the children or could not provide them with the necessary education or discipline. There are also cases where both parents were living but could not afford to have the child remain at home.[20]

Minors were always bound out until adulthood, usually 21, although reduced to 18 by contract in a few cases. As a result, a child bound during the period when he would have to be considered a negative asset, before the age of 11 or 12, would have to compensate for the costs of upbringing with his labor as an adolescent. Children bound at an early age, then, seldom received an education from their masters in anything except the rudimentary housekeeping and husbandry skills necessary to set up a household in the colony. When released from their first indenture, they had only the barest skills to offer future employers.

Except for orphaned children and those from indigent families, children were seldom bound out before they were old enough to pay their own way. When a child over the age of 10 was bound, his parents were compensated in some fashion, usually at the time of binding, although some agreements specified payments later in the child's servitude. A request that the child be taught to read the Bible might reduce the monetary compensation for his services. Because all minors, no matter what their age, were bound until adulthood, a child bound at 12 had more years to serve than an adolescent bound at 15, but the latter presumably had a higher quality of labor to offer.[21]

When an adolescent was bound as an apprentice to

learn a trade, the direction of compensation reversed. An apprentice's family generally compensated the master for the education the child would receive, although occasionally the apprentice's value as a worker was considered sufficient compensation. Apprenticeship has generally been associated in the colonial world only with cities; however, apprenticeship was common in the Chester County countryside. The court records reveal adolescents having been assigned as apprentices in Chester County in a wide variety of trades: carpenter, cordwainer, fuller, joiner, smith, weaver, and spinning-wheel maker. Girls could be bound apprentice as well, although the trade was limited to "tayloress." An apprenticeship provided a valuable stock of human capital which sometimes only a fairly well-off family could afford for the children.[22]

Several adolescents willed landed estates by their fathers were also ordered bound out as apprentices in their fathers' wills. Joseph Townsend willed a saw mill and 212 acres to his three sons, but ordered them to be "put to trade at 15." Richard Morris was also to be bound apprentice at 15, despite the legacy of 260 acres he was to receive at 21. Job Pyle of Marlborough willed £150 to his daughter Ann and considerable real estate to his two boys, but he still ordered that "my two sons when they arrive to the sixteenth year of their age to be put to some good and benefishal trade." Job Harvey, a wealthy fuller with £569 in personal estate and land in Darby, Charlestown, and Berks County, left money so that his grandson could be put apprentice to a trade he desired.[23]

When an apprentice ended his period of indenture, his acquired human capital enabled him immediately to set up on his own. A young adult with a trade was in an excellent position in colonial society to begin accumulating a stock of physical and financial capital to go with his skills; practicing artisans who died young in Chester County frequently owned financial assets totally out of proportion to their physical assets. Many farmers doubled as artisans, practicing their trade in the slack agricultural seasons or hiring servants to work the farm. Having an artisan in the extended family added to the total amount of income the family could produce, and a farmer/artisan was later in a good position to acquire labor cheaply on the promise that he would train his own servants in his "mystery." It is easy to see why Chester County families were willing to pay a great deal to acquire a trade for their sons, even when their sons would inherit sufficient real estate to set up a plantation as adults.

Unlike apprentices, most bound adolescents emerged from their indenture, however, without skills to support themselves and insufficient capital to set themselves up in independent households. They joined the large, young-adult labor market, which consisted not only of former bound servants, but also of adults who had left their father's household or whose household had dissolved early due to death or misfortune. Adults could sell their labor on a daily basis; they could informally bind themselves out at fairs for a specified sum; or they could sell themselves for a period of two to three years for a given amount of money and the usual freedom dues. Or they could combine the options: James Harmon had himself indented apprentice to a cordwainer in 1746 with the proviso that he "be allowed two weeks in every harvest to work for himself."[24]

Judging by the estate accounts filed in the Chester County Archives, there was a floating population of day laborers who offered their services at a daily wage. Furthermore, there were people who classified themselves in court, debt, or estate records as "labourer." A common laborer could clearly not earn as much as a skilled artisan, but if he stayed away from the alehouses and other "entertainments," he could save enough to set up a household in his late twenties or early thirties. There were young "labourers" in the Chester County inventories whose estates contained both financial assets and real estate.[25]

Another way to earn a living and perhaps save for future independence was to sell one's labor on an annual or semi-annual basis, without benefit of written contract. This practice, common in England, apparently occurred regularly at the fairs in the Pennsylvania countryside, although it is hard to track down precisely because the agreements were verbal. A former servant, well known in the area as a steady worker, could probably earn quite a bit in this fashion. Adults could enter into long-term contracts as well as adolescents. Free adults could bind themselves out for a fee to be paid at the end of the indenture or at the assumption of the servants' already acquired debts by the new master. The courts also bound out debtors who had spent over six months in the jail and could not pay their debts.[26]

Immigrants fell naturally into this last category of indentured servants, as they came to the region with a debt to pay. Immigrants came to the country in one of three ways. First, they paid their own passage, as most married immigrants or those with families did. Second, they bound their labor to the ship-master or a general labor importer at the dock in Europe, and he sold the indenture upon arrival in America. Finally, they came as "redemptioners," who gave their personal bond for the price of passage at the port of departure and then sold themselves up for payment of debt when they arrived in Philadelphia, as would any other indigent debtor in the colony.[27]

Of the two methods, the redemptioners appear to have had the better deal. Irish servants who arrived as bound labor in New Castle were usually bound for a period of five to seven years. In contrast, the average redemptioner paid only four years for his passage. The difference is probably accountable for by one of several explanations. Irish servants may have been bound as minors. Hence, their indentures were until 21 and would probably have been longer than those for adults. Most German immigrants apparently had funds to pay part of their passage, which would reduce their debt upon arrival. And the passage from Germany may have been less as more ships had reason to go to the Continent.[28]

As a rule, judges usually allowed male immigrants to discharge the debts of passage at a rate of £4 per year. In contrast, during the period 1730 to 1750, a native adult male servant who had incurred a debt would generally have had time added to his servitude at the rate of a year for every £7, a figure 75 percent higher than the effective "wage" granted the new arrivals. This discrepancy reflected both a lack of experience on the part of the immigrants concerning the value of labor in America, and uncertainty on the master's part about an immigrant's natural abilities and knowledge of Pennsylvania husbandry. After this first indenture, immigrants would be treated in the same fashion as native labor in the market.[29]

When problems arose between the two parties to the labor contract, the master and the servant, either one turned to the courts for redress. Employers usually turned to the court for legal authorization to extend a servant's indenture as reimbursement for costs incurred by the servant's misdeeds. The most common complaint, of course, was runaways. A runaway servant could be charged five times the days spent away from home and ordered to pay expenses; if he could not pay expenses, they were calculated into days and that time as well was added to his contract. In most cases, the expenses formed the bulk of the punishment time added to the original indenture. William Pallet ran away from Jeremiah Colet seven times over the course of the year 1729, losing twelve days of service in all. He was charged sixty days extra servitude to make up for the runaway time, but he was also ordered to reimburse his master for the £4.5.6 his master incurred bringing him back each time, which added ninety more days to his servitude. Richard Pearce was missing from his master's service for only ten days in 1735, but he was ordered to serve two extra years to repay his master £11.9.10 in search costs, in addition to the fifty days assigned as punishment for his absence.[30]

The second most common source of complaints stemmed from the possibility that a female servant might get pregnant. Pregnancy was no small matter for any unmarried girl, but at least a free woman could get married once she realized she was pregnant. Servants were prohibited by law from marrying without their masters' consent; of course they rarely were granted that. A pregnant servant girl was subjected not only to social disgrace, but also to economic burdens stemming from her status as a servant. Inevitibly, she and her named accomplice (as confessed in childbirth) were charged with fornication at the next session of the county courts. The girl was charged with lost working time during her lying in (made up without adding extra days, however, as it was considered not absenteeism but illness); the cost of a nurse; the cost of raising the child (or burying it); and the cost of her fines in court. If she (or her good friend) could not pay the fines, her servitude was lengthened accordingly, generally for one and a half to two years. If she was unfortunate enough to be a servant when the child was weaned, the family might have the child bound out as well.[31]

A final source of extra servitude was debts incurred by the servant which the master had to pay, with court debts providing the greatest of those. The unfortunate Oliver Plunkett was found innocent of a capital crime in 1729, only to have his servitude lengthened to reimburse his master for fees of prosecution and his time in the county jail. Pregnancy could also result in a longer indenture for a male servant if, for instance, he was named as the father in her childbed, as his master would end up paying his fine for fornication. Job Harvey's servant Joseph Fisher, who married without his master's permission, was ordered to serve an extra year as punishment. His wife was also ordered to pay Harvey £6, or to serve him a year with her husband.[32]

Servants in turn sued their masters when they felt the agreements in the indenture had not been met. The most common complaints were that a servant's time was up but that the master would not let him go, or that the master refused to pay the servant his freedom dues (two sets of clothing, one of them new, including shoes). In many of the cases, the problems arose when the servant's indenture had been sold to several masters in a row, and one or more of them down the line refused to abide by the commitments made with the original master. Several masters who bought the last year of a servant's time were sued in court for reneging on the freedom dues. One other common source of complaint was that a master had refused to provide promised education in a trade. If the promise was written into the indenture, the servant generally won the case, and the master was ordered to turn his indenture over to another. In some cases, however, the servant claimed he had been verbally promised a trade, with no witnesses to the agreement. In those cases, the servant lost.[33]

Only the fringe of the system can be seen through the courts. On average, four servants a year were brought to the Chester County Court between 1720 and 1750, either as runaways or as petitioners themselves. Of these 125 servants, 64 were runaways whose length of servitude was increased; 61 requested to be released from their master or had not received their freedom dues; and six others, plus two of the runaways, involved female servants who had given birth. The runaways included only the most serious cases—most had run away several times before—but they included all of the servants whose time was increased because of a debt or having missed time during their servitude.[34]

Many minor problems were handled informally. In the case of a master who refused to pay freedom dues, a servant could first turn to his neighbors or to a local justice of the peace. The town of New Town petitioned as a group on behalf of Francis Culbert, who "hath not been kept to his Trade according to the Tenor of his Indenture but hath been Imploy'd in Common Labour upon his Masters Plantation." As a result, Thomas Moore, his master, was "Enjoynd to keep the sd Servant to the trade of a Weaver And not for the future to Imploy the said Servant in plantation work or otherwise then at his said Trade," or he would be discharged from his servitude the next session of the Court after the violation.[35]

There were, of course, other sources of labor in Pennsylvania besides children, adolescents, and young adults. Slavery was legal, although attempts were made from time to time to make it expensive to import slaves into Philadelphia (ostensibly for moral purposes). Slavery simply was not common, however, particularly in the countryside. At no time between 1717 and 1751 did the proportion of inventories in Chester County with slaves reach 7 percent, and those seldom contained more than one slave (the maximum was five; see table 1.6). In contrast, the number of slaves per household in All Hallow's Parish in Maryland averaged ten during the same period, and

Table 1.6. Bound Labor in Chester County, Pa., and All Hallow's Parish, Md.

Chester County, Pa.	1717–1721	1732–1737	1748–1751
Number of estates	83	185	304
Percent of estates with bound labor	19.3	23.5	20.7
Mean number of servants, all estates	0.20	0.28	0.27
Mean number of slaves, all estates	0.07	0.09	0.07
Mean number of servants, estates with bound labor	1.06	1.16	1.29
Mean number of slaves, estates with bound labor	0.38	0.30	0.33
All Hallow's Parish, Md.	1711–1720	1731–1740	1751–1760
Number of estates	54	54	52
Percent of estates with bound labor	48.1	63.0	82.7
Mean number of servants, all estates	0.30	0.35	0.17
Mean number of slaves, all estates	3.80	6.32	7.92
Mean number of servants, estates with bound labor	0.62	0.56	0.23
Mean number of slaves, estates with bound labor	7.89	10.03	9.58

SOURCE: Chester County Wills and Imventories, Chester County Archives. The data for All Hallow's Parish were taken from Carville Earle, *The Evolution of a Tidewater Settlement System*, p. 41.

four-fifths of the estates inventoried contained slaves. Slavery was more common in the city of Philadelphia, but still not usually more than one or two household servants were slaves. The vast majority of householders did not own any slaves at all.[36]

Since slavery was legal, it is open to question why it was not more common, as it was in the colonies on Pennsylvania's southern border. The most obvious explanation is that slaves were expensive. The average price from inventoried estates appears to have been about £45 for an adult slave, either male or female. Native adult servants could be fairly expensive, costing as much as £8 to £10 per year. But immigrants could be bought in Philadelphia for only £4 a year. At that rate, it would take a slave eleven years of work to make up the investment, and there was no guarantee he would live that long. Technically the slave's progeny would become the property of the owner as well, but there does not seem to have been a large enough slave community to have guaranteed that sort of return on the investment. Householders in Pennsylvania seldom used more than one servant of any kind, in strong contrast to Maryland, where slaves appeared with sufficient frequency to have been expected to keep a slave community growing.[37]

Furthermore, wheat farming in general did not lead to the sort of labor requirements that would best be served by slavery. As we have seen before, the preferred production unit included no more than five or six older teenagers and young adults; a household would thus have no reason to own more than that number in bound labor. In addition, unlike tobacco, wheat did not require constant care and attention. A large year-round work force proved of little use in Pennsylvania. The preferred alternative to indentured servants was to hire wage labor, reflecting a preference for increasing the labor force during harvest time rather than year-round. Several historians have noted that when some areas of the Chesapeake substituted wheat for tobacco as their chief cash crop, the incidence of slavery declined rapidly.[38]

Some Pennsylvanians were clearly unhappy about the whole idea of slavery. Several owners freed their slaves in their wills. Christopher Taylor of Tinicum ordered that four of his five slaves be set free at the age of thirty. The fifth, a "mulatto boy," was to be set "free as soon as his mother pay to my Executors" £25. Deborah Nayle of Thornbury ordered in 1751 that her executors give "her freedom from any person or persons whatever: to my Negro Woman called Bella." Bella, in her own will ten years later, gave enough money to a nephew to buy his freedom.[39] Quakers as a whole had misgivings about the morality of slavery, but not enough yet to forbid ownership of slaves to members of the sect. As early as 1719, the Quaker Discipline Book showed guarded disapproval of slavery in its instructions to members, but stopped short of its prohibition:

It is desired that friends do not buy or sell Indian Slaves, also that
none among us be concearned in the fetching or Importing negro
Slaves from their own Country or elsewhere. And it is the advice
of this Meeting that all friends who have any of them do treat
them with Humanity and in a Christian manner.[40]

As the price of indentured servants increased at the
end of the eighteenth century, the incidence of slaveholding rose
in Pennsylvania. Pennsylvanians appear to have been reluctant
to become involved with slavery, some for religious reasons. But
the major reasons for the relative lack of slavery in Pennsylvania
before 1755 were the expense of owning a slave compared with
the cost of immigrant indentured labor, and the relative incom-
patibility of slavery with wheat farming as opposed to other cash
crops.

While the majority of labor in the market was supplied by single persons, married householders occasionally offered their service in the labor market, although virtually never
as bound labor. There are some incidents of married immigrants
bound together to the same master, but they are rare. Day laborers who appear in the accounts of estates and tradesmen could
very well have been married. The court records include people
who referred to themselves as "labourers" and who were married; some had children. Many of these, no doubt, were living
on other people's property, exchanging specified services for the
right to a tenement, a plot of land, perhaps a cow and some
sheep. It is these people who show up in the tax records as
"inmates."[41]

The category of "inmate" in colonial Pennsylvania
has recently been redefined through the work of historian Lucy
Simler. At one time it was believed that "inmates" referred generally to tenants. Thus, the relative number of landowners among
all householders could be calculated easily by taking the lists of
all taxpayers (thoughtfully provided and retained in the four pre-
1750 counties in Pennsylvania) and dividing them between inmates and everyone else. In the process of researching a study
of Marple township in Chester County, Simler discovered that

tenants paying rent either did not show up on the records at all or were recorded as landowners. Inmates, dependent people living on another's land, were something else again. Most appear either to have been living on a landowner's property as a charity case, such as widows, or to have been servants with separate households.[42]

WAGE LABOR IN PENNSYLVANIA

In addition to local and immigrant supplies of bound labor, laborers working for wages appear in Pennsylvania records almost from the colony's beginnings. The account books of Coventry Forge in northern Chester County, one of the first successful iron foundries in the colonies, provide ample evidence of the use of wage labor in the first half of the eighteenth century. Samuel Nutt established his first bloomery in 1717 on French Creek in upper Chester County. A full set of his account books exists from 1726 until his death in 1737; the account books were continued by his heirs as the family's holdings increased to include Warwick Furnace and Reading Nos. 1 and 2. The Nutt family intermarried with the Potts family to begin a dynasty in iron- and steelmaking in Pennsylvania.[43]

A variety of laborers were employed at Coventry Forge to perform a variety of functions. Some, such as woodcutters, miners, and the highly skilled ironworkers, were paid by the piece. The company carters were paid by the month. Several carters outside Coventry had regular contracts to take a load of pig iron or bar iron down to Philadelphia at a standard rate throughout the period of £2 per ton.[44]

Unskilled laborers with steady employment at the forge were paid by the month, the week, or the year. The wage generally included board, although some of them were paid an extra allowance of 5s. a week for "dieting," or 3d. a week for washing. When an extra chore had to be done on the premises, someone was called in to be paid by the day. At harvest time the company also hired agricultural workers by the day.[45]

The highest paid workers at the forge were the men who actually worked with the iron. During this period the group included Thomas Feldon, William Shuell, Thomas Savage, and Thomas Minion. As they were working by the piece, their wages could vary greatly, and when there was down time at the forge they were not compensated at all. However, they were all paid very well by colonial standards. From the summer of 1728 to the summer of 1729, for example, Savage earned almost £50 and Shuell over £57. The company also paid them by the day when they were required to perform some chore outside of their usual job. Savage was paid 3s. a day for "work about the Bloomery Bellows" in the fall of 1728; in the spring of 1729 he was paid 3s. 4d. a day for working on the "great hammer." The wrought hammer gave Nutt quit a bit of difficulty that spring; he hired several skilled outsiders at wages ranging from 2s. 6d. to 3s. 4d. a day to fix it. Finally he sent Thomas Savage to Joseph Rutter's, paying him 3s. 4d. a day to do Rutter's work while Rutter came and fixed the wrought hammer.[46]

Most of the people who worked on a regular basis at Coventry Forge were paid by the month. It is probable that these people were semiskilled workers, not as proficient as the blacksmiths, yet experienced in the other tasks necessary around the forge and foundry. The standard rate was 40s. a month, including diet, with "absent" days deducted. For example, Sam Cambell worked from September 1729 to June 1730 at 40s. a month, but amounts were deducted from his pay for three weeks and four days "absent Time" in the winter and 1s. 3d. of a month in the summer. Even with the absent time deducted, however, Cambell earned over £20 a year working for the company. In all, over seventeen men worked at Coventry at various times from 1730 to 1755 at the rate of 40s. a month. Seven more earned 45s. in the period 1737–1755. A few earned only 30s. a month, which was more commonly given out as a wage at Pine Forge in northeastern Pennsylvania. Several earned more, including James Guest and Martin Kinsula, who each earned over

£3 a month in 1743. "Negro Hercules" was originally hired at
20s. a month in the 1730s. Midway through his first year, however, a note appeared in his account that the salary had been
raised "by agreement" to the standard 40s.[47]

Some workers were paid by the week. After having
worked for 40 s. a month in 1726, Thomas Savage was paid 20s.
a week (or over £4 a month) through 1727 and 1728 for "work
at the finery and Bloomery". Samuel Harris was paid 20s. a week
for coaling and keeping the furnace, 23s. a week with diet for
filling at the furnace. John Hartshorn was paid 12s. 6d. per week
for eleven weeks "at the mines and at the Dam and at the hay."[48]

Still others preferred to be paid by the year. John
Gregory received £50 per annum in 1727 and 1728. James Speary
was paid "after the rate of £32 per annum," including diet, with
only a week and a half deducted for one year's service. Speary
found ways to supplement his income as well: he wrote bonds
for a few pence apiece, and he also frequently offered his services as bleeder, charging 9d. per "bleeding." John Kent received £155 for five years work from 1743–1749; later he received £50 a year from September 1750 through September
1752.[49]

While the monthly and annual workers apparently
drew their main source of income from the forge, there were
others who appear in the accounts who worked for the company by the day, whenever some special work had to be done
at the house or on the farm. The standard wage for a day's work
by an adult male throughout the period was 2s., in most cases
with food provided. Day laborers worked at a variety of chores:
"10 dayes work for Mr. Nut making a wood fence and ditching
and other business"; "2 dayes work making a Road for Sam
Harris"; "1 dayes work picking stones in the orchards"; "15 1/2
dayes work in the meadow and at the furnace"; "24 days work
upon the Bank and makeing hay and sundry other business";
"6 dayes grubing and stubing in the New meadow"; "3 days
going for a pair of Oxen to Concord;" "6 dayes worke spreading
dung in the meadow fenceing and carting."[50]

Two shillings was the standard wage for a day's la-

bor, but more often had to be paid at harvest time. Some laborers still charged 2 *s.* for mowing or haying, but many charged
2*s.* 3*d.* or 2*s.* 6 *d.* This figure is consistent with those in the
Chester County estate accounts. Richard Hayes, a flour miller in
Haverford, paid 2*s.* 3*d.* a day for harvest work as early as 1715.[51]

Women were also paid to work at harvest. In July
1749, Barbara Goodbread and Catherine Rumford were each paid
2*s.* 3*d.* a day for four days reaping. Margaret Hughes was paid
2*s.* a day for two days reaping in 1742. Margaret Enters, "harvest girl," and Barbara Hildebrand were both paid 1*s.* 6*d.* a day
for harvest work in the summer of 1742.[52]

The company also had to pay more when the ser-
vices of a skilled worker were required. Henry Hockley received
4*s.* a day for three days plowing—presumably part of that was
for rental of the oxen. James Cassel and "his man" were each
paid 3*s.* a day for construction work "at the forge and furnace"
in April 1730. When Nutt was building a new house in the spring
of 1729, he paid Frances Edwards, Sam Cambell, and William
Dodd and his man each 3*s.* a day for carpentry work, "daubing
the new house, and corking and about the leanto chimly." (He
also purchased 2200 shingles and 250 "clap boards.") James
Barton was paid 3*s.* a day for mason work in 1748. James Burn
was paid 3*s.* 6*d.* a day in 1753 for carpenter work. Paul Custard
was paid £3.15.0 for building the chimneys at "Cold Spring" in
1749 and 4*s.* for a day's work at the Milk House. Evan John
was paid 5*s.* a day for smith work in 1744 and 1746; Joseph
Shaver 4*s.* a day for carpenter work in 1745; John Kirling received 5*s.* a day for smith work and "stealing the Gudgeon" in
1744. Walter Wash received £3 in 1742 for one-third part of
building a house, £2 in 1743 for one-third of another house,
and £3 a day for "work at the forge" and "carpentry work" in
1743 and 1744. Hugh Ben also received 4*s.* a day for carpentry
work in 1745 and 1748. Henry Shepard received 3*s.* 6*d.* a day
in 1738 for "mending the Tayler House," building a shed, "laying a heart", "walling a well," and other business.[53]

There are also a few cases where the company paid
for the time of a bound laborer. In August 1726, the Nutts paid

John Robeson 16*s*. 6*d*. for "yr Negro at Hay making 6 dayes at
2 sh. per Day and Diett." In 1728 the company paid George
Dandison £7.10.0 for "his man coaling," and there are several
cases where the company paid a neighbor 2 shillings a day for
his time plus 2*s*. a day for "his man," or 1*s*. 6*d*. for "his boy."[54]

A few people were able to put together combinations
of jobs from Nutt and Grace in such a way that they always
appear to have been working for them, although never at one
task consistently. Over the course of the year 1729, Thomas Price
collected between 17*s*. and £11/16/1 a month at a variety of
chores, including cutting wood, "grubing and stubing," "wheel-
ing and setting" wood, fencing, burning brush, coaling, and
carting. His wife earned money for making shirts and teaching
sewing skills to Anna Nutt's daughters, Rebecca and Ruth. Patrick Judge and Thomas and Mary Cloward also earned a steady
income from the company in this haphazard fashion.[55]

As the cases of Mary Cloward and Thomas Price's
wife demonstrate, there were many women on the company
payroll. Mary Cloward was one of several women who washed
clothes at 2*s*. 6*d*. a week. In 1728 she received annual wages of
£6 for unspecified duties. She also knit stockings, spun wool and
flax, and made shirts, as did Rebecca Goheen, Elizabeth Edwards, Elizabeth Thomas, Susanna Hopkins, Lydia Cloward,
Margaret Allen, Mary Dodson, Ann Evans ("Widow in the for-
est"), Jane and Sarah Butler, Jane Goucher, Jane Mulcastle, and
William MacBeen's wife. Margaret Night was paid 2*s*. 6*d*. a week
for washing and £1.10.0 a month for general work. Rebecca Harris
received £2 in 1749 and 1750 for three quilts and 8*s*. 2*d*. for one
bedstead. Elizabeth Smith received 5*s*. a week for keeping school
in 1750.[56]

The wages, as depicted in the family account books,
continue in the same vein with very little change in amounts
received until the Seven Years' War. The number of people
working for wages in Coventry in the first half of the eighteenth
century, as well as the variety of wage arrangements, strongly
suggests that wage work was compatible with the economy of
the region as early as the 1720s. A matching set of wages exists

for Thomas Rutter's forge in northeastern Pennsylvania. A similar pattern of wages in the Chester County estate inventories and Richard Hayes account book suggests that the practice of paying wages at Coventry Forge was not an isolated occurrance, but fairly common to Pennsylvania.[57]

The wages in Chester County were extremely high by British standards. The conversion rate during the period 1726–1730 was £150 Pennsylvania currency to £100 British sterling. Thus the monthly wages of 40s. Pennsylvania currency would amount to 27s. in British currency, or £16.4.0 a year. This compares to annual wages in southern England ranging from £4 a year to £6 a year during the same period. The Pennsylvania wages included diet, so boarding costs will not account for the discrepancy. Even allowing for major differences in skills or work requirements, the wage differential is stunning.[58]

Equally interesting are the very high rates paid to the skilled ironworkers working by the piece. Nutt was known to have gone to England several times in search of skilled workers to use in his forge; if these wages are higher than those in England then this would provide evidence as to the relatively scarcity of skilled labor. And yet, even with the high costs of labor for Coventry Forge, the foundry was profitable. At the time of Nutt's death, he was planning to expand with two new furnaces. His heirs carried out his plans and continued to expand through the century.[59]

The labor market in Pennsylvania thus appears as a curious mixture of the traditional and the modern. The long-term indenture with which children, adolescents, and young adults were bound, while negotiated in a market context, still represented a system of labor based on social role. On the other hand, the labor market of young adults appears to have been heading toward a more modern concept, with shorter and shorter contracts leading to an early wage system.

In the case of children and adolescents, binding out appears to have been almost as much a social institution as an economic one: rather than allowing minors to live outside the household, society found a way to provide them with one. The practice enhanced social stability, both for the minors whose households for whatever reason could no longer support them, and for the community which could keep the discipline and care of adolescents in the type of social environment considered best— the household.

The system worked to the advantage of immigrants who came to the country as minors. In essence, they incurred no real penalty for the cost of their passage, for an unattached minor who had paid his passage would probably have been bound out by the courts upon arrival anyway (depending on his ability to pass for 18 and stay out of the way of authorities). Adult immigrants were aware when they could not pay their passage that they were facing three to seven years of bound labor, but they generally seem to have believed that economic opportunities were better in Pennsylvania than the region they were leaving. They were not cheated. Eighteenth-century Pennsylvania bore little resemblance to seventeenth-century Virginia, where indentured servants seldom lived long enough to see freedom. Land could be acquired at virtually any price, depending on how far one wished to go from the trade routes; labor received higher wages than abroad; capital appears to have been no more expensive. Taxes were certainly lower. The quality of life, as represented by the life expectancy of an adult and his ability to raise a complete family, was much higher in Pennsylvania than at home.

Local laborers, not making the same tradeoff as an immigrant, found little reason to bind themselves voluntarily to a long-term agreement. The major reason for getting caught in a long-term indenture was indebtedness. Servitude was preferable to time in jail, and no matter how great the debt, the courts did not require servitude longer than seven years. The long-term contracts appear to have benefited both employers and employees when there was education involved—employers could risk the time of educating because they received work in return; employees were willing to work for a long period if they came out with a greater supply of human capital. Otherwise, both parties seem to have been happier with shorter-term contracts, which gave both the choice to continue or move on.

As in the English countryside, the move toward shorter contracts represented a movement toward a modern wage system of labor. Unlike England, however, it would appear that many more youths remained within the family unit, never leaving the household to join the open labor market.[60] Others perhaps contributed wages earned outside the household to the household budget when they returned home again. Whether or not a youth spent his adolescence in his own household or another's, however, he always returned to the household as mode of production once he had married and had his own children. And as long as the household remained the basic unit of production, traditional social roles and chronological age would strongly influence the choices available for both sides of the labor market.

The labor market formed the most traditional aspect of the Pennsylvania economy. The fact that production was organized on the basis of households rather than firms, however, did not affect the market for products between households. As will be apparent from the evidence presented in the following chapters, Pennsylvania households produced a variety of goods and services for the domestic as well as the international market. Land (and the improvements made upon leased land) was bought and sold freely. Paper money printed by the colonial legislature allowed Pennsylvanians to escape the more cumbersome aspects of barter. A lively capital market enabled householders to lend or borrow money at interest in the countryside as well as in the city; country householders in need of capital were not necessarily dependent upon implicit loans from their neighborhood storekeeper. The option of applying for mortgages through the Pennsylvania General Loan Office added to the general availability of credit. Pennsylvania households were never confined to their own boundaries when making choices concerning production, consumption, or investment.

CHAPTER TWO

Uncertainty, Diversification, and Economic Performance

Pennsylvania householders augmented the goods available for consumption by trading in the market. The economy quickly reached a level of diversification whereby all were not producing the same goods at the same time. This left a high degree of flexibility in the options available both for production as well as consumption. In addition, diversification lessened the risks associated with trading in the market. Risk was further reduced by the close-knit family, community, and religious ties of Pennsylvania householders. Ironically, it was precisely those elements of Pennsylvania society that were the most traditional and community-oriented that *enabled* householders to feel free to participate in the market.

METHODS OF COPING WITH UNCERTAINTY

Risk was a constant factor in the economic decision making of the Pennsylvania household. Most of the uncertainty stemmed from four sources: the vagaries of life and death; of climate and weather; of the market; and of individuals wielding power. Pennsylvanians coped with these problems by acquiring knowledge or relying on the knowledge of experienced individuals; by an extensive network of family and friends to fall back on in times of need; by diversification of production; by using the government to maintain order and stability; and by keeping a close eye on institutions and individuals who might develop a powerful influence over the economy.

Because the household was the unit of production as well as of consumption, the household economy was easily disrupted by any natural disaster which truncated the growth of the household before it reached "optimal" size—that is, mature family with several productive young adults. Widowhood, injury, or disease could leave the family outside the normal operations of the economy. Young families with small children at home were especially vulnerable to the loss of either parent. Not only would the producing unit itself be torn apart, but, as noted in chapter 1, these families were most likely to have been in debt at the time of the loss.

The community provided various forms of insurance for such situations. The first recourse was the horizontal extended family. Uncles, brothers, and brothers-in-law appear frequently in the records as guardians of estates or orphans. Provided there was enough land to place adult children in operating households, the advantages of having a large family extended beyond the productive capabilities of young single adults in the family unit. Long after the original household broke up, the siblings could be counted on to share the risks of life and death among them.[1]

Families could differ greatly in their ability or willingness to come to each other's aid. Historians implicitly assume that fear is the only mechanism by which families remain unified. Fathers controlled sons by refusing to give out land while the father was still alive. But the father-son relationship was not the only family tie operating in colonial Pennsylvania, nor was the threat of denying an inheritance the only mechanism by which a family could keep a son involved in the welfare of the whole. Relationships that developed between siblings could last through their respective lifetimes. Some family members operated out of genuine concern and a sense of responsibility for each other, which was carried into adulthood.[2]

Whether drawn to each other from fear or affection, from a desire to keep up appearances or genuine regard, the family that was able to provide a support network of grown siblings distributed the risks of an uncertain world among each other. Spreading risks among a large group, a function served today by the institution of the insurance firm, can greatly decrease individual costs, to the benefit of the whole. On the other hand, however, irresponsible behavior on the part of one sibling could risk the fortunes of all. An economically unwise love match, or careless behavior, could result in an elder sibling being called in to straighten out the mess. Families took a lively interest in each other's marriages, as an in-law became part of the group.

While the family was expected to provide a first line of defense for one another, there were times when the fortunes of the extended group could not cover the problems of a difficult household. The community and the church could be counted on to come to the aid of a family beset with unexpected misfortune. The Society of Friends (Quakers), in particular, considered it their responsibility to aid members of their group who had fallen into hard times. While they did not feel a similar responsibility to those who did not join them in "orderly Walking, honesty and plainness," the Quakers were responsible for the enactment of poor relief legislation from the beginning of Pennsylvania's existence as a colony.[3]

The final recourse was the township. A household that was forced to turn to the township, however, completely lost its identity. The children would be bound out to be raised in other households, and the adults would become inmates or servants with no independence of their own. With the family members separated and placed into other homes, the household would cease to exist. Much more fortunate the family that could turn to relatives or friends in times of trouble.[4]

The Quaker meetings not only stood between the householder and the unexpected misfortunes of life, but also attempted to lessen the uncertainties that resulted from participation in the market place. Quakers were required to conduct their business affairs with honesty and integrity. Irresponsible business practices could result in a member's ejection from the "Fellowship of Friends." According to the Book of Discipline distributed by the Philadelphia Yearly Meeting:

> It is the Business of the Oversears or other weighty Friends to Speak to and deal with [those, among others] . . . such as trade by sea or land or buy bargain or contract beyond their ability and such as keep not their words promises or Engagements in their dealings, or do not pay or Satisfie their Just debts according to time agreed on, those being a reproch to Truth, and a manifest Injury and Injustice.[5]

At no time does the Book of Discipline mention prices or interest rates, fair or otherwise. The sin was not in asking too high a price or usurious charge of interest, but in not living up to one's contract.

The insistence upon honesty in business dealings gave Friends an edge in international business. Any Friend who traveled abroad was required to obtain a Certificate of Removal from his monthly meeting certifying that he was a Friend in good standing. The certificates were used to demonstrate that no one was attempting to commit bigamy or otherwise abandoning a family elsewhere, but they were also helpful in the information they provided prospective business partners. Anyone in good standing with his Monthly Meeting clearly could not be under a cloud for illicit business dealings or heavy debts, either at home or abroad. A professed Quaker could be trusted in business.[6]

The Pennsylvania householder also had to face the vagaries of nature. The colonial economy was highly dependent upon agriculture, which in turn was highly dependent upon unpredictable changes in the weather and climate. The first response to this source of risk was knowledge. When a newcomer to the area came as an indentured servant, he was not only paying for his passage, but also learning the methods of husbandry useful to the area. In a similar manner, the "apprenticeship in husbandry" to which many locally born youths were bound involved the transmission of human capital in the ways of Pennsylvania agriculture: the "apprentice" learned not only his father's methods, but also those of the family with whom he was positioned for a while.

It is easy to see why almanacs were so popular during this period. The typical eighteenth-century Pennsylvanian was less inclined to pray for good weather than to study the signs and try to predict it. Almanacs purported to give certainty to an uncertain science: long-term prediction of the weather. In a more scientific effort to reduce uncertainty, the naturalist John Bartram, a Chester County farmer, gained international fame for his contributions in the new science of husbandry. Other colonists, less well known, also experimented with agriculture and husbandry. The less adventurous copied their better educated neighbors after such experiments proved successful.[7]

DIVERSIFICATION

Diversification of production provided the strongest hedge possessed by the Pennsylvania householder against risk. Diversification stemmed from a desire to make use of disparate resources to the fullest degree possible. At the same time, however, diversification lessened one's dependency on nature by decreasing the importance of a particular crop in total income. Diversification could also provide insurance against an unpredictable market in the same manner: by reducing dependency on one item.

Diversification of household production is not synonymous with self-sufficiency. The nature of Pennsylvania agriculture led to the production of a variety of agricultural products, some of which were marketed abroad, some marketed at home, and some indeed consumed by the household itself (as has always been typical of farm households). Two harvests of wheat were varied with the production of other grains, of fruits, of non-food crops, and of animals. But the Pennsylvania household also manufactured a variety of items, not only for home consumption, but also for sale. Despite large exports of flour, bread, and other foodstuffs to the West Indies and Europe, and despite the steady importation of manufactured items from abroad, the early Pennsylvania economy was sufficiently diversified to encourage internal trade to flourish much earlier than has been normally presumed.[8]

The typical Pennsylvanian was not a jack-of-all-trades, but rather master of two. Many city artisans were also shop-keepers, and in the countryside most artisans practiced husbandry as well. Adding the practice of a skilled craft to the usual two harvests of spring and summer wheat enabled an artisan/farmer to smooth out the flow of income. With older sons or bound labor to run the farm, the artisan could practice his craft year-round. Furthermore, labor could be acquired cheaper if an employer could offer education in a desired skill.

Many artisans whose estates were recorded in the Chester County inventories appear to have been practicing husbandry as well as their craft. Artisans known to be practicing a trade represent from 18 to 29 percent of all of the inventories; the true proportion could be higher, as an artisan/farmer was as likely to call himself a yeoman as to use his occupational designation. The frequency and value of livestock and grain in artisan's estates nearly duplicated that for the population as a whole (see table 2.1). Clearly artisans were practicing husbandry on the side. The personal estates of artisans averaged lower than that for the population, however, although some specific artisans held higher amounts of personal estate and weavers as a group appeared to have done well (see tables 2.2–2.4).[9]

The diversity of production in Pennsylvania was determined not only by comparative advantage in particular agricultural products in demand abroad, but also by the human capital brought to the region by the immigrants. Within a generation, immigrants had duplicated the pattern of the northwestern European countrysides from which they had migrated. Colonial Pennsylvanians showed no fixed attachment to farming as the only occupation, or to land as the only investment. Production decisions seem to have been determined by trade, by the market, and by individual decisions of households.

Table 2.1. Grain and Livestock Owned by Artisans in Chester County Inventories

	1717–1721	*1732–1737*	*1748–1751*
Livestock			
Average value, artisans only[a]	28.54	30.86	32.52
Percent of personal estate, artisans only	22.8	18.6	16.3
Percent of personal estate, all inventories	23.7	21.1	20.1
Percent of artisans with livestock	95.1	84.8	84.6
Percent of all inventories with livestock	88.0	85.0	83.0
Number of artisans	20	28	78
Artisans as percent of all decedents with known occupations	51.3	28.9	46.1
Total Grain			
Average value, artisans only[a]	2.64	6.11	5.99
Percent of personal estate, artisans only	2.1	3.7	3.0
Percent of personal estate, all inventories	3.0	2.9	4.6
Percent of artisans with grain	40.0	46.4	43.6
Percent of all inventories with grain	45.0	46.0	46.0
Number of artisans	20	28	78
Artisans as percent of all decedents with known occupations	51.3	28.9	46.1

SOURCE: Chester County Wills and Inventories, Chester County Archives. There were 83 valid cases in 1717–1721; 185 valid cases in 1732–1737; and 304 valid cases in 1748–1751. The values given are in pounds Pennsylvania current money, recalculated to control for changes in the price level using the Pennsylvania pounds to British pounds sterling exchange rates in John J. McCusker, *Money and Exchange in Europe and America, 1600–1775*, table 3.7, pp.183–185.

[a] Converted to pounds British sterling.

The primary industry throughout the colonies was agriculture, and Pennsylvania proved no exception. By the time Pennsylvania was settled, farmers in New York and New Jersey had already discovered the profitability of growing foodstuffs for the West Indies; Pennsylvania's first settlers immediately adopted the behavior of their neighbors and began growing wheat for export as flour and ship bread. Wheat remained the staple of the Pennsylvania economy throughout the century. Rapidly rising

Table 2.2. Value of Personal Estate by Occupation of Decedent in Chester County
Inventories, 1717–1721

Occupation	Value of Personal Estate[a]	Number of Inventories	Percent of All Applicable Inventories
Yeoman	131.73	11	28.2
Husbandman	51.66	1	2.6
Widow/spinster	140.84	8	20.5
Merchant	60.27	1	2.6
Carpenter	81.18	1	2.6
Shoemaker/cordwainer	103.32	2	5.1
Innkeeper	140.22	1	2.6
Joiner	64.23	1	2.6
Laborer	45.51	2	5.1
Smith	136.53	1	2.6
Tailor	105.78	1	2.6
Weaver	158.56	9	23.1
All applicable cases	144.51	39	47.0[b]
All inventories	159.60	83	

SOURCE: See table 2.1.
[a] Converted to pounds British sterling.
[b] Percent of all inventories.

demand for grains in Europe resulted in continually rising prices, particularly after 1750, despite the entry of additional farmers into wheat production along the colonial seaboard. Increasing returns for flour shipped abroad enabled millers to pay more for wheat, in turn covering the costs of greater and greater distances traveled by land or water to reach a mill. Immigrants pouring into the area could buy cheaper land farther out from the city without sacrificing their access to the international market: by the 1750s, even settlers in the Shenandoah and over the major mountain ridges in Pennsylvania were producing wheat for eastern millers. Planters on Maryland's eastern shore were producing wheat as well as tobacco, and other parts of the Chesapeake would follow suit as the century progressed.[10]

　　If increasing returns to wheat production meant the addition of producers who were farther away from the ports and

Table 2.3. Value of Personal Estate by Occupation of Decedent in Chester County
Inventories, 1732–1737

Occupation	Value of Personal Estate[a]	Number of Inventories	Percent of All Applicable Inventories
Yeoman	246.10	49	50.5
Husbandman	154.00	1	1.0
Farmer	158.00	2	2.1
Widow/spinster	162.67	9	9.3
Merchant	509.00	1	1.0
Gentleman	237.00	2	2.1
Carpenter	199.00	2	2.1
Cooper	138.00	1	1.0
Cordwainer/shoemaker	262.17	6	6.2
"Framework knitter"	133.00	1	1.0
Glazier	374.00	1	1.0
Joiner	283.00	1	1.0
Mason	174.00	1	1.0
Miller	91.00	1	1.0
Schoolteacher	40.00	1	1.0
"Shoemaker/tanner"	42.00	1	1.0
Shopkeeper	293.00	1	1.0
Smith	148.00	2	2.1
Tanner	344.00	1	1.0
Tailor	73.00	2	2.1
Turner	77.00	1	1.0
Weaver	106.00	10	10.3
All applicable cases	210.70	97	52.4[b]
All inventories	179.57	185	

SOURCE: See table 2.1.
[a] Converted to pounds British sterling.
[b] Percent of all inventories.

who thus had higher transportation costs, it also resulted in increased profits for those who already were producing wheat closer to Philadelphia and the major millers. These producers could have increased their own production of wheat, incorporating land either previously unused or employed in some other crop, but it does not appear that they did. Estate inventories from prosperous Chester County show that the average acreage planted in

Table 2.4. Value of Personal Estate by Occupation of Decedent in Chester County Inventories, 1748–1751

Occupation	Value of Personal Estate[a]	Number of Inventories	Percent of All Applicable Inventories
Yeoman	234.29	56	31.5
Husbandman	175.82	3	1.7
Farmer	188.18	3	1.7
Widow/spinster	161.54	28	15.7
Merchant	1403.51	2	1.1
Gentleman	361.73	1	0.6
Minister	226.68	2	1.1
Captain	219.38	1	0.6
Brazier (brassworker)	31.20	1	0.6
Carpenter	131.38	4	2.2
"Clothworker"	425.10	2	1.1
Coffinmaker	82.88	1	0.6
Cooper	61.91	2	1.1
Cordwainer/shoemaker	85.02	5	2.8
Fuller	119.93	1	0.6
Glazier	65.33	1	0.6
Innkeeper	456.30	1	0.6
Joiner	321.75	1	0.6
Laborer	47.04	4	2.2
Miller	146.25	1	0.6
Sadler	53.63	1	0.6
"Sawyer/turner"	176.48	1	0.6
"Shoemaker/tanner"	807.30	1	0.6
Shoekeeper	322.63	10	5.6
Smith	129.68	7	3.9
"Spinning wheel maker"	271.05	1	0.6
Surveyor	95.55	1	0.6
Tanner	376.35	2	1.1
Tailor	179.08	6	3.4
Turner	85.08	2	1.1
Weaver	213.56	25	14.0
All applicable cases	218.11	178	58.6[b]
All inventories	189.58	304	

SOURCE: See table 2.1.
[a] Converted to pounds British sterling.
[b] Percent of all inventories.

wheat actually declined slightly from 1720 to 1750, although the total acres planted in grain increased (see table 2.5). The average value of wheat in inventories rose dramatically, however—from £9.11s. to £14.8s. in the estates where wheat was present. Higher wheat prices meant higher incomes for the farmers in the developed areas. But high incomes to the west would also have encouraged developed areas to find their comparative advantage in diversification rather than staple production.[11]

As first noted by historical geographer James Lemon, crops other than wheat were grown throughout the period, mostly for domestic consumption. Indian corn was used for cattle feed and corn meal. Rye could be found on many estates along with wheat, although the value of planted rye per acre was much lower than that for wheat. Virtually every farm had a patch growing flax, as most households produced linen as well as woolen yarn. Some farms also grew hemp, encouraged by the legislature and London, with the intention of producing rope as a naval store. Without the subsidies, however, hemp could not be grown profitably in the colony. Some inventories included turnips, which were supposed to add to the ability of dairy cows to produce milk. Many farms also included apple orchards; about 10 percent of inventoried estates in Chester County included cider mills or presses.[12]

A well-developed farm in colonial Pennsylvania always had meadowland, cleared land used for the cattle. Throughout the period 1717–1751, livestock represented over a fifth of the total personal estate of a typical decedent in Chester County (see table 2.6). Cattle were used both for dairy products and meat, much of which was consumed at home, although some was exported abroad and some sold in local markets. Even town and city dwellers tried to find a place to keep a cow for milk. There appears to have been a growing local market for meat, and by the end of the period, the occupation of drover seems to have been on the increase, with meat packers near the city keeping large stocks of cattle to fatten up for slaughter. Hay appears in the inventory as a sizable item only toward the end

Table 2.5. Grains in Chester County Inventories

	1717–1721			1732–1737			1748–1751		
	Value[a]	Percent of Inventories	Percent of Deceased	Value[a]	Percent of Inventories	Percent of Deceased	Value[a]	Percent of Inventories	Percent of Deceased
All Inventories									
Harvested crop total	4.85	3.04	45	5.24	2.92	46	8.63	4.55	46
Wheat	2.96	1.86	41	2.99	1.67	42	3.69	1.95	38
Indian corn	0.05	0.03	13	0.21	0.12	17	0.35	0.18	17
Hay	0.09	0.06	2	0.00	—	—	1.37	0.72	26
Value of all grain on the ground	4.05	0.03	35	4.18	2.33	43	4.60	2.43	41
Value of wheat on the ground	1.77	0.01	34	2.22	1.24	41	2.57	1.36	41
Inventories with Grain									
Harvested crop total	10.87	6.81	45	11.41	6.35	46	19.03	10.04	46
Wheat	9.56	5.99	41	10.49	5.84	42	14.42	7.61	38
Indian corn	3.69	2.31	13	2.62	1.46	17	3.07	1.62	17
Hay	3.69	2.31	2	0.00	—	—	6.03	3.18	41
Value of all grain on the ground	11.58	7.26	35	9.67	5.39	43	11.55	6.09	41
Value of wheat on the ground	12.57	7.88	34	9.49	5.28	41	12.54	6.61	41
Acres planted in grain, total		12.8			15.6			16.0	
Acres planted in wheat		14.0			16.2			12.7	

SOURCE: See table 2.1.

[a] Converted to pounds British sterling.

Table 2.6. Livestock in Chester County Inventories

	1717–1721			1732–1737			1748–1751		
	Value[a]	Percent of Inventories	Percent of Deceased	Value[a]	Percent of Inventories	Percent of Deceased	Value[a]	Percent of Inventories	Percent of Deceased
All Inventories									
Livestock	37.86	23.72	88	37.91	21.11	85	38.12	20.11	83
Horses	17.04	10.68	83	17.17	9.56	82	19.35	10.21	79
Cattle	15.68	9.83	76	16.02	8.92	75	13.65	7.20	70
Sheep	3.10	1.94	49	3.07	1.71	57	2.47	1.30	54
Swine	1.41	0.88	47	1.35	0.75	46	1.46	0.76	51
Oxen	0.69	0.43	6	0.70	0.39	7	0.40	0.21	5
All Inventories with Livestock									
Livestock	43.10	26.97	88	44.39	24.72	85	46.02	24.27	83
Horses	20.60	12.91	83	20.83	11.62	82	24.57	12.96	79
Cattle	20.82	13.05	76	21.29	11.86	75	19.78	10.43	70
Sheep	6.43	4.03	49	5.42	3.02	57	4.81	2.47	54
Swine	3.09	1.93	47	3.04	1.69	46	2.95	1.55	51
Oxen	11.07	6.94	6	9.36	5.21	7	8.62	4.54	5

SOURCE: See table 2.1.

[a] Converted to pounds British sterling.

of the period. While early inventories contained almost no hay at all, the proportion of estates with hay jumped to about one-fourth by 1748–1751. A sudden interest in flooding and draining low-lying fields for the production of hay in the 1750s and 1760s appear to have been related to the appearance of meat packers near the city. The end of the period also saw an increase in dairying for the market. Butter was packed in kegs for the international market as early as the 1710s. Several Chester County farmers regularly sold butter and cheese to Coventry Forge. The inclusion of a butter print in one Chester County estate from 1751 suggests the household was marketing butter locally under their household trademark. Despite the increase in market activity for cattle products, however, the price of cattle remained about the same throughout the period.[13]

Sheep and pigs were also common items in eighteenth-century inventories, although the former were kept mostly for the production of wool rather than as a food. Pigs do not appear to have been permitted to roam as they were in the South; few inventories referred to swine presumed to be in the woods. The price of neither pigs nor sheep seems to have changed over time. While a few oxen appear in the inventories, most households used horses for animal power. "Working cattle" were present in some inventories, but were outnumbered by "working horses."[14]

Horses, unlike other livestock, appear both as a production and a consumption item in the typical colonial household. By the 1750s the price of a young horse could vary dramatically, from £2 for a "working horse" to £25 for a stallion. A "riding horse" was calculated as a separate item in most inventories, and the value increased steadily through the century. Some households seem to have been raising horses for profit: for example, William Kirke's estate contained an "interest in partnership of a Mare." Horsebreeding, and livestock husbandry in general, were effective methods for saving capital stock for adult children. A young household beginning husbandry frequently started out with livestock donated by their families.[15]

While agriculture was the main economic activity of colonial Pennsylvania, it was by no means the only industry. A wide variety of manufacturing industries were well established in Pennsylvania early in the century, not only in the city, but also in the countryside (see table 2.7). The manufacture of cloth and clothing, furniture, household and husbandry tools, buildings, processed food, and metal goods occurred throughout the province. Highly specialized craftsmen produced items for the market in Philadelphia, while more general manufacturers worked out of market towns, crossroads shops, and even on their own farms far away from the city. Major centers of iron production had developed by the 1720s and continued to grow dramatically in Coventry, Reading, and Manatawny, producing not only pig iron but molded products and nails. The foundation for the prosperous manufacturing industries of Pennsylvania in the nineteenth century could be found in the city and the countryside almost from the colony's inception.[16]

The most common manufacturing industries in the countryside were food processing and the production of cloth. Waterpowered grist mills served two functions in Pennsylvania. Farmers had millers custom grind their wheat for their own use, and millers bought wheat from the farmers to market as flour in Philadelphia. At first most millers performed both services. By the end of the period, however, a class of large-scale commercial millers had appeared in distinction to those who concentrated on custom work. Special stones imported from France produced superfine flour greatly in demand abroad. For example, Strode's Mill, built in 1723, used French stones to grind high-quality flour (see figure 2.1). Registered brands and the Philadelphia inspection system guaranteed that high quality would be rewarded with high prices in the overseas market. The high prices in turn enabled commercial millers to keep their mills open nearly year-round with wheat bought from as far south as Virginia and as far north as New York.[17]

Second to flour milling, but probably involving more people, was the production of cloth. As early as the 1720s, a

Economic Performance

Table 2.7. Variety of Occupations in Colonial Pennsylvania, 1717–1755

	Philadelphia		Loan Office Mortgages 1725–1755	Chester County Inventories		
	Freedom List 1717	Tax List 1754		1717–1721	1732–1737	1748–1751
Selected Occupations						
Yeoman	—	1	2033	11	49	56
Husbandman	—	—	—	1	1	3
Farmer	1	1	—	—	2	3
Laborer	4	78	5	2	—	4
Widow/spinster	3	58	69	8	9	28
Gentleman	—	9	59	—	2	1
Merchant	10	174	47	1	1	2
Professional						
Clerk/scrivener	—	10	4	—	—	—
Lawyer/attorney	—	20	5	—	—	—
Minister	—	9	—	—	—	1
Pharmacist	1	1	—	—	—	—
Physician	1	25	5	—	—	—
Schoolmaster	—	13	1	—	2	—
Surveyor	—	1	1	—	—	—
Cloth/Apparel						
Blew dyer	—	—	1	—	—	—
Brass button maker	—	—	1	—	—	—
Clothier	1	—	1	—	—	—
Clothworker	—	—	1	—	—	2
Collarmarker	1	1	1	—	—	—
Feltmonger	6	—	4	—	—	—
Framework knitter	—	—	—	—	1	—
Fuller	2	—	10	—	—	1
Glover	—	2	1	—	—	—
Hatter	—	33	2	—	—	—
Shoemaker	18	96	1	—	—	—
Silk dyer	—	—	1	—	—	—
Staymaker	—	8	1	—	—	—
Stockingweaver	—	13	—	—	—	—
Tailor	16	75	60	1	2	6
Weaver	3	6	87	9	10	25
Woolcomber	1	1	2	—	—	—
Woolmaker	—	—	1	—	—	—
Food						
Baker, male	8	61	2	—	—	—
Baker, female	1	2	—	—	—	—
Bolter	2	1	—	—	—	—

Table 2.7. (Continued)

	Philadelphia		Loan Office Mortgages 1725–1755	Chester County Inventories		
	Freedom List 1717	Tax List 1754		1717–1721	1732–1737	1748–1751
Brewer	3	5	8	—	—	—
Butcher	—	27	10	—	—	—
Malster	1	—	—	—	—	—
Miller	—	5	47	—	1	1
Slaughterer	5	—	—	—	—	—
Victualer	—	—	4	—	—	—
Vintner	—	11	1	—	—	—
Other food	—	10	—	—	—	—
General Trade						
Carter	9	11	4	—	—	—
Cooper	19	50	44	—	1	2
Porter	3	10	—	—	—	—
Trader	1	—	—	—	—	—
Wagon maker	—	—	1	—	—	—
Waterman/shallopman	—	14	—	—	—	—
Wheelwright	2	5	9	—	—	—
Retail						
Barber	6	22	1	—	—	—
Haberdasher	—	—	1	—	—	—
Innkeeper, male	10	5	17	1	—	1
Innkeeper, female	1	1	—	—	—	—
Shopkeeper, male	21	58	8	—	1	10
Shopkeeper, female	6	35	—	—	—	—
Stable keeper	1	—	—	—	—	—
Tavern keeper	1	64	1	—	—	—
Tobacconess	1	—	—	—	—	—
Tobacconist	—	13	2	—	—	—
Construction						
Bricklayer	3	19	6	—	—	—
Brickmaker	9	7	1	—	—	—
Carpenter	19	58	91	1	2	4
Glazier	3	6	3	—	1	1
Mason	1	—	43	—	1	—
Plasterer	3	10	2	—	—	—
Wood						
Cabinetmaker	1	—	—	—	—	—
Carver	1	1	—	—	—	—
Chairmaker	1	12	1	—	—	—

Table 2.7. (Continued)

	Philadelphia		Loan Office Mortgages 1725–1755	Chester County Inventories		
	Freedom List 1717	Tax List 1754		1717–1721	1732–1737	1748–1751
Joiner	15	38	20	1	1	1
Sawyer	3	5	5	—	—	1
Spinning wheel maker	—	—	—	—	—	1
Turner	3	5	14	—	1	1
Leather						
Bootmaker	1	—	—	—	—	—
Cordwainer/shoemaker	18	96	89	2	6	5
Currier	3	—	—	—	—	—
Leatherdresser	1	1	—	—	—	—
Sadler	10	13	21	—	—	—
Skinner	—	14	12	—	—	1
Shoemaker/tanner	—	—	—	—	1	1
Tanner	5	10	25	—	1	1
Metals						
Blacksmith	11	18	—	—	—	—
Blockmaker	2	6	1	—	—	—
Boltmaker	—	—	2	—	—	—
Brazier/brassworker	2	4	—	—	—	1
Cutler	4	6	2	—	—	—
Founder	2	3	—	—	—	—
Goldsmith	3	3	—	—	—	—
Gunsmith	—	2	5	—	—	—
Hammerman	—	—	1	—	—	—
Ironmonger	—	1	2	—	—	—
Locksmith	—	1	2	—	—	—
Nailmaker	—	2	—	—	—	—
Pewterer	2	2	—	—	—	—
Silversmith	—	12	—	—	—	—
Smith	4	16	84	1	2	7
Stonecutter	—	3	2	—	—	—
Tinsmith	—	4	1	—	—	—
Whitesmith	1	—	—	—	—	—
Shipping						
Boat maker	—	5	—	—	—	—
Captain	—	58	—	—	—	1
Mariner/seaman	10	68	7	—	—	—
Rigger	1	2	—	—	—	—
Ropemaker	3	3	1	—	—	—

Table 2.7. (Continued)

	Philadelphia		Loan Office Mortgages 1725–1755	Chester County Inventories		
	Freedom List 1717	Tax List 1754		1717–1721	1732–1737	1748–1751
Sailmaker	6	5	—	—	—	—
Ship carpenter	—	5	—	—	—	—
Shipwright	27	6	22	—	—	—
Miscellaneous Manufacturing	19	74	14	2	—	5
Artisan as percent of all persons listed[a]	100.0	88.9	26.4	21.7	17.8	27.6

SOURCE: Philadelphia Tax List, 1754, Philadelphia City Archives; for the mortgages, see table 5.1; for the inventories, see table 1.1. For the freedom list, "Minutes of the Common Council of the City of Philadelphia."

Note: The freedom list was a list of applicants for the "freedom of the city" of Philadelphia, or the right to practice a trade. Of the 425 applicants, 82, or 19.3 percent, did not list an occupation.

[a] All trades except husbandry, "widow/spinster," gentleman, and merchant.

report intended to soothe the Board of Trade's fears of illegal cloth manufacturing in the colonies contained the following:

> in the Colonies of New England, New-York, Connecticut, Rhode-Island, Pennsylvania, and in the County of Somerset in Maryland, the People have fallen into the Manufacture of Woollen and Linen Cloth for the Use of their own Families; but we could not learn that they had ever manufactured any for sale in those Colonies; *except in a small Indian Town in Pennsylvania* [emphasis added], where some Palatines had then lately settled.[18]

Home production of cloth with professionals providing custom services in weaving and fulling existed side by side with the production of cloth and clothing for the market. Production of wool cloth for the market was of course illegal throughout the Empire after 1699; wool was the primary manufactured product of England and a subject of some of the earliest mercantilist regulations. Recent historians of the Pennsylvania German population have found that the Germans, many of whom had been practic-

Figure 2.1. Strode's Mill, Rte. 52, Chester County, Pennsylvania. Built in 1721, Strode's Mill was used to grind wheat as late as the 1950s. Reproduced with permission of the Chester County Historical Society, West Chester, Pennsylvania.

ing weavers back in Germany, manufactured and sold wool and linen products in the market; evidence from county records show that cloth manufacture flourished among all the settled nationalities. Coventry Forge bought and sold locally produced linen.[19]

Many households kept sheep for wool or grew flax to make linen. Female members of the household were generally responsible for breaking and combing raw flax and wool and spinning it into yarn, although there were women who were paid for spinning. Household members seldom did their own weaving, however. A local weaver either custom wove the material for a household or bought spun yarn and sold the finished product. If the material was wool, it might then have to be "fulled," another job usually done by a professional. Fulling mashed the dampened wool until the fibers blended together; the wool cloth might then also be "tented" or stretched on racks to dry in the air. Some frontier households apparently fulled material themselves, with all household members and perhaps neighbors gathering to stamp the material in "bees" not unlike a quilting bee. But such activities seem not to have persisted for long. Water powered fulling mills, with stones to do the work of the pressing, appeared in the colonies as soon as grist mills; in fact they were frequently in the same location. The same mill race that powered one mill stone could be employed to power two as well. Customwork fulling was replaced early in the nineteenth century by the influx of cheap cotton cloth produced both locally and in Britain. Fulling mills, common throughout the Pennsylvania countryside until the mid-nineteenth century, gave way to factories that brought the various parts of the wool-manufacturing process together.[20]

After the linen or woolen cloth was manufactured, it could either be returned to the household to be made into clothing or sent off to a local taylor or seamstress ("tayloress"). The option was also available to employ a professional dyer to color or add a pattern to the cloth. Finished clothing was seldom sold in shops, although one widowed shopkeeper in Lancaster County sold shirts on the side. Stockings, on the other hand, could be purchased through the various country and city shops. Stocking manufacture, common in the British countryside a century earlier, apparently flourished in Pennsylvania during this period. The same producers easily manufactured stockings for their own households, on specific order from neighbors, or to sell to peddlers and shopkeepers. While most stocking knitters in the account books were women, at least one professional "stockinweaver" practiced his art in Chester County before 1715, and a "framework knitter" worked at his trade until the 1730s. Finally, while some householders apparently kept the tools and possessed the knowledge to make shoes, shoemakers and cordwainers operated shops and roamed the countryside practicing their trade. Samuel and Anna Nutt at Coventry Forge bought large numbers of shoes (as many as thirty to fifty at a time) from local shoemakers at 6s. 6d. They sold the shoes through their store at 7s. 2d.[21]

The woodworking trades provided a third major line of manufacturing. Waterpowered sawmills produced chestnut and walnut lumber for the manufacture of a variety of furniture items; one Chester County artisan even imported mahogany. Chairs, tables, and bureaus, in a wide range of qualities and prices, were manufactured in the countryside as well as in the city. Both John Moore and Joseph Hibberd manufactured spinning wheels. The latter's estate also contained 228 unfinished chairs. In fact, chairs were manufactured in large numbers all over the colony; Francis Swaine of Caln in Chester County operated a turning mill as well as a sawmill, presumably for the manufacture of chairs in bulk.[22]

A variety of construction professions could be called upon in the countryside a well as in the city by the established householder who wished to build a substantial house. Not surprisingly, most professional builders lived in Philadelphia or in the major trading towns in the countryside. Even those who built their own houses, as most farmers undoubtedly did, could call on the services of a glazier to mount the windows.[23]

Metalworking provided the last major industry in the colony. As in the case of the millers, the industry early split into two types of practitioners—the local smiths and metalworkers who manufactured goods on custom order, and the owners of the large ironworks built in the Coventry and Manatawny regions of the province. In Philadelphia, metalsmiths produced a variety of silver, brass, pewter, gold, and iron products; almost as many different types of goods (although most likely not anywhere near the quality) could be found produced in the countryside as well, with steel added by mid-century.[24]

By the 1720s another form of metal manufacturing had already become well established in the colony. Iron furnaces supplied pig iron as ballast for Pennsylvania shipping. Coventry Forge also sent iron west to Conestoga and Donegal, receiving linen in return. A variety of cast iron products were produced and sold locally. The iron mines, foundries, forges, and even slitting mills for nail manufacture of Anna and Samuel Nutt, William Branson, Thomas Potts, John Taylor, and others quickly made them both wealthy and powerful in the province. In contrast to the metalworking artisans who continued to practice in the cottage system, the owners of large ironworks in the Coventry and Manatawny region early developed large communities of dependant workers in a preshadowing of the nineteenth-century company town. Unlike the southern iron works, which employed slaves on isolated plantations, the Pennsylvania foundries and forges used large numbers of wage laborers.[25]

Ironmongers wielded a great deal of power in Pennsylvania. The foundry owners, for instance, were able to have passed an early law prohibiting the sale of liquor within two miles (later expanded to five) of a foundry. Furthermore, in the only two cases appearing in the evidence where the General Loan Office exceeded its legal limit, William Branson and John Taylor were loaned £350 and £460 respectively.[26]

In addition to these major industries there were in the Pennsylvania economy many specialists in trade, ranging from peddlers who roamed the countryside to international merchants and shippers. Both historians and contemporaries have been fascinated by the rapid development of the merchant class in Philadelphia in contrast to its slower emergence in some southern colonies. The cause has most frequently been attributed to the nature of Philadelphia's staple export. Wheat made use of several secondary industries before shipment. While there is something to be said for this argument, milling, the most important of the secondary industries, operated outside the city and did not by itself produce Philadelphia's merchant class.[27] Rather, the very diversity of Pennsylvania's products and their destinations probably enabled a merchant class to develop within the colony. Rarely did any one person own an entire shipment, and rarely did the ships all head to the same destination. In the Chesapeake, entire ships were filled with tobacco and sent straight for London or Liverpool. The tobacco trade could easily be directed by the already developed merchant houses in England. Because of the diversity of origin and destination for shipments from Philadelphia, however, location became an advantage to the Pennsylvania merchant.

GROWTH, EQUITY, AND EFFICIENCY

There are a variety of yardsticks that can be used to measure an economy's performance. The three most common are growth, equity, and efficiency. Economic growth refers to sustained changes in income per person, where income is the flow of goods and services available to an economic unit over time—nation, province, household, or individual. When the economy grows steadily the income available in each generation increases, leading to a range of expectations about life and the future that will be far different from those in a society where the economy is stationary or declining. An economic boom is a period in which income per person grows rapidly; in a decline or a depression income levels fall. An economy may experience long-term growth despite a series of short-run dislocations every few years, although the short-run bouts of negative growth will affect people's experiences and perceptions of well-being.

Equity will be used here to refer to the distribution of income and wealth in a society. Clearly a society with a high level of economic growth, but a great deal of inequality in the distribution of income, will be different from one in which the level of economic growth is not perhaps quite as high, but the distribution of income is more equitable. Equal levels of growth would have been perceived quite differently in Pennsylvania and in the West Indies, where the institution of slavery resulted in highly inequitable distributions of wealth and income.

Finally, an economy's performance can be judged on the basis of its degree of efficiency. Economic efficiency results when the goods and services desired of the economy can be produced at the lowest possible cost to the community. In general, increases or decreases in economic efficiency will be positively correlated with changes in the rate of growth of the economy. Relationships which promote growth may have the reverse effect on equity, and vice versa; a growing economy might not be as efficient as it could, or an efficient economy might stagnate.

The economy of colonial Pennsylvania, however, can be judged to have performed well by all three standards.

The Chester County inventories supply insights into the growth in wealth in colonial Pennsylvania before 1755, provided the sample is limited to families in the same stage of the life cycle. Eighteenth-century estates were inventoried when a will had been registered or a court case was involved. Householders with children were most likely to have wills to govern the distribution of their estate: those without wills were likely to have estates end up in court over the guardianship of the children or the handling of the estate. As a result, there is a much greater proportion of inventories for these groups than would be expected by their frequency among all decedents. The eldest householders are well represented by inventories, but it is difficult to determine whether they were still operating a working productive unit (that is, whether the decedent remained the head of the household with adult children at home), or whether they had given up that function. Limiting the study to households in stages three and four—young and mature families—will be the closest we can come to comparing a homogeneous group over time.[28]

The figures on the young and mature households suggest that the increase in personal estate found for all inventories concealed some dramatic variations over time (see table 2.8). There appears to have been little change in the average real personal estate between the period 1717–1721 and 1732–1737. Average values of the personal estates jumped dramatically from 1732–1737 to 1748–1751, however, increasing by 23 percent for the mature families and by a stunning 71 percent for the young households. The value of livestock actually fell, as households continued to diversify away from husbandry. On the other hand, the value of financial assets in the estates, along with the estimated value of cash, rose steadily through the three periods.[29]

The relationship between increases in wealth and increases in income is not always stable, however. If the increases in wealth represented increases in the capital stock, then the

Table 2.8. Young and Mature Households and Personal Assets

	Stage 3[a]	Stage 4[b]	All Inventories
1717–1721			
Personal estate	181.89	194.08	159.60
Financial assets	7.16	23.10	43.70
Cash	—	—	2.97
Livestock	32.18	33.46	43.05
Number of inventories	17	14	83
1732–1737			
Personal estate	171.63	203.71	179.57
Financial assets	41.11	33.14	64.05
Cash	—	—	4.47
Livestock	22.60	29.43	44.39
Number of inventories	46	21	185
1748–1751			
Personal estate	293.54	250.29	189.58
Financial assets	106.44	85.02	69.36
Cash	—	—	7.09
Livestock	20.23	26.96	47.32
Number of inventories	48	24	304

SOURCE: See table 2.1.

Note: Personal estate, financial assets, cash, and livestock converted from value in pounds Pennsylvania currency to pounds British sterling to control for price movements over the time period.

[a] Young household: minor children only.

[b] Mature household: adult children at home and adolescents.

added productive capabilities of the economy should have resulted in increases in income in later years. To some extent the increases in value of personal estates of young and mature households represented an increase in items used for consumption, such as books and clocks, rather than production. The inventories also show an increase in household items used to produce other goods—spinning wheels, cheese presses, cider mills, and beehives (see table 2.9.) Not only were the items produced with the household tools used within the family, but yarn, stockings, cheese, butter, cider, and wax were regularly sold in the market to buy other goods, presumably also for consumption.[30]

Table 2.9. Frequency of Selected Items from Chester County Inventories

	Percent of Inventories with Specific Item		
	1717–1721	*1732–1737*	*1748–1751*
Spinning wheels	34.9	47.8	57.1
Wool	22.9	22.6	32.7
Flax	22.9	22.0	32.7
Clock	3.6	14.5	17.8
Cheese	7.2	5.4	7.6
Cheese press	10.1	8.6	15.5
Churn	14.5	7.0	19.8
Cider mill	3.6	8.1	12.9
Bees	6.0	11.6	9.9
Books	38.6	43.0	49.2
Number of inventories	83	185	304

SOURCE: See table 2.1.

Financial capital, physical capital, and human capital all increased during this period, showing the degree to which the community was able to add to its stock of wealth. The increase in financial assets far exceeded that in personal wealth, quadrupling for the mature households and mushrooming by a factor of fifteen for the young households. Investment also occurred on the land. The ratio of developed to undeveloped land increased throughout the period as farmers continued to divide holdings. While the amount of cleared land for each plantation remained the same, the concurrent rise in number of plantations resulted in an increase in the amount of cleared land for the same region. Investment in human capital should not be forgotten as well; when possible, a household tried to buy a trade for a son through an apprenticeship.[31]

It would appear then that both the ability of Chester County households to save as well as the amount they were able to consume rose over the period from the 1730s to the 1750s. The increased wealth shown in the estate inventories was the result of an increased capacity on the part of households to produce income; they divided that additional income into additional consumption as well as additional savings.

If the proportion of income devoted to wealth accumulation did not increase over the time period in question, then increases in wealth accumulation can be used as a conservative proxy for increases in income. The assumption will also have to be made that the value of real estate holdings increased at the same rate as the value of the personal estate, as there are no accurate sources of data for the nominal value of real estate. Using changes in holdings of personal wealth to estimate growth in income per capita, then, it must be concluded that the Chester County economy experienced substantial growth between the period 1717–1721 and 1748–1751. Income per capita grew at a level of .6 percent a year on average. When the analysis is limited to families with children, to control for the variance in inventoried estates across age groups, the growth rate is even higher. Income per capita grew at a rate of .9 percent a year for mature families and 1.65 percent a year for young families. This last figure is comparable to growth rates found in the nineteenth century, when income per capita grew at the rate of 1.4 percent a year.[32]

The most important aspect of economic prosperity in Pennsylvania in the mid-1700s, however, was probably not the size of the increase in per capita income, but the experience of increasing income itself. The absence of severe bouts of negative growth due to famine, disease, or war, was probably at least as important as the rate of growth itself. Pennsylvanians consumed higher incomes in the enjoyment of large, healthy families, the individual members of which enjoyed a life expectancy far in excess of that in Europe. Except in Philadelphia at the end of the period, serious epidemics were unknown, and historical demographers by and large agree that the population was very healthy by eighteenth-century European standards.[33]

Equity can be measured by the distribution of wealth in a society. Inventories omitted too many people on the bottom end of the economic scale to provide a reliable source for the distribution of wealth. Counties in Pennsylvania were permitted to levy taxes on their residents at the rate of 1 to 3 shillings per pound assessed holdings of real estate and livestock. However, assessed value of real estate holdings as recorded by the county fell so short of the known value of real estate holdings of residents that, unfortunately, it had to be concluded that the tax rates could not be used to calculate the actual value of holdings of physical wealth. They are probably fairly accurate, however, in the sense that they provide a *ranking* of the wealth-holders in the county. That is, the proportion by which real estate was severely undervalued in the rates was probably similar for all residents, so that the relative values are reliable even if the nominal values are not.[34]

Historian Lucy Simler has observed that another problem with the tax lists is that often tenants were included as landowners, as they, not the landlord, frequently paid the tax on the land. To the extent that a tenant owned the improvements on the land (see chapter 3), as well as the livestock, the distribution would not be terribly skewed because of this practice.[35]

An analysis of Chester County tax lists suggests that, for most county residents, the distribution of wealth changed little between 1729 and 1754 (see table 2.10). When calculating the distribution of wealth and income, the most difficult segment of the population to trace is the mobile population at the lower end of the scale. Indentured servants did not appear in the tax records at all during this period. Single householders on their own would have appeared as "freemen" and would have been expected to pay a special 6s. to 9s. head tax because they had no dependents (a tax higher than that paid by 90 percent of the other householders). The very poorest families appeared under the designation "poor" and paid no taxes at all; there were no householders so listed in 1729 and only 2 percent were considered "poor" in 1754. Inmates also paid no taxes. As defined by Lucy Simler, inmates were "dependent" people living on another's land, generally with a family of their own to support. Freemen were not included in the calculation of wealth distribution, as there is no way to judge how much wealth they possessed. Those labeled poor, and inmates, were included as potential taxpayers who were so poor they were assessed no taxes at all.[36]

Table 2.10. Wealth Distribution in Chester County

Percent of Taxpayers	Percent of Assessed Wealth[a]
1729	
Top 10 percent	31.8
Top 25 percent	47.6
Top 50 percent	69.1
Bottom 10 percent	7.5
Bottom 25 percent	10.9
Bottom 50 percent	31.9
Total number of taxpayers = 1,498	
1754	
Top 10 percent	27.5
Top 25 percent	46.5
Top 50 percent	73.2
Bottom 10 percent	5.4
Bottom 25 percent	10.7
Bottom 50 percent	26.8
Total number of taxpayers = 3,384	

SOURCE: Chester County tax lists, Chester County Archives.

[a]The freeman's tax of nine shillings per head in 1729 and six shillings per head in 1754 was not included, although inmates and the poor were included as possessing no wealth. The tax was ordered at a rate of 3 pence per pound assessed wealth in improved real estate and livestock in 1729, and 2 pence per pound in 1754. However, the rates seriously underrepresent wealth holdings. As a ranking, they are probably fairly accurate.

The number of inmates increased substantially over the period 1729–1754. The effects of this increase, however, depends on who these people were and why they lived as inmates. Some inmates were apparently unfortunates—widows, householders with disabilities—who could still avoid poor relief by working for a wealthier householder. Others were householders with families who could not afford to live elsewhere and were probably trapped as inmates through the cost of having to support their children. A large group of the inmate population appears to have derived from the very large numbers of formerly bound youths able to earn sufficient levels of income (room and board and perhaps daily wages) to keep them out of bondage, but without enough capital to set up their own households. To the extent that it was a temporary, and probably expected, part of the life cycle, this period of dependency as an inmate did not restrict either future opportunity or present sense of well-being. And to the extent that immigration of bound labor was increasing throughout the period, the added numbers of freed young people is sufficient to explain much of the expansion in the number of inmates listed in the tax records.

These categories are obviously quite different in nature. It makes quite a difference which kind of inmate is appearing in the statistics: those who became inmates through misfortune; those simply passing through the category of inmate as an expected part of the life cycle; and those living in the company towns at the iron works. Until the dimensions of the category of "inmate" are better understood, it is hard to tell what the increase in the number of inmates means. Does it signify a breakdown in the family insurance system, the beginnings of industrialization, or merely a rise in the number of young people in the population?

As can be seen from the above discussion, inequities could be found in the distribution of wealth in Chester County. Furthermore, as time passed, wealth differences became more noticeable between the settled upper portion of the population and the newcomers. On the other hand, Pennsylvanians enjoyed a system far more equitable than that in Europe. There were very few who could be called a landed aristocracy (the Penn family and other owners of manor lands lived in England, not in Pennsylvania). While there were groups of landless and dependent people, they were by no means comparable to the roaming bandits in the French countryside or the beggars and street people in eighteenth-century Paris. The stereotype of the colonial Pennsylvania countryside as a relatively equitable society before 1755 is not far from the truth.[37]

The final measure of the performance of the Pennsylvania economy is that of efficiency. When compared to other economies of the time, indeed, when compared to Pennsylvania as a state one and two hundred years later, the Pennsylvania economy seems to have been extremely flexible and efficient. While we do not have any means of directly measuring the economy's productivity, one measure of its success was its degree of diversification. For a society which had been established for only one generation, Pennsylvania enjoyed a respectable level of diversification, and as the economy continued to develop—as more people poured in, as more roads were built, and as the city of Philadelphia continued to grow—the economy continued to diversify. There were very few institutional barriers to trade. Unlike the Puritans, the Quakers had few philosophical objections to merchant activities or to earning interest from money loaned. As for the government, the long arm of Britain was not long enough to reach across the Atlantic Ocean effectively. The provincial government of Pennsylvania was too weak to hamper trade against the wishes of the majority of the population, and the local governments were never asked to do so.

For the majority of the population, the basic economic goal was not the strength of the nation or the glorification of their religion but the prosperity of the family unit. If families were to pass on their way of life to all of their children (in a very prolific society), the economy had to grow. As will be seen in the following chapters, Pennsylvania colonists used government basically as a rule-setter and arbitrator. When government action increased the ability of families to add to their own income, it was welcome and obeyed. But laws which impeded plans for family prosperity were simply ignored.

CHAPTER THREE

Land Use in Pennsylvania

The household economy of Pennsylvania depended heavily on land distribution, which in turn was determined by government policy. Land policy derived first from the law. When legal mechanisms interfered with the household goal of settling all adults on arable land, however, the community created its own land policy by using the court system and the rule of custom.

LAND POLICIES OF THE PENN FAMILY

All land in Pennsylvania that had not already been granted under Swedish patent became William Penn's when he was named proprietor of Pennsylvania. Land policy in Pennsylvania thus stemmed originally from William Penn's own policies toward the province. As the century progressed, land policy would continue to be the Penn family's major interest in the government and would spark most of the conflicts between the settlers and the proprietary family.[1]

William Penn's own land policies derived from three sometimes conflicting purposes: his need for a source of income and store of value in the land for his family; his desire for an ideal community of Quakers built along the Delaware; and his awareness that both goals would be better met if development of the area occurred rapidly. Penn's desire to earn income led him to reserve the right of quitrents when he released land to settlers. This practice was a major source of contention with the provincial government throughout the colonial period. His need for a manorial preserve of land to hold for future generations led him to keep some land off the market entirely. Meanwhile, his plans for an ideal community of Quakers resulted in attempts to force immigrants to settle the land in the English village pattern, with homes close together in a village community surrounded by working fields. Plans for township grids yielded almost immediately to the need to develop the region rapidly and the settlers' adamant refusal to adopt such a restrictive pattern. Manors and quitrents were a continuing source of tension. But the final result of Penn's settlement plans and the rapid development of the area was a wide variety of options in landholding patterns.[2]

The manorial lands kept by the Penn family were intended to preserve a base of income and power for future generations. Penn and his heirs did not use the manors as a source of current income. That is, they seldom leased them on a long-term basis to tenants. To the contrary, they were fearful of devaluing the land by defoliage or rough treatment by tenants and occupied much of their agents' time fighting off squatters and trespassers. Each of the manors was settled with an overseer or a ranger whose duty it was to report attempted settlements, round up livestock, and prevent the cutting down of timber by neighboring planters. The major manors included Rocklands in northeastern New Castle County, Richland and Perkasie in Bucks County, Moreland and Springfield in Philadelphia County, and Conestoga and Paxton on the frontier. The Penns also owned manors in New Jersey. Conestoga gave them the most problems. Because Conestoga was so far removed from normally traveled routes, settlers could live there several years before the Penns found out. As the region developed it became increasingly impossible to keep settlers off the manorlands. By the 1740s, the Penns were ready to settle tenants on the manorlands and sell parts of others, ordering their agents to prepare long-term leases in the style of the other manors in the colonies.[3]

The Penns were not the only owners of manorlands in Pennsylvania. At the beginning of the settlement of Pennsylvania, William Penn had followed the usual practice in England of selling off entire townships to developers who promised to bring settlers into the region. Two major blocks of land were settled in this fashion. The first, the Cox-Vincent-Thompson purchases of six townships, much of which was later bought by the West New Jersey Society, was the source of a bitter suit throughout the second half of the century between the Penn family and the Society. The second, three townships in Chester County owned by the London Company (London Grove, London Brittain, and New London), appears to have developed early into an area favored by the artisan-farmers described in chapter 2. These manors, Pikeland, Vincent, and the London townships, were run in the same fashion as manors in New York and Maryland. Tenants developed sizable farms on the land on a long-term, informal basis, with rights to all improvements and negotiable leaseholds.[4]

The manors proved successful as income-producing property as long as the company had reliable agents. If the owners wished to liquidate, however, the manors could present a problem. John White, a London merchant and early manorial landlord, experienced unexpected difficulties trying to sell off his property in the 1740s. His nephew, John Swift, sent as his agent to disburse the land, was soon informed by neighbors that he would have to offer tenants the first choice of purchase at a price the tenants considered reasonable—that is, not including improvements. Otherwise, Swift informed his uncle, they would "burn their fences and go away into Virginia, and never be heard of more."[5] The difficulty of removing tenants and reaping the gain in land value from development led Penn agent James Steel to write to John Paris in London in 1737,

> Thy Project of Settling a number of Familys will not as yet answer any purpose to advantage, and therefore in my opinion it will be better to let the Land ly as it is, under the care of some honest person dwelling near it to preserve the Timber from spoile, than to place a number of People on it that will at the End of a Term of years render it less Valuable than the same would be without any such Settlem[en]t. We have in this Prov-

ince seen several Instances of the same kinde but scarce one turn out to the advantage of the Owner of the Land, and therefore I think it will be adviseable to have a little Patience while the Inhabitants in that Part of the Province [upper Bucks] may be Encreased which in a few Years will undoubtedly come to pass. . . . I make no doubt but this Tract, when the adjacent Lands are settled, will Increase in Value much more than by putting Tennants on it.[6]

One of the few times the Penn family tried to use its power as proprietors in an obviously illegal manner to acquire more land occurred over what was called "Cox's Land" in Chester County. In 1686 Penn sold two townships each to three of his friends—Matthias Vincent, Major Robert Thompson, and Dr. Daniel Cox, then Governor of West New Jersey—with the promise that they would settle the land in 500 acre plots within twelve months. Five years later, Cox sold his portion to the West New Jersey Society, a collection of land speculators already involved in similar transactions in the Proprietorship of West New Jersey. The land was settled shortly after the colony was established, although settlers apparently were aware that they could not purchase the land. No formal leases were signed, but as the West New Jersey Society's agents paid taxes on the land, most likely they were collecting rents as well. In 1738, an agent from the West New Jersey Society began making rounds through the area agreeing with the tenants there on a rent. According to common law, such verbal agreements were as good as contracts—once the tenant had paid rent and the landlord accepted it, a long-term contract was assumed unless the parties had agreed in writing to the contrary. It was the usual practice for the landlord's agent to renegotiate the rent regularly with the tenants, as a certain amount of turnover took place. Thomas Penn, however, took this as an opportunity to add to a perceivedly inadequate stock of proprietary manorlands—and a particular lack of manorial property in prosperous Chester County.[7]

Shortly after the visit of the society's agent to Vincent, Penn sent the sheriff of Chester County to inform both the agent and the residents that the proprietors knew of no claim by the society to those lands and that they were still owned by the proprietors. Deputy surveyor Samuel Lightfoot was then sent to survey all the lands in the township. Lightfoot first refused to survey the lands of the long-term tenants of the society, instead returning surveys of the surrounding areas that were not occupied. Sent back by the proprietors in 1743, Lightfoot finally surveyed the tenants' properties, under the protest of the tenants. Naming the property Callowhill Manor, the Penns sent an agent with preprinted, three-year leases for all the tenants to sign. At least 89 of them did, after a few had been arrested by the sheriff for trespassing. Three-year leases were produced again by the Penns in 1746, and the West New Jersey Society appeared to have been defeated. In 1758, however, the society signed formal obligations with all the tenants, agreeing to reimburse them for all expenses incurred in the battle with the Penns. The society then went to court.[8]

The society offered a better deal to the tenants than the Penns. All the Penns would give were three-year leases, with no right of ownership of improvements. All along, the society had permitted ownership of improvements and agreed to long-term leases, which were negotiable in the market. As a result, the tenants testified for the society in court and the Penns lost. The Penns had a technical loophole in their favor—Cox had not settled the land within twelve months as agreed; but the courts ruled that custom had determined that the land was indeed Cox's to sell to the West New Jersey Society. The Penns had waited too long to use the loophole. Even then, the case was not finally settled; there would be more lawsuits. But custom in the country won over the Penns' presumed powers as proprietors.[9]

The land the Penns reserved to themselves as proprietors and that which William Penn sold to his friends for manors represented only a small part of the land available in Pennsylvania. By and large, most land was sold to settlers themselves, with the reservation of the quitrent. The Penns believed that legally *all* the settlers were their tenants; indeed, in much of their correspondence the word "tenant" is used freely to mean almost any resident of Pennsylvania. When William Penn first sold land in Pennsylvania, he reserved for himself the right to an annual payment, or "Quit Rent," in lieu of other feudal rights to which a feudal landlord was legally entitled. Quitrents varied in amount depending on the year that the land was patented but generally ran about a penny per acre. Payable in wheat or flour in addition to "ready money," quitrents were never a very large percentage of average colonial income—and because no provincial taxes were levied from 1711 to 1755, they were much less of a tax burden than a settler's counterpart would have had to pay in England. Penn saw the quitrent as a tax on the inhabitants for the duties he performed as proprietor. Given his expenses to acquire the charter from the king and protect it from Lord Baltimore, he did have a claim on reimbursement. More than that, however, Penn felt that he was a benevolent lord to his constituents and that they should *want* to pay him some sort of reward for his kindnesses. The "tenants," on the other hand, believed that they had paid enough by incurring the risks of settling an undeveloped colony. If greater lobbying was necessary in London, it should come out of the normal costs of government and be voted by the representatives. The settlers were well aware that Penn had other sources of income if he chose to use them (i.e., he could settle the manorlands with tenants rather than leave them empty); they had bought the land and felt he was entitled to no more payments. Under pressure from his agent in the colonies, James Logan, Penn agreed to sell quitrents in a lump sum under certain circumstances, but he adamantly insisted on his entitlement, as did all successive generations of Penns.[10]

In a colony where the provincial government could not collect general taxes because of noncompliance, quitrents predictably proved extremely difficult to collect. A provincial law restricting collection to the spring harvest, when farmers would have the wherewithall to pay, exacerbated the difficulties inherent in the situation. There was not enough time, nor enough agents, to go from door to door every year, so planters were supposed to travel to well-advertised central places where an agent would be posted to collect the payments. Poor record keeping did not help, either. At times, it was very difficult to prove whether someone had or had not actually paid. Finally, given the complete dislike of quitrents throughout the colony, it was nearly impossible successfully to prosecute for avoidance of payment.[11]

When Thomas Penn arrived in Pennsylvania in 1733, one of his primary goals was to straighten out this difficulty and secure the steady source of income to which he felt he was entitled. By then, the southeastern portion of the colony had been sufficiently settled that a system for collecting quitrents could be more easily developed. Penn selected specific townships, prosecuting for collection and forcing targeted settlers to pay. Then Penn's agents went from township to township making up quitrent lists. Whenever a land transaction occurred, an agent was usually there to make sure quitrents were paid. The Penns and their agents eventually even used the General Loan Office to collect some of the quitrents. Whenever a mortgage was made, quitrents in arrears were deducted before the sum was given out to the mortgagor. Even as quitrent collection was being improved in the settled southeast, however, James Steel was having all the old problems collecting them in newly settled Lancaster County. Every year for six years, from 1734 to 1740, he wrote to a deputy in Lancaster County that this would be the year when a list would be made up so that quitrents could be collected; every year passed with no such list made. He sent his agent a stack of printed announcements informing the countryside to appear in Lancaster Town on the appointed days to pay; but every year, without specific lists to go by, the agent reported that few appeared to pay. Until transportation and government networks were well enough organized to force compliance, the settlers' view of the payments as an unfair tax won over the Penns' legal rights.[12]

One final restriction on the general purchase of land by settlers did not even last into the eighteenth century. Penn was not alone among colonial planners in his dreams for township settlement with a little community of neighboring houses surrounded by patches of farmland. There appears to have been a nostalgic desire on the part of many seventeenth-century religious utopians for a particular kind of supposedly communal "English village." Penn's ideal village appears in plan very similar to the ideal village of the Puritans in New England earlier in the century. Presumably, high moral and religious standards could best be maintained in a physically close-knit community, where everyone lived together in mutual self-support (and criticism). Both the Puritans and Penn, however, were foiled by the practical needs of the pragmatic colonial farmers. They preferred the time saved in not having to walk to distant fields to the warm togetherness earned by living in the town. Penn's settlers accomplished in less than one generation—in a later period of time, and without the authoritarian discipline—what New Englanders took three generations to achieve. Despite the formal plans for township grid settlement, Pennsylvanians soon adopted the isolated farm plan that would epitomize the American countryside for the next three centuries. As late as 1751, Thomas Penn would write to James Hamilton complimenting him on his settlement of a new township, but wondering why the blueprint of central town settlement had not been followed when the region was actually settled. The township was settled as the residents, not the Penns, wished.[13]

The only lasting effect of the Penn's explicit land policies were the quitrent battles, which were really very minor in terms of actual income lost, and the manorlands reserved for the Penns and their friends. Settled late in the colonial period in the middle of an already successful economic region, Pennsylvania never needed the protection that other colonies needed in the formative stages of their growth. In the end, implicit land policy as developed through custom by residents themselves proved more important in terms of the amount of land in use and the number of people affected.

LAND USE AND THE COURTS

William Penn envisioned a clear set of steps by which land would be sold to individual buyers. First, a prospective settler would request a warrant for a survey from the Land Office. The warrant referred to a number of acres of uncontested land in a specific region of the colony. After inspecting the area and determining exactly where he wanted to settle, the buyer would have the property surveyed by one of the official surveyors or their deputies. Once the survey was returned to the Land Office, the land could be formally bought from the proprietors. The purchase price would be paid, sometimes in installments, and the settler would receive a patent signifying he owned the land. At the time he would make arrangements for payment of quitrents, and under certain circumstances he could buy the quitrents outright. The last step, as required by law in all land transactions, would be registration of the deed in the county seat.[14]

While Penn expected all of these steps to proceed smoothly, there were problems inherent in the number of requirements. Each step required payment of a fee and often a trip to Philadelphia or the county seat. The surveyor and his retinue needed room and board and transportation as well as the fee. Furthermore, because it was so difficult to predict how much time each of these steps would take, no formal deadline for completing any of them was established. As a result, no one noticed if the process dragged on for generations. It was thus easy for landowners to put off the inconvenience and expense of going through all the steps to own the land clear of all incumbrances.[15]

There were temporary blocks to the formal purchase of a settler's land as well. In 1705 William Penn mortgaged the entire colony, not including the government; until his heirs paid the mortgage off in the 1720s, even his agents could not legally grant title. Furthermore, throughout the colonial period the Three Lower Counties, Lancaster County across the Susquehanna, and southwestern Chester County were tied up in litigation with Lord

Baltimore over whether they belonged in Maryland or in Pennsylvania. The practice of accepting lesser property rights began during this period of uncertainty. Only a very small portion of the colony was afflicted with these land contests after the mortgages were paid off in the 1720s. However, a precedent had been set. The Penns' agents and the courts had accepted settlers' rights of ownership in cases where no patent had been bought nor a deed registered.[16]

Because of the uncertainty surrounding Penn's rights to grant lands in the first two decades of the century, a survey was usually sufficient to prove ownership of land. There was, of course, an element of risk associated with ownership of land on any level beneath that of clear title and formally registered deed. In practice, however, once a settler had acquired a survey which clearly delineated his metes and bounds, for all practical purposes he possessed the land. A resurvey could take away land not formally patented, but the courts and the Penns discouraged encroachments, siding with earlier settlements. In several disputes the Land Office gave a later arrival a new warrant to find some more land upon the discovery that a prior settler had surveyed land—without recording the survey or taking out a patent—and developed it. Before the Seven Years War, an outsider simply could not purchase a patent to land already under another's warrant if the prior owner had developed the land. Furthermore, the Penns and the courts always turned to the neighbors of the earlier landowner for consultation before settling disputes when two claimed to have developed the same land; ownership by custom always won over ownership by a piece of paper. After the Seven Years War, through a period of decades from 1760 to 1790 in different areas of the province, the deed would replace custom in determining true ownership, causing more than a few conflicts between absentee owners of patents and settlers with surveys whose land had been passed down to them through wills and articles of lease and release. Before 1760, however, declared intent to purchase, through a warrant, the testimony of neighbors that everyone *believed* the householder did own the property, and productive development of the land formed the strongest proof of ownership a household could possess.[17]

The lowest level of land rights was that of "quiet possession," what later generations would call "squatters' rights." Quiet possession, or uncontested settlement for a period of at least seven years, essentially gave a family rights of first purchase. If they could not or would not purchase the land, the household considered itself entitled at least to payment for the improvements, and custom upheld that right. Improved land was almost always worth considerably more than unimproved land: the rule of thumb was £50 per 100 acres for unimproved land, and from £100 to £200 per 100 acres for improved land. Improvements included cleared land, fences, barns and other outbuildings, houses, meadows, ditches, and orchards. The value of the improvements could be diminished by poor treatment of the property such as deforestation, poor crop rotation practices, or shoddy building. In general, however, improvements added rather than detracted from the value of the property. A clear legal distinction was made at the time between the land itself and the improvements upon the land. The improvements did not automatically belong to the true landowner if another placed them there with the owner's tacit consent. Hence the "quiet" in quiet possession: a letter denying the settler's right to occupy or improve the land was sufficient to demonstrate the possession was less than quiet. The absentee owner of large tracts of land placed that ownership in jeopardy if he did not keep watch for squatters.[18]

Settlers felt they had rights of ownership to improvements they had placed on the land; they also firmly believed they were entitled to convey that ownership to another settler through an article of agreement or a will. For squatters, however, this right was never positively acknowledged in the courts. While improvements during a period of quiet possession entitled the original settler to compensation, settlers who later bought those improvements found themselves in a weak position when their ownership of the improvements was contested by a later purchaser of the land itself. That did not keep squatters from selling their improvements, nor others from purchasing them. Ulster Scots seemed to be particularly prone to buy and sell improvements on land to which they had no legal rights. Along the western and southern boundaries of settlement, Ulster Scottish families had a reputation for spending a few years developing the land, selling to an incoming family, and moving on, eventually down the line into Virginia. The Ulster Scots were even known to sell improvements on the Penns' manor lands, lands which were not supposed to be occupied at all.[19]

While quiet possession gave fairly clear rights to the family which originally made improvements on the land, it was highly risky to buy such improvements, and it could be difficult to prove that one's family had indeed been the original owners. Furthermore, the land could not be surveyed, as the surveyors were strictly forbidden to work on land which had not been previously warranted in the Land Office, no matter how long the settlers had occupied or developed it. As a result, the safest route was to purchase the warrant. Even the Ulster Scots were willing to purchase such insurance. There are several cases in the warrants where the same Ulster Scot family can be seen moving along every three to five years, taking out another warrant to develop a new patch of land after selling the improvements on the first. A warrant was uncontestably assignable. Warrant rights could be bought, sold, and passed on to designated heirs. Warrant rights thus represented a marked improvement over quiet possession.[20]

The settler who purchased a warrant right now owned the improvements and could sell them, but he still did not own the land underneath them. Warrant rights, or "improvement rights," were valued in inventories at a much lower rate than ownership of the land outright. Ranging in value from £50 to £150, however, the rights to improvements were nothing to scoff at and formed a major source of investment for beginning homesteaders. The right to sell this investment proved to be important for two reasons. The settler was not confined to one geographic location. He could move on to a new township or move to a better farm. Moreover, the settler's heirs were able to inherit the value of the investment he had made during his lifetime, even if for a variety of reasons they were unable to live on the land themselves.[21]

Once a certain level of development had been reached by both the settler and his neighbors, however, it was considered wise to have a survey made. A survey prevented encroachment, by a neighbor's planting improvements on a section of land claimed by the settler, or by another's survey encompassing some improvements already made by the original settler and unnoticed at the time of the survey. Once a survey had been made and returned to the Land Office, the land was considered to belong to the householders, even when they did not buy a patent and register the deed. It has been estimated that about half the landowners at the time bought and sold land through articles of lease and release, believing they and their purchasers owned the land outright, and never bothering to complete the final steps of patent and deed registration. Some patents remained unpurchased well into the next century, although a series of land disputes in the 1760s and the 1790s pushed most landowners into the final step of buying their patents.[22]

There were other ways to hold land in Pennsylvania besides routes leading to eventual land ownership. As noted above, long-term leases were available on the large manor lands owned by various land speculators, including the London Company and the West New Jersey Society, the Vincent family, and the Pike family. For our purposes, a long-term lease will be distinguished from a short-term lease not by the actual number of years but by the question of ownership of improvements. If the tenant owned the rights to the improvements through the length of the lease, then it will be considered a long-term lease. If the landlord owned whatever improvements were made on the land, then it was a short-term lease. There appear to have been three major varieties of long-term tenancy arrangements: informal lifetime agreements; leases specifying a certain number of years, 21 or 35 being common; and 99-year or 3-lifetime leases.

According to common law, a tenant was presumed to have occupancy of the land for his own lifetime or the lifetime of his landlord, barring other formally written agreements. Once a tenant paid his rent and the landlord accepted it, an informal agreement was presumed to have been made for lifetime for that amount of rent, providing the land was not abused. Improvements made by the tenant belonged to the tenant. When the tenant died, or when he sold his improvements to a newcomer, the informal lease was automatically renewed the moment the landlord accepted payment from the new occupier of the land, whether an heir or an assign. This was apparently the arrangement that existed in Vincent and Pikeland in the early 1700s. The West New Jersey Society sent an agent around to collect the rent, and he did so from everyone in general, thus automatically establishing new arrangements with newcomers as they paid their rent. These absentee landlords do not appear to have been particularly concerned about who occupied the land, how many improvements had been made, or who had bought or sold these improvements. As long as the land was not "abused," and their rent was collected on time, it was immaterial to them who was on the land.[23]

When the Penns brought suit over their Chester County lands, the society moved from informal agreements to signed 35-year leases. The leases guaranteed a certain rent for 35 years, no matter how much the land was developed. Under the leases, all improvements belonged to the tenant for the period of 35 years; after that time, however, the improvements apparently reverted to the landlord. It would have been interesting to observe how landholding patterns shifted to adjust to the changing ownership of the improvements as the end of the 35 years approached and new leases were negotiated; by that time, however, the society was getting out of the landlord business and had sold the land to the tenants.[24]

A third variety of tenancy, common throughout the colonies but apparently only introduced in Pennsylvania at the end of the period, when the Penns finally decided to lease out some of their manor lands, was the 99-year or three-lifetime lease. The name is a little deceptive because the leases never actually lasted 99 years. The tenant was asked to nominate three people whose "lives" would be entered into the agreement. The lease was good for as long as any one of the three "lives" was still valid—that is, until all three were dead—or until 99 years had passed, whichever came first. "Lives" could be substituted for a variety of reasons, specifically if a nominated "life" intended to move, but only if the "life" being replaced appeared to be in good health.[25]

Richard Peters, one of the Penn family agents, instructed his deputies to make out 99-year leases by using any three lives the tenants wished to nominate. The rent would be calculated by valuing the land, including improvements then standing, and estimating its price in fee simple on the open market. The deputy would then calculate 5 percent of that price as the annual rent that would be charged for the property. Peters wrote:

> When a Tenant pitches upon a Tract, and desires to have a Lease thereof, Estimate, in Sterling Money of Great Britain, the true and exact value of the Fee Simple of that Tract, at that time. . . . Then, the Quantities of the Yearly Rent, . . . must be exactly what would be one years Interest at the Rate of £5 Per Cent Per Ann. Sterling, upon the Sum that such estimated value shall amount to.[26]

Renegotiation of the lease, upon sale of the improvements or death of one of the "lives," involved a complicated formula for determining the new rent. The market value for the land, including all improvements that were then standing, was reestimated, and a new "rent" calculated as 5 percent of the new valuation of the land. The original rent was then subtracted from the new "rent," and that sum called the "rule." The "rule" was multiplied by a given number of "years," depending on how many of the original "lives" were still around, and that calculation determined the "fee" which was owed the proprietors within four years of the renegotiation of the lease. For example, if a piece of property was originally valued at £100, the annual rent was £5 no matter how many times the lease was renegotiated. Twenty years later, the property might be worth £200, and two of the three lives might still be around. The annual rent would remain £5, but the "rule" would be £5. Multiplied by, perhaps, 2 (the multiplier is not given in Peters' instructions, unfortunately), the "fee" would then be £10 to renegotiate the lease. The proprietors were thus capturing a percentage of the value of the improvements, and their portion depended on how long the tenants had been on the land and presumably benefited from the improvements themselves. But the tenants still captured most of the value of the improvements and the rise in land value, if it was due to reasons other than the addition of improvements.[27]

On land other than manors, short-term tenancy was far more common than long-term tenancy. In short-term tenancy, the tenant did not own the improvements, either because the landowner already owned the basic set of improvements necessary to run a farm or because the landowner wished to keep the building of improvements under his control. In either case, however, the tenant was compensated on the spot for any improvements he himself made on the property with the permission of the landlord. Short-term tenancy could occur in four cases: local investment in land intended for resale as land values rose during development of the region; local investment in land to secure a future plantation for a householder's sons; lands tied up in estates where minor sons could not yet put the land to work; and, in the cities, lots owned in large blocks by investors capturing both the expected long-term rise in city land prices and the annual rents from city tenants.

In practice, most long-term investors in undeveloped land did not place tenants on their property. As Steel commented to John Paris, tenants had an unfortunate propensity to behave as if the improvements did belong to them, making it very difficult to sell the land if the tenants were not compensated. Furthermore, tenants could actually lower the value of the land through careless use. James Logan tried to solve these problems by using twenty-one-year leases which left no doubt as to who owned the improvements and clearly stated Logan's expectations as to how the land was to be developed:

> before the Expiration of the Said [21-year] Term build a good substantial dwelling house of at least Twenty four feet in length and Eighteen feet in breadth with a good Barn and sufficient outhouses for the Use of Such a Plantation; That he or they [the tenant] shall within three Years after the date thereof plant an Orchard of at least One Hundred Apple Trees of good fruit and keep the Same well trimmed under a good Fence to the end of the said Term[.] That he or they shall not clear or occupy in cleared Land above the Quantity of One Hundred Acres in the whole on the said Tract[.] That he or they shall enclose all their cleared fields with Substantial Splitt Rails and as far as in them lies endeavour to raise Quickset hedges of Thorn Locustwood Privet or other woods proper for that purpose planted on the banks of Ditches cast up under the fences. That he or they Shall not plow or Sow any of the said Land after the first two years oftener than once in three years Save for Buckwheat only. That he or they Shall not on any pretence sell or dispose of any Timber or Wood from off the said Land, except such as can be spared from the fields to be cleared after a sufficiency is reserved for fencing such fields, nor commit any Waste or fall any Timber or wood on the Land reserved for wood save what shall be absolutely necessary for their own firewood and fencing, And That he or they shall at the Expiration of the said Term quietly and peaceably quitt and resign the said Land with all the Buildings and Improvements thereon made or to be made in good and sufficient Repair and all the fields Meadow and Orchard under good Substantial fences.[28]

The twenty-one-year lease does not appear to have been particularly popular either with tenants, who generally had more attractive opportunities, or with landowners, who disliked the idea of tying their land up with tenants for twenty-one years. Far more common were three- to five-year leases. Land leased on a short-term basis was usually already cleared, the heaviest burden in the process of improvement. Estate accounts where a plantation was being readied for short-term leasing sometimes also charged the estate with building a barn, repairing a house, or erecting fences. In the accounts the tenant himself charged the estate with digging ditches or other repair work, and simply paid an outright rent. When a widow remarried and remained on the estate, her husband was charged rent for the estate, and he in turn was reimbursed for the cost of raising his stepchildren. Lands were not permitted to remain vacant by death or temporary displacement for very long. If the owner would not sell, someone was usually willing to rent. A short-term tenant did not own the improvements; he merely leased the land. Houses, shops, bakeries, brewhouses, etc., in the city, were leased in this manner, as were mills in the countryside.[29]

Tenants in all the above-described cases generally owned enough in personal estate to be considered freeholders. They were often taxed for the land they were renting. In the case of the long-term tenants, this was a fair arrangement because the bulk of the value of the land came from the improvements. In a society which has at times been described as divided between "independent" and "dependent" people, tenants did not fall into the category of "dependents." As will be made clearer in the discussion of the economic effects of Pennsylvania's landholding patterns, tenancy was merely one of many options available for a householder to acquire the means to earn an income and to accumulate or spend capital.[30]

ECONOMIC EFFECTS OF LANDHOLDING POLICIES

The economic effects of the explicit land policies of the Penn family must be judged against the yardsticks of equity, efficiency, and economic growth and development. Policies could have made the distribution of income and wealth in the province more or less equitable. They could have enhanced or detracted from the economy's efficiency. They could have promoted or hindered economic growth (the increase in total income per capita over time) or economic development as reflected in the increase in population and trade.

Manors existed in Pennsylvania because of the privileged position of the Penn family and their friends. As elsewhere in the colonies, owners of enormous tracts of land acquired them through purchases at a price lower than the going rate per hundred acres for smaller tracts. The owners of large pieces of land were either friends of or agents for those in power in the government. William Penn acquired his lands because of his courtier relationship with the king. Members of the London Company were friends of the Penns in England, as were Vincent and Major Thompson; Cox and members of the West New Jersey Society were Penn's associates in the West New Jersey Proprietorship. The major local landholders included the Hamiltons (Andrew, Speaker of the House 1727–1739; James, Governor of the Province 1747–1754); William Allen (Chief Justice, 1750–1774); and James Logan (chief agent for William Penn, Chief Justice, Secretary of the Council, Acting Governor 1736–1738).[31]

Investors held onto large tracts of land for long periods of time because they expected to sell the land for a higher price eventually; to be successful they understood they had to realize a profit higher than the 5 percent or 6 percent annual interest they could have received had they loaned their money out at the going rates. The relative value of land, as opposed to other assets, could be expected to rise over time for a variety of reasons, including (1) if the economy experienced a period of inflation, increasing the value of real assets as opposed to financial assets, or (2) if the real productive value of the land rose, or (3) if population rose relative to the amount of land available, increasing demand for land relative to its productive value. There were no major periods of inflation after the introduction of paper money restored prices to their pre-recession level at the end of the 1720s. Land prices rose in Pennsylvania during this period mostly for the last two reasons: because the productive value of the land rose; and because of the increasing scarcity of desirable land close to Philadelphia. The rise in the productive value of land was attributable in part to the development of the region, as increases in trade allowed farmers to concentrate on the agricultural products for which their land was best suited. It was also attributable during this period, and even more so after 1750, to rising wheat prices, as Pennsylvania began to feed Europe as well as the West Indies. Finally, the productive value of land rose because of the improvements that had been placed thereon by the colonists.[32]

To the extent that Pennsylvania land speculators captured this increase in prices, it was simply a windfall gain and not because of any economic services they performed. Unlike Shenandoah Valley speculators in the 1750s and midwest land developers in the nineteenth century, Pennsylvania landholders did little or nothing to settle the land they owned; they simply held on to it until it rose in value. Their gain in wealth as a result of land speculation must be seen as an inequitable redistribution of wealth from the general landowners who settled the land and paid slightly higher prices for it as a result. Landowners who lived on and developed the land they owned also benefited from the general rise in land prices over time, but their profits could be seen as returns for the risks they took in settling a less-developed area. Indeed, in their early fights with Penn over the quitrent issue, this was apparently precisely the view they took.[33]

Land speculation did not always affect economic growth or development, however. The Vincent-Pikeland ("Cox's Land") and London Company lands were settled by tenants who developed the land as rapidly as the surrounding areas so that neither population growth nor growth in trade was curtailed by the use of those lands as manors. A few local land speculators did perform the function of a real estate developer as well, encouraging settlement in a previously undeveloped area to occur rapidly to the threshold point where advantages in specialization and trade could occur. The most notable example of this sort of development was the Hamilton family's activities in Lancaster Town. While near the Susquehannah, the Conestoga, and the Great Road to the frontier, Lancaster was not actually situated on any of the three. The Hamiltons' aggressive settling of large numbers of people with general skills in the town, coupled with the naming of the town the county seat (a result of their political connections), quickly took it to that "threshold" point where it became worthwhile to go the short distance from the river and the wagon road to pass through the town. By the mid-1700s Lancaster was the major terminal on the route west and the largest inland town in the colonies. It would eventually be the destination of the nation's first turnpike. Other towns developed in like fashion in the area included Chester and Darby in Chester County and Newport and Wilmington in New Castle County. Bristol in Bucks County, on the other hand, proved a dismal failure. It was too close to Philadelphia and too far from the rapidly developing southwest region.[34]

Those speculators who held large tracts of land off the market while refusing to permit settlers did for a time retard development and growth, however. Most prominent in this regard was, of course, the Penn family itself, with several sizable manors off limits to potential settlements. As the colony developed, however, the settlers refused to permit such prime land to go empty and pushed the Penns to take action. Faced with having to evict large numbers of squatters who intended to settle the land anyway, the Penns acquiesced and began leasing their land by the middle of the century.[35]

Tenants captured part of the windfall gains of the large land companies. It is doubtful that long-term tenancy as an institution would have existed in Pennsylvania without the prior grants of land in large amounts to Penns' friends; long-term tenancy did not exist in the province except on the original manorlands. As historian Sung Bok Kim first pointed out, long-term tenancy offered settlers the opportunity to earn income as farmers, even though they lacked sufficient capital to buy land. Improvements on the land represented capital investments, or savings, which they could recapture in selling the improvements to the new tenant. Furthermore, to the extent that the landlords were careless and failed to increase rents in proportion to the rising value of undeveloped land in general, the windfall gains from a regional increase in land value would also accrue to the tenant when he sold his improvements.[36]

Leases in Vincent (the West New Jersey Society

manor) actually sold for considerably more than many warrant rights did. Matthew Reading owned the "Right of an Improvement of 105 Acres of Land in Vencent [Vincent]" worth £80 in 1758; Thomas and Daniel Griffith each owned £100 worth of improvements on leased land in Vincent and Pikeland, respectively. Joseph Muckleduff owned improvements worth £95 in Springtown Manor (owned by the Penns). Peter Highet's "improvement" in New London (part of the London Society tract) sold for £108 after his death in 1750. And William Thomas willed 100 acres in Coventry, which he owned outright, to a younger son, giving the eldest son his "plantation on Pikesland," which he apparently valued higher.[37]

Tenants in Vincent also owned sufficient financial assets that, had they so chosen, they could have owned land elsewhere; some of the tenants in Vincent did indeed own land in other parts of Chester County. One enterprising "tenant" owned the lease and *rented* the lease out. Again, long-term leases could be a bargain for tenants, for not only did they capture the increase in land value from the improvements they made, but if the rents did not go up over time, they also could capture the part of the value of the general rise in productivity of the land resulting from increasing development of the region as a whole.[38]

Given that the proprietors permitted the purchase of large chunks of land before settlement, an inherently inequitable arrangement, long-term leasing did not retard either economic growth or development and probably reversed a little of the inequitable distribution of wealth. Tenants were never "dependent" on landlords because they were always free to sell their improvements at a market rate comparable to the value of improvements elsewhere in the colony. Furthermore, there is no evidence that tenants as a class owed substantial amounts of money to their landlords, another historical source of tenant dependency. There was always an affordable price for land if a settler was willing to live far enough out. As James Lemon has noted, long-term tenancy actively encouraged development by allowing settlers without sufficient capital to live on land close to trade routes. Tenancy was the option for those who wished higher incomes than those available in the areas where they could afford to buy land. Tenancy also provided an opportunity to diversify holdings of wealth to include financial and working capital, and not to be limited to real estate alone.[39]

Short-term tenancy was one step further along the spectrum away from investment in real estate and toward higher incomes along trade routes. It was no accident that the highest incidence of short-term tenancy could be found in the towns and cities. Artisans invested money in human capital (learning their trade), tools, inventory, raw materials, and accounts receivable (the revolving credit any successful artisan had to offer his customers). In the early stages of an artisan's career, he could not afford also to invest in real estate. Later on, some apparently chose not to, holding greater amounts of financial assets such as bonds and entering into commercial transactions by buying pieces of ventures abroad. The Wharton family can be considered a prime example of an artisan family (Joseph Wharton, the founder, was a cooper) which from the beginning demonstrated a preference for commercial and financial ventures over real estate. In terms of the options available, it is interesting that the London Company townships (London Grove, London Brittain, and New London) seem to have held a disproportionate share of artisan-farmers, who invested part of their capital in the running of a manufacturing business rather than putting it all into real estate.[40]

Short-term tenancy was only one option for a young householder with little in the way of capital. Undeveloped land in Lancaster County and down into the Shenandoah was always inexpensive during this period. Mortgage money was available to buy improved land in any part of the colony (see chapter 5). Tenants acted out of choice from a preference for using land solely to produce income (as artisans rented a shop), choosing either to save or not, and to invest their savings elsewhere rather than either go into debt to buy land or to buy land outside the Philadelphia trade routes—"away from the Philadelphia market," as Lancaster County residents described themselves. Given unequal endowments, from inheritence, from length of time in the colony, from fortune or misfortune, tenancy offered a means of acquiring a capital stock while earning income at a high rate and without going into debt. To reiterate, tenants were not considered dependent upon their landlords, not by tax collectors nor by pollsters nor by their neighbors. Tenancy increased the rate at which the colony developed; to the extent that tenants used their increased income to accumulate capital, the distribution of wealth and income was probably improved as well.[41]

The varieties of landownership resulting from the customary land policies in the Pennsylvania countryside also increased the development of the colony. Virgin land could be acquired cheaply in Pennsylvania on a promise of future payment and the payment of a few fines. The usual cost of effective landownership was the cost of a warrant, purchased from either the Land Office or the prior owners, and a survey or resurvey. Those purchasing developed land had to pay for improvements as well, which could triple the cost of buying the land. But four-year mortgages were common, as were intergenerational transfers. As previously noted, the family with grown unmarried children acquired capital swiftly to enable each member successfully to set up a landowning household upon marriage and dispersal.

The practice of allowing quiet possession obviously increased the rate of development, as those who could not have afforded to purchase land were able to develop it quickly. The practice of selling those improvements, however, appears to have resulted in a class of specialists in land clearing, families adept at working the land to an initial state of income-producing readiness. The Ulster Scots seem to have had a talent for land clearing, selling their services to incoming families who had enough capital to avoid the backbreaking and low-income first years of starting a farm.

In terms of land distribution, colonial Pennsylvania probably met the economic goals of equity, growth, and efficiency better than any of the other colonies. To a large extent, this was true not because of specific policies developed by the Penns but because the economy was able to benefit from the already developed economies of New York, Maryland, and the

West Indies, skipping the period of economic dependency other colonies had experienced upon settlement. The land polices developed in the colony as the settlers chose; when they conflicted with the plans of the Penns, the settlers went ahead anyway. In their implicit land policies, Pennsylvanians rewarded economic development and growth which would benefit future generations. Furthermore, Pennsylvania settlement patterns would provide a model for the land policies applied to most of the new nation as the population moved west in the next century.

CHAPTER FOUR

The General Loan Office and Paper Money

All was not well with the economy of Pennsylvania in 1720. The first boom in the flour trade overseas had ended. Entrepreneurial profits gained in the early years of the West Indies trade disappeared as other competitors entered the field. The growth of domestic trade had presented the colonists with a new problem: the money supply was not increasing as fast as trade, and further specialization of domestic output threatened to be choked off as colonists found themselves without a usable, efficient medium of exchange. To make matters worse, the South Sea Bubble caused a credit crunch in England with reverberations in Pennsylvania. As the crisis unfolded, colonists were at first bewildered and then dismayed by the effects on colonial trade of the financial crash in London.[1] Philadelphia merchant Jonathan Dickinson wrote to friends:

> Running into Stocks and Bubbles . . . [may] prove fatall to us in all the Plantations for when this Devouring Stock hath Destroyed the Bubbles . . . who will Govern Trade in all its Branches? [September 1720] . . . The produce of all america is sunk in its value since the Nation of Great Britain hath ever into Stock and Jobbing which is said to advance some men's fortunes and sink others what the thing is in itself or wherein the Great Benefits that may accrue Is a mystery to us at present. But we are thus sensible that the Products of all the Plantations are Greatly Sunk and Trade Declining. [October 1720] . . . The deplorable calamity that has happened by South Sea Stock has ruined Trade Sunk

the Currency of money and by our last account all things were at a Stand. [May 1721][2]

Contemporary observations and the little information we have on the Pennsylvania economy point to the severity of the depression of the early 1720s. Flour prices were low, both in absolute terms and in comparison to prices of New York flour. Shipbuilding came nearly to a halt, and early iron works failed. English immigration had slowed, and while some German immigrants were beginning to arrive, the very large numbers of German and Ulster Scottish immigrants would not come until later.[3] As Benjamin Franklin would write in his autobiographical papers:

> I remembered well, that when I first walk'd about the streets of Philadelphia, . . . I saw most of the houses in Walnut-street, between Second and Front streets, with bills on their doors, 'To be let;' and many likewise in Chestnut-street and other streets, which made me then think the inhabitants of the city were deserting it one after another.[4]

The Pennsylvania legislature responded with an unusual burst of activity, producing more economic legislation than was enacted in any other two-year period in the colony's history. The legislatures of 1722 and 1723 enacted laws to tax imports from neighboring colonies (a defensive measure: Maryland and New York had already enacted similar laws); lowered the usury ceiling from 8 to 6 percent; established a bounty for the production of hemp; prohibited the use of molasses in manufacturing beer in order to encourage the use of locally grown hops; expanded the liquor excise to include a tax on imported molasses, cider, hops, and flax; established an inspection system for export flour and ship bread ("biscuits"); printed £45,000 paper currency; and created a loan office to lend the paper money to owners of land and houses at 5 percent interest.[5]

By the end of the decade, when the economy had recovered from the depression, the bounty on hemp, expanded import duties, retaliatory duties against New York and Maryland, and molasses restriction were either repealed or permitted to lapse. The usury ceiling remained in effect, technically, but aroused little discussion. Inspection of flour and bread, printing of paper money, and issuance of long-term loans at below-market interest rates survived the depression of the 1720s to remain the central focus of explicit economic policy in Pennsylvania up to the Seven Years War.[6]

The primary policy response of the Pennsylvania legislature to this depression was to print fiat money and issue it on long-term loans at 5 percent simple interest to owners of land and houses. Printing paper money in Pennsylvania involved more than an increase in money supply. Fiat money itself can be seen as a financial innovation, a type of money more efficient for the purposes of domestic trade than the sorts of money already in use in the colony at the time. The printing of controlled amounts of paper currency in Pennsylvania in the mid-1700s led to increases in real income both because it enabled the money supply to meet the needs of an expanding economy and because of the decreases in transaction costs brought about by the replacement of awkward forms of commodity moneys by paper.[7]

A variety of moneys were used in trade in Pennsylvania in the first decades of the 1700s. A distinction can be made between money that was negotiable abroad and money used solely in domestic trade; a further distinction should be made between money which held its value over time and money which was liable to fluctuations, in some cases extreme fluctuations. The most high-powered form of money in the colonies was, of course, specie, gold and silver. Specie could be used in transactions anywhere, was not particularly difficult to ship in the amounts used in colonial trade, and during the eighteenth century did not suffer wide fluctuations in value. Coin could be clipped, it was true, but merchants were well aware of the problem and had developed satisfactory mechanisms for dealing with it.[8]

The problem with specie was that it was in chronically short supply throughout the colonial period. Historians and contemporaries alike have blamed the balance of trade with

Britain, but the problem lay elsewhere.[9] While colonists imported more goods from abroad than they exported, the difference was made up in the amount of capital exported to the colonies from Britain. Had colonists consistently made all the payments they were supposed to according to the level of trade, they would eventually have been forced to curtail that trade because they lacked the means of payment. But merchants carried the colonists on their books for decades, rolling over debts or transferring them to others, in an informal financing scheme by which the capital formation of the developing colonial economies was financed through the savings of the more developed British economy. The returns were not in explicit interest rates but in the high charges for imported goods which made it worthwhile for British merchants to continue carrying the debts: most assuredly, London merchant houses would not have kept the colonists in a debtor relationship for generations had they not been profiting by the arrangement.[10]

The lack of specie was thus not the result of an adverse balance of payments. When English merchants bought Chesapeake tobacco, instead of sending back to America the payments in specie, the London merchants credited the planters with a positive balance in their running account in London. Given that much of what the planters wished to buy with the proceeds from tobacco production came from London, the system worked fairly easily and avoided constant transfers of specie from one side of the Atlantic to the other. A planter who wished to make a purchase from someone other than the buyer of his tobacco would simply draw a bill of exchange on his account in London, using his merchant house as a bank. The only problem was that the merchant in London had use of the funds until the planter's bills of exchange came through; the planters were well aware of this, however. They, too, most likely received implicit interest when their balances were positive; it showed up in the services a merchant house typically rendered for the American planter in arranging purchases, ferrying about visiting relatives, and otherwise performing the services of an agent.[11]

Bills of exchange drawn on London merchant houses

passed as money in the colonies from an early period. Bills were endorsed and passed from hand to hand, with their main drawback being their lack of easy divisibility. In practice, bills of exchange were often used for large purchases and specie for small. While some danger always existed of a bill being returned, actual cases where bills were contested were relatively rare, given the volume in use. Most merchants only dealt with bills of which they were sure. Between bills of exchange and coin, the latter mostly Spanish dollars, the money supply was generally adequate for the expanding international trade.[12]

The problem came when the domestic trade began to grow as settlers poured into the region and the economy began to diversify. Colonists found themselves forced to use a variety of commodity moneys in local trade as transactions increased far more rapidly than the money supply. When commodity moneys were inadequate, colonists changed their methods of meeting payments, thereby increasing velocity. When that failed, the colonists found economic growth stunted as transaction costs mounted in the absence of a more efficient form of money.

To understand the problems caused by an inefficient money supply, it is necessary first to summarize why money is useful. Money can be said to perform the following functions in an economy: (1) unit of account; (2) medium of exchange; (3) store of value; and (4) standard of deferred payment. Forms of money can also vary in degree of portability, durability, and acceptability. In Pennsylvania, the standard unit of account (even before the paper money emissions) was "pounds Pennsylvania currency," based on a legal exchange rate. Pennsylvania account books do not show any other unit of account at any time in the colony's history.[13]

Pennsylvania's problem in 1722 was the lack of a medium of exchange:

> nor need we dive any farther than into our own Pockets, to convince us, that a running Stock of Money now wanting is the Cause of this Decay [in trade]: The common Necessities for Families brought to the Market are, not to be bought, because Change (as *Silver* and *Copper* is commonly called) is not to be had.[14]

It was as a medium of exchange that paper money would prove such a useful innovation. All mediums of exchange serve in some manner to reduce the search and delivery costs of trading. When some commodity is acceptable in exchange by all possible partners, no time need be wasted searching for a possible trading partner with exactly the right good to offer: any buyer of the trader's product will do, as will any seller of the desired good. An efficient medium of exchange should reduce delivery costs as well, requiring fewer indirect transactions than an inefficient medium, and it should be physically least costly to transfer of all the options.

A variety of commodity moneys were used as mediums of exchange in the colonies, some more successfully than others. Pure barter was not common practice in the colonies. Pure barter takes place without a medium of exchange: the commodity produced is exchanged directly for the commodity consumed. Every producer must find a potential consumer who in turn produces exactly what it is that the first producer wishes to consume. The result is only a minimal amount of trade, which is restricted by the immense information and transaction costs of matching up precisely the right buyers and sellers—if they exist at all.

While it is true that the staple products of most of the colonies were used at one time or another as money, this practice was not the same as barter. The situation is rather that of near-barter, or of commodity money. An item is chosen because it will satisfy a number of purchasers, and it is used as money in most transactions. In near-barter, the chosen item is accepted as money generally because most consumers feel that others will also accept it in trade, not because it is a specifically desired item at the time. A commodity money can represent an improvement over barter because it reduces the search costs associated with finding the right purchaser of a good; commodity moneys vary, however, in their ability to decrease other costs of exchange.

The type of commodity that best performed the functions of money was, of course, specie—gold, silver, and copper. Specie was available in the colonies, however, only in direct proportion to trade conducted with specie-holding countries. Specie was a product that had to be purchased from abroad. It could be acquired only in exchange for exports of goods or services. Thus tied to the international market, specie could not be acquired in sufficient amounts to service the fast-growing domestic market.

Faced with insufficient supplies of specie, colonists relied on other commodities as mediums of exchange. Tobacco functioned quite effectively in the Chesapeake as a form of commodity money throughout the colonial period. Always negotiable abroad, tobacco was used in so many transactions that contemporary account books from the Chesapeake frequently include a column for tobacco drawn in after the usual ones for pounds, shillings, and pence current money. Nearly everyone marketed tobacco, so it was widely acceptable for use in transactions. Tobacco's usefulness as a form of money in the Chesapeake was enhanced by laws drawn up in the mid-eighteenth century in Virginia and Maryland requiring the exchange of export tobacco for inspection notes at government warehouses; the inspection notes circulated quite easily as money. In fact, as long as increases in the quantity of tobacco produced coincided with the increase in population in the Chesapeake, the tobacco colonies had no problems with that part of the money supply used for local transactions.[15]

Sugar products and tobacco, in demand abroad, thus functioned quite well as commodity moneys. These goods served as money much the same way as did specie, although specie was more portable and, during this period, held its purchasing power better. Other forms of commodity money used in the colonies, however, met with less success. The middle colonies used flour and other forms of "country produce" as money; New Englanders even tried fish. For a variety of reasons, however, these products proved less satisfactory than did sugar products or tobacco.[16] As Pennsylvania merchant Francis Rawle wrote in 1721:

> What would they do [in Boston] without Paper-Money? Must every Gentleman, Tradesman, etc. turn *Fish Merchant?* What an

odd kind of Running Stock must stinking Fish make? Instead of
a Bag, or Pocket, they must have a Cart to carry Home *Fifty Shillings;* and after all, the intrinsick Value of their Running Stock
would be daily in Danger of rotting or wasting some way or another.[17]

Wheat never functioned well as a form of money in
Pennsylvania. One drawback was that it was not negotiable
overseas. Tenants did pay some rents in wheat, and farmers would
take notes from local millers for their processed flour to use as
payment elsewhere, but the flour market worked best when
everything moved quickly; it was awkward to tie up large portions of "country produce" in a payment mechanism system.
The worst problem with relying on wheat or flour, however,
was that not everyone grew wheat in Pennsylvania. Unlike the
Chesapeake, where growth in the economy was directly tied to
growth in the quantity of tobacco produced, throughout the 1700s
economic growth in Pennsylvania came from diversification into
other forms of production. The transition to wheat production
by farmers along the eastern shore of the Chesapeake and in the
western portions of Virginia would lead to increased demand for
paper money in Maryland and Virginia, as it had in Pennsylvania. Apparently wheat and flour were poor substitutes for specie
or even tobacco as a commodity money.[18]

In the absence of either specie or usable "country
produce," farmers turned to book credit. An increase in book
credit should be viewed not as an addition to the money supply,
but rather as a change in the velocity, or rate, at which the money
already in circulation was used for transactions in a given period
of time. When cash was available, farmers seldom used their
accounts with one set of merchants to pay off debts with another. Even when cash was unavailable, instead of using notes
on book credit as money, farmers would confine much of their
trading to a few local storekeepers, alternately running positive
and negative balances as they sold goods on one date and bought
others on another.[19]

The extensive use of book credit created other costs

of trading. When a farmer bought goods from a local merchant on credit, with the promise eventually to pay, he was doing no more than taking out a loan, with an effective interest rate being charged in the price of the goods. If no such interest rate was being charged, the merchant could not have afforded to remain in business, because he would have tied up his working capital for considerable periods of time in these consumer loans. Pennsylvania storekeepers often made these arrangements explicit, requiring an interest-paying bond from customers whose debts remained on the books more than one or two years.[20]

The result of increased costs of transacting in the market would be a reduction in market participation. Increased market costs would lead to higher costs to specialization and a slowing down of diversification within the economy. Pennsylvanians would then lose the gains from trade they had acquired through diversification. Skilled artisans would be forced to become less-skilled farmers; skilled farmers would have to waste part of their time producing the goods they could have bought from specialists (or do without).

The already unpleasant situation was only made worse by the international credit crunch brought about by the South Sea Bubble of 1720. Considered by many the first modern stock market crash, the South Sea Bubble involved the London money market in a "can't lose" investment bubble. For a time, purchasers of "South Sea Stock," stock in trading projects in the South Seas, were willing to pay any price in the belief that the price could only rise in the future. At some point, bears began to outnumber bulls and the bubble burst, resulting in a temporary shake-up of the London financial market. As interest rates rose in Britain, loans to Americans looked less desirable. With British merchants less willing to export capital to America, consumer credit was called in and payments requested. By 1721 money in Pennsylvania was scarce.[21]

Pennsylvanians petitioned their legislators for an increase in the money supply. Paper money could perform the same function as specie in terms of a medium of exchange; furthermore, while specie was of use in transactions abroad, paper money was not. Using it in domestic trade would keep specie in circulation where it was needed in the international trade. The choice of paper money resulted in part from previous failures to bring in specie through legislation and from other colonies' experiences with the use of paper money to pay for military expenditures.

When the only efficient form of money was perceived to be specie, the problem of increasing the money supply as local trade increased seemed almost insurmountable, because Pennsylvania and indeed the colonies as a whole had no source of local gold or silver with which to augment that which came from abroad. At one time or another, most of the colonies, Pennsylvania included, tried to bring specie into the colony by the rather shortsighted practice of overvaluing coin.[22] In effect, the government of Pennsylvania tried to purchase specie from abroad by offering a discount on Pennsylvania products in return. Without an enforcement mechanism, however, the Pennsylvania government was powerless to change the market rate of exchange sufficiently to attract much specie. If the government had a powerful enforcement mechanism (as Britain did in the Bank of England), it still would have taken a dramatic overvaluation of coin to bring in enough extra specie to match even the small amounts of paper money issued in a much less costly fashion by the Pennsylvania government.

Colonial governments turned to printing paper money of their own, at first quite by accident. Desperately in need of funds with which to finance government expeditions against the Indians, the Massachusetts government printed one of the first issues of fiat money to finance government expenditures in the history of finance. At the same time, it inadvertently solved the colony's chronic problems with the money supply. Rhode Island learned the lesson so well that New England's money supply was thrown into havoc as the colony attempted to finance its expenditures through arbitrage—printing paper money, permitting it to depreciate, and benefiting from the lag in response on the part of the other colonial legislatures in readjusting their legal exchange rates to the new market exchange rates. Both the advantages and disadvantages of fiat money were thus brought home to the colonies at once. Paper money could serve adequately as a form of money as long as people believed it could be exchanged for a real commodity. But unchecked emissions of paper money could lead to price inflation. In the depression of 1722 Pennsylvanians thought they would prefer to take their chances with the latter problem.[23]

The Pennsylvania legislature in 1721 was deluged with petitions from the countryside and the city of Philadelphia calling for the issue of a paper currency. Governor William Keith, ever attuned to popular sentiment, supported paper money; most of the merchants in Philadelphia did as well, contrary to the progressive historians' hypothesis that as debtors, farmers always supported paper currency and, as lenders, merchants always fought against it. The only true enemies of paper currency seemed to have been the Penn family (not without irony, for William Penn had supported the idea of printing paper currency a generation earlier, when overvaluation of coin had been chosen instead) and members of the governor's council, specifically James Logan and Isaac Norris.[24]

The Penn family opposed paper currency for two reasons. The Board of Trade disapproved of paper money, and the Penns could lose the colony if the Board felt its wishes had been disobeyed. Of more concern to the Penns, however, was the status of their quitrents. Because Pennsylvania paper money would not be negotiable in England, the proprietors wished to continue to receive quitrents in specie. As the Penn family agent in Pennsylvania, Logan opposed paper money not only because his principals did but also because he was probably the person who would end up having to transform quitrents paid in paper currency into payments to the Penns in specie; if the paper money depreciated, Logan would have to make up the difference. Logan mounted an attack on paper money that probably cost him his political standing within the colony.[25]

Pennsylvania's most articulate proponent of paper money was the Quaker merchant Francis Rawle. In response to the economic crisis, Rawle published a pamphlet in 1721 delineating a plan of action for the Pennsylvania Assembly that appears in retrospect particularly prescient. Rawle's suggestions of staple inspection and paper money emissions for ending the depression would become the major supports of explicit Pennsylvania economic policy in the eighteenth century. Rawle died in 1727, however, before seeing the full results of his plan.[26]

By the opening of the Pennsylvania Assembly of 1722–23, there was no doubt that a paper money bill would be passed. Even Logan had finally yielded to the inevitable. The remaining problems with paper money were its acceptibility by all, durability, and functions as a store of value and standard of deferred payment. Paper money would perform poorly in the last two respects if allowed to depreciate. Thus the major questions remaining were how much would be printed and how it would be "secured." The first question—how much to be printed—has plagued policymakers before and since. The Pennsylvanians thought they knew how much money was too much; New England had been providing an unfortunate example for a generation. They also knew how much was too little. There was no doubt trade in the colony was suffering from a lack of circulating medium. But how much was enough? It should "exceed not in Quantity the Running Stock of Money a Country demands in its Trade," Rawle answered vaguely. Logan pleaded "that the whole sum struck be small, and just sufficient to pass from hand to hand, for a currency." The Assembly finally decided to begin with a very small amount, £15,000. By December 1723, it had tripled that sum, but the amount still remained small compared to paper issues in other colonies at the time or to the amounts Pennsylvania would release during the war years later in the century. Between 1755 and 1759, the legislature would order printed £485,000 Pennsylvania paper currency, six times the total printed in the thirty years before the war.[27]

The Assembly believed that it was important to prevent depreciation of the bills' value by providing assurance to the public that the bills would be redeemable in the future for a real sum comparable to their face value. If they passed the test of acceptability, they would perform better as a store of value and standard of deferred payment. The bills would be made legal tender, of course, and payable in all transactions within the colony. But when Thomas Penn arrived in the colony, he refused to allow paper currency to be used in payment of quitrents. The legislature then struck a deal with Penn in 1739 whereby the Pennsylvania government paid the Penns an annual lump sum of money and the Penns agreed to take paper currency in payment of quitrents.[28]

Paper money could be "secured" in one of two manners: promise of future tax receipts or assurance that the money was backed by real property. According to contemporary economic thought, backing the bills with real property was considered the more sound course; there was always uncertainty that the government might not come through with the tax money, particularly in the colonies, where tax collection was never efficient. Ideally, theorists believed, paper money should be secured with gold or silver. The colonists were intrigued, however, by cases in England where country banks had loaned money on land as security rather than on specie. "As Bills issued upon Money Security are Money," Benjamin Franklin would write in support of another currency bill in 1729, "so Bills issued upon Land are in Effect Coined Land." Land was the one form of real wealth the colonists possessed in abundance. Furthermore, it was reasoned, rising land prices would ensure that the Loan Office would always have access to funds with which to redeem the paper bills as they became due. Pennsylvania was not the first colony to consider the creation of a "land bank," as it was called; in fact, Governor John Blackwell, the unpopular Puritan brought in unsuccessfully by Penn in the 1690s to corral an insubordinate legislature, had written a pamphlet on the subject. A land bank was attempted on a private basis in New England at about the same time. But Pennsylvania was the first to put the plan into action and the first for whom the plan succeeded.[29]

The legislature passed three money bills issuing a total of £45,000 in 1723. Unsure how the Board of Trade would react, the legislature included a provision that within a certain number of years all the money would have been recalled and "sunk," or burned, and thus taken out of circulation. As it turned out, the Board of Trade was not at all pleased. But by the time it received the law the money was already in circulation, and it was powerless to do much about it. The Penns, who were also displeased that the bill had passed, removed Governor Keith in 1726 and replaced him with Patrick Gordon. The Penns and the Board gave Gordon explicit instructions not to authorize any more paper money emissions without a provision in the law suspending the printing of the money until the Board had had time to rule on the legitimacy of the law. Gordon brought the instructions to the legislature. He explained that he simply could not sign any paper money bills, but to no avail. He soon found that if he did not approve the issuing of £30,000 more in 1729 the legislature would refuse to appropriate any money for his support. Gordon signed, after including a token clause suspending the printing of the money for a few months, not nearly enough time for the bill to be received and acted upon in London.[30]

By the next decade, Thomas Penn was in Pennsylvania and he permitted no more major emissions. When he returned to England, he made his governors put up security against passing any law the proprietors disapproved of, with paper money bills explicitly in mind. James Hamilton, governor from 1748 to 1754, took the issue to Attorney General Dudley Ryder in London in 1753. Told that he would risk forfeiting his bond if he signed a paper money bill disapproved of by the Penns, Hamilton acquiesced and vetoed the bills. In their quarrels with Keith and Gordon, the Penns had objected to paper money itself. This time, however, their opposition stemmed from the disposition of the interest money from the Loan Office. The legislature reserved the income from the loans for its own use, and Penn wanted a clause inserted to give him partial control as well. Before the issue could cause further trouble, however, the Seven Years War erupted, and the legislature was permitted by the Penns to print money for defense.[31]

For thirty-three years, the General Loan Office printed paper money and loaned it out with land as security. During this time the Assembly made four original emissions: £15,000 in

March 1723; £30,000 in December 1723; £30,000 in 1729; and finally £11,110.5*s.* in 1739. These emissions brought the sum in circulation to £80,000 Pennsylvania currency, or about £49,000 in British sterling. The format of all the emission laws was similar. Loans could be made on land at double the value of the loan or houses at treble. Provision was also made for loans on a stream of income from rental property and one-year loans with silver as collateral, but instances of both were rare. The loans were set at 5 percent simple interest and were not to be made for less than £12.10*s.* or greater than £100. There was also a provision for loans up to £200 under certain circumstances, but they also were rare.[32] Of 3,111 loans for which we have records, only 55, or less than 2 percent, were for more than £100. The average loan was for £64.13*s.* (see table 5.1 in the following chapter). The purpose of the restriction on the size of the loans was to enable more landholders to have access to mortgages. The laws expressly forbade assigning land on trust to relatives with the purpose of acquiring more loan money:

> whereas the aforesaid Bills of Credit are chiefly intended for the Benefit of the poor industrious Sort of the People of this Province, at an easy Interest to relieve them from the present Difficulties they labour under; which End cannot be so well performed if any one Person should be allowed to take up too great a Sum of the said Bills of Credit upon Loan: Therefore to prevent the Splitting of any one Man's lands into sundry Parcels by dividing the same to divers Persons in Trust [loan applicants were required to affirm otherwise].[33]

The loans were to be paid back in annual installments to the due date. The due date itself was the same for all loans under the same law. Thus the due date was 1736 for all loans made after the re-emission act of 1725; a mortgagor in 1724 had twelve installments at 1/12 each; a borrower in 1728 had eight installments at 1/8 each. It is clear to see why pressure mounted for a new law as the due date approached. The colonists were concerned about loss of circulating currency, and the long-term loans had become short-term loans. As the principal came into the office, it was originally supposed to be "sunk," or burned; the interest was to be used for the support of the government, and eventually it provided half the operating revenue for Pennsylvania.[34]

Four re-emission acts were also passed, in 1725, 1731, 1739, and 1746 respectively. Easier to pass than bills adding to the total money supply (neither the Penns nor the Board of Trade objected to re-emission), the re-emission acts performed several functions. First, they provided for the printing of new money to exchange for old "worn, torn, and ragged" bills, solving the problem with durability. They also provided that payments of principal be reloaned rather than sunk, and they set a new due date for the reloaned mortgages. Money was loaned to provincial and local governments, in some cases with interest and in some cases without. Philadelphia City spent its loans immediately on previously incurred debts; Bucks and Chester County hoarded theirs and were chastised by the legislature for not putting the money into circulation fast enough.[35]

By 1755 the nature of the paper money had changed. The Assembly had voted £5,000 to the "King's Use" in 1746 in exchange for the approval of the re-emission act of 1746. This issue, unlike the others, was not to be secured by loans but to be "sunk" over a ten-year period through annual payments of £500 from the excise fund. A three-year effort from 1752 to 1755 to extend the mortgages and to issue £20,000 to £40,000 more failed after heated quarreling among the legislature, governor, and proprietary family. This altercation resulted in the resignation of Governor James Hamilton, who, as a good Quaker, did not wish to vote money for the use of troops. He was also sick of the bickering over paper money. After 1755, all paper money issues were dedicated to the war effort and backed by the promise of future tax money. The Loan Office ceased to function as an experiment in economic development and became instead an instrument of war finance. Much larger sums of money were issued. After experiencing 35 years of price stability, Pennsylvania eventually suffered the adverse effects of inflation as a result.[36]

EFFECTS OF THE PAPER CURRENCY

What were the effects of the paper money issues? Obviously, they increased the money supply. The actual amount of paper money was small when compared to the Massachusetts emissions or to the amounts printed in Pennsylvania during the Seven Years War and the Revolution. The amount of the money, however, did not have to be large to have a large effect on real income; specie and paper currency, for example, account today for less than one-tenth of the money supply.[37] In fact, the paper money emissions seem to have accomplished their purpose. That is, they provided a money supply for local transactions, which is all that anyone ever wanted them to do.

It has generally been assumed that many colonial transactions were made using local bills of exchange, with the Hancock papers being given as the source for this conclusion. But the Hancock accounts come from a period in Massachusetts history when paper money was banned by the British government and New England was forced back to a less efficient form of money, conditions similar to those in Pennsylvania before 1723. Pennsylvania account books tell a different story, contradicting the evidence from both the Hancock books in Boston and from other account books in the Chesapeake, which show large numbers of transactions taking place using tobacco as money.[38] Admittedly, all transactions took place through the original extension of credit, even if it was only for a few weeks. On the other hand, large numbers of transactions were cleared out within a year. Whether the account was cleared and the debts paid in months or in years, however, the majority were paid in Pennsylvania currency. In a sample taken from Samuel Powell's unusually complete accounts (see figure 4.1), a random sample of 72 accounts from the period 1727–1731 show that 73.6 percent of the amount paid was paid in Pennsylvania currency. Five percent of the payments, involving fourteen cases, were made through transferring money from someone else. One customer paid in coin (0.2 percent of the payments). Slightly less than 2

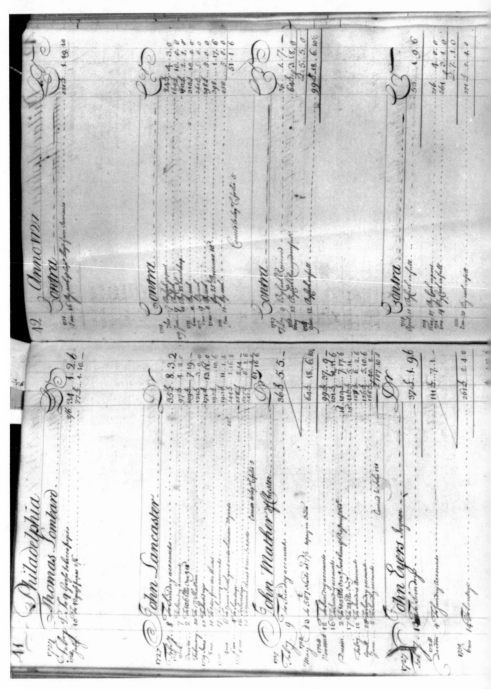

Figure 4.1. Sample from Samuel Powell's accounts.

percent of the total amount involved rebates on poor quality merchandise. That leaves 20 percent, or one-fifth, that was paid in kind—half in wheat or flour, half in goods ranging from "taylor's services" to beeswax and soap. Of the £3,758 Pennsylvania currency the 72 customers owed Powell, 70 percent was paid within three years and 30 percent was carried to another set of books. Similarly, when farmers near Coventry Forge sold produce to the company, they were paid in cash. (For an example, see figure 4.2.) The fact that most accounts were closed out within two years using Pennsylvania currency argues strongly that the Pennsylvania legislature had succeeded in printing just enough to "pass from hand to hand, for a currency."[39]

The final question as to the effects of the paper currency concerns the relationship between the paper currency issues and real income. An identity can be postulated whereby the amount of money in circulation (M) times the velocity with which it circulates (V), that is, the number of times the same money changes hands within a given period, exactly equals the average price of goods (P) times the number of transactions (T): $MV = PT$. The identity becomes a behavioral equation if we make assumptions about velocity and use data on two of the remaining variables to estimate a fourth. In this case, we will assume that velocity was stable—that is, that it did not change over the period in question. Then we can use changes in the price level (dP) and changes in the money supply (dM) to estimate changes in the number of transactions (dT): $dM/dP = dT$.[40]

An assumption of stable velocity over this period will, if anything, overestimate the effects of changes in the money supply on the price level, as velocity, when it changed at all, probably moved in the same direction as money and prices. The introduction of paper money probably led to a decline in the use of book credit and thus a decline in velocity. However, this decline was more than offset by the increase in explicit loan activity for investment due to the growing economy. As there appear to be no changes in bookkeeping or payment practices beyond the initial introduction of paper currency, velocity most likely remained relatively stable throughout the period.[41]

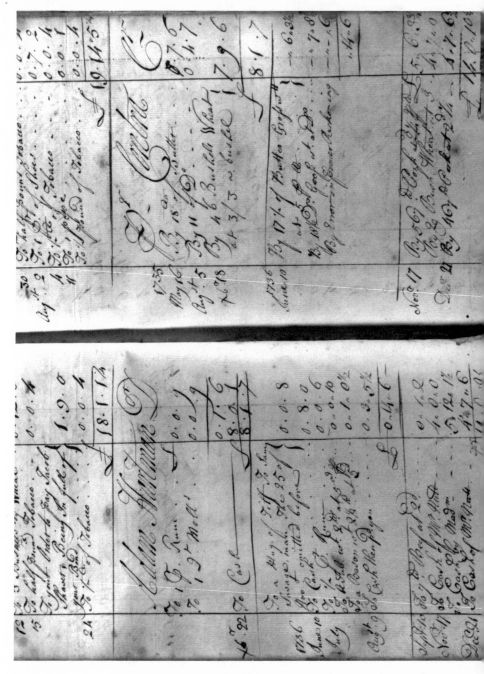

Figure 4.2. Cash payments for produce.

The major primary emissions of paper money were made in 1723 and 1729—£45,000 and £30,000, respectively. The money was not issued in a lump sum. It was loaned at an average of £67.13s. per loan, and it took at least three years for the original amount to come into full circulation. Thus the money supply rose from 1723 to 1726, from 1729 to 1732, and again slightly from 1739 to 1741 as the £11,110 issued in 1739 were loaned. The paper money supply remained stable in the interim.[42]

Drawing upon Anne Bezanson's index of wholesale prices for twelve commodities in Philadelphia (see table 4.1), we find that a period of mild deflation just before the first paper money emissions in 1723 was reversed. Prices jumped 8.7 percent from 1724 to 1725 and 4.6 percent from 1725 to 1726. Prices then fell slightly and leveled off. The £30,000 emission of 1729 caused prices to rise by only 6 percent from 1729 to 1730, followed by a decline of 11 percent to 1731. Prices remained relatively low during the 1730s, jumping again dramatically by 29 percent in 1741. After the re-emission of 1739 went into effect, prices then fell, but to a level higher than in the 1730s. As most of Bezanson's commodities were agricultural, there is a problem with the series because agricultural products are normally subject to erratic jumps in prices. Bezanson was aware of the problem and used a moving average, but that does not help us in looking for changes which probably were in effect for only a year or two.[43]

A better criterion of the stability of the purchasing power of the paper money would probably be the exchange rate between Pennsylvania paper currency and British pounds sterling (see table 4.2). In fact, this was the criterion the colonists themselves used. The British pound was relatively stable during the eighteenth century. Furthermore, although domestic production was growing, a large portion of goods were still purchased from abroad, which required that Pennsylvania currency be converted. John McCusker's exchange rates, drawn from merchant letterbooks and account books, show that the Pennsylvania currency did depreciate in its first years, trading at

Loan Office and Paper Money

Table 4.1. Annual Indices of Wholesale Prices of Commodities in
Philadelphia, 1720–1755

Year	Price Index	Percent Change Since Previous Year
1720	86.2	—
1721	78.6	−8.8
1722	81.6	+3.8
1723	84.3	+3.3
1724	88.9	+5.5
1725	96.6	+8.7
1726	101.0	+4.6
1727	97.6	−3.4
1728	92.8	−4.9
1729	92.5	−0.3
1730	98.0	+5.9
1731	87.1	−11.1
1732	83.6	−4.0
1733	90.0	+7.7
1734	87.2	−3.1
1735	87.8	+0.7
1736	83.6	−4.8
1737	91.1	+9.0
1738	91.1	—
1739	82.2	−9.8
1740	87.3	+6.2
1741	112.6	+29.0
1742	108.3	−3.8
1743	95.6	−11.7
1744	90.9	−4.9
1745	92.7	+2.0
1746	99.7	+7.6
1747	110.6	+10.9
1748	124.7	+12.7
1749	121.5	−2.6
1750	113.0	−7.0
1751	112.8	−0.2
1752	111.9	−0.8
1753	109.9	−1.8
1754	109.1	−0.7
1755	107.3	−1.6

SOURCE: Index of twelve commodities (base: monthly average 1741–1745) in Anne Bezanson et al., *Prices in Colonial Pennsylvania*. The index is based on an unweighted average of the following commodities: beef, bread, corn, flour, molasses, pitch, pork, rum, salt, sugar, tar, and wheat.

Loan Office and Paper Money   137

Table 4.2. Rate of Exchange: Pennsylvania on London, 1720–1755

Year	Rate[a]	Percent Change Since Previous Year
1720	138.75	—
1721	137.50	−0.9
1722	135.01	−1.8
1723	140.37	+4.0
1724	143.11	+2.0
1725	139.34	+2.7
1726	—	—
1727	149.58	+7.3
1728	150.62	+0.7
1729	148.61	−1.3
1730	152.03	+2.3
1731	153.28	+0.8
1732	160.90	+5.0
1733	166.94	+3.8
1734	170.00	+1.8
1735	166.11	−2.3
1736	167.00	+0.5
1737	170.25	+1.9
1738	160.42	−5.8
1739	169.69	+5.8
1740	165.45	−2.5
1741	146.14	−11.7
1742	159.38	+9.1
1743	159.79	+0.3
1744	166.67	+4.3
1745	174.77	+4.9
1746	179.86	+2.9
1747	183.78	+2.2
1748	174.12	−5.3
1749	171.39	−1.6
1750	170.60	−0.5
1751	169.86	−0.4
1752	166.85	−1.8
1753	167.49	+0.4
1754	168.35	+0.5
1755	168.79	+0.3

SOURCE: John J. McCusker, *Money and Exchange in Europe and America, 1600–1775,* table 3.7, pp. 183–185.

[a] Pounds Pennsylvania currency per one hundred pounds British sterling.

£135.01 Pennsylvania currency to £100 sterling in 1723, and jumping to £150 Pennsylvania currency per £100 sterling by 1727. The rate rose to £166.94 per £100 by 1733, then fluctuated at £166 to £170 per £100 for the next several years. Intriguingly, the year prices rose the highest in Pennsylvania (1741), exchange rates dropped lower than they had been in over a decade—surely reflecting a year when demand for Pennsylvania exports hit an unusual high. In fact, both the price series and exchange rates leave one with the impression that short fluctuations in both were due less to changes in the money supply than to changes in trade relations. This experience must be contrasted with that of Massachusetts during the same period, when Massachusetts currency depreciated from £219.43 per £100 sterling in 1720 to £516.67 per £100 in 1736 and £1,033.33 per £100 by 1750.[44]

If prices in Pennsylvania did not rise appreciably while velocity was stable and the domestic money supply increased, then the number of domestic transactions must have been on the increase as well. As noted in chapter 2, income per capita increased at a rate between 0.6 and 1.65 percent a year. The population of Pennsylvania increased, in part because of the growing reputation of the colony as a profitable site for an immigrant, whether planning to farm or to practice a trade.

By the end of the 1740s trade was beginning to be pinched again by the lack of a medium of exchange. The Assembly was flooded with petitions calling for an increase in the money supply. By this time, the bond required of Governor James Hamilton prevented the sneaking of another money bill past the Board of Trade, as had been done in the first two cases. The issue was taken so seriously in Pennsylvania that the government was deadlocked for three years in the mid-1750s after having argued for nearly a decade over the necessity of printing more money. The possible long-term effects on the economy cannot be known, however, because of the effects of the Seven Years War. The large issues of paper currency during the war did not cause a rise in prices to the extent of the size of the issues, however. Nor did exchange rates fluctuate dramatically as they had in Massachusetts. While the war issues are beyond the scope of this study, the evidence appears to support the hypothesis that Pennsylvania made out quite well financially during the war.

By creating a medium of exchange that was not needed for either consumption or investment (being worthless for either), was easy to transport, was acceptable in all transactions, and was stable in value over time, the paper money issues of the General Loan Office increased real income in the colony over the years 1723–1755. The issues seem to have decreased the cost of transacting in the marketplace and thus increased the gains resulting from specialization in trade. The depression caused by a "glut" in the West Indies food markets (see chapter 6) and the credit crunch in the English-speaking world following the South Sea Bubble greatly reduced aggregate demand, and the injections of spending caused by printing paper money and releasing it in the economy helped reverse the decline in demand that was causing a decline in real income.[45] But both contemporary description and the ongoing effects of the benefits from the increase in the money supply would point to financial innovation as the greater of the causes of the increase in real income resulting from the paper money issues. Finally, while the monetary effects of the General Loan Office are the most evident, the Loan Office itself contributed to economic growth by distributing the paper money through long-term loans on real estate at below-market interest rates. The Loan Office thus also promoted capital formation, a subject that will be discussed in detail in the next chapter.

CHAPTER FIVE

The General Loan Office
and Capital Formation

Furnishing the Country with a Medium of
Trade, and of a Kind that could not, to any Purpose,
be exported, as it facilitated mutual Commerce, lessened our Taxes by the Interest it produced, and made
it more easy for every one to obtain ready Pay for his
Labour, Produce our Goods (a Medium so evidently
wanted at the Time Paper Money was first issued) has
doubtless been one great Means of the subsequent En-
crease of our Trade and People, by inducing Strangers
to come and settle among us, But your Committee
conceive, that the manner of issuing this Medium contributed no less to those happy Effects than the Medium itself. It was by the Law directed to be emitted
on Loan, in Sums of *Twelve Pounds Ten Shillings,* and
upwards, not exceeding *One Hundred Pounds* to one
Person, for a long Term, on easy Interest, and payable
in yearly Quotas; which put it in the Power of many
to purchase Lands, and make Plantations, (the Loan
Office enabling them to pay the Purchase so easily)
and thereby to acquire Estates to themselves, and to
support and bring up Families; but who, without that
Assistance, would probably have continued longer in
a single State, and as Labourers for others, or have
quitted the Country in Search of better Fortune. This
easy Means of acquiring landed Estates to themselves,
has, we suppose, been one principal Encouragement
to the great Removal hither, of people from *Ireland* and
Germany, where they were only and could scarce ever
expect to be other than Tenants. And that happy Con-
trivance in our Money Laws, by which the yearly

Quotas are, as fast as paid in, re-emitted to other Borrowers, makes the same Quantity of Currency service-
able in their Turns to a much greater Number of People; thereby lessening the Necessity and Demand for
striking great additional sums, which, if carried to Excess, might depreciate the Value of the Currency.
>   —Excerpt from the Report
>   of the Committee appointed by the Assembly
>   to enquire into the State
>   of our Paper Currency, August 19, 1752.
>   Benjamin Franklin, Richard Walker,
>   George Ashbridge, Evan Morgan,
>   and Peter Worrall[1]

As Franklin and his committee made clear in 1752, the
operations of the Loan Office had effects on the Pennsylvania
economy beyond those on the money supply alone. The Loan
Office reduced the cost of capital in a developing economy by
offering long-term loans at below-market interest rates; it realized gains through economies of scale made possible by its government backing. The Loan Office was, however, not the only
source of investment capital in mid-eighteenth century Pennsylvania. Before examining the office, we need to look at the general dimensions of the capital network in colonial Pennsylvania.

To return to the tables in chapter 1, inventories recorded in Chester County in the mid-eighteenth century contained a far greater proportion of financial assets than a student
of the colonial economy would have been led to believe (see
tables 1.2–1.3). Colonial lenders were by no means limited to
merchants and shopkeepers. Two-fifths of inventoried householders in Chester County had some money out on loan at the
time they died. The figures are biased upward because the inventories exclude those in the lowest segment of the population.
Nonetheless, the countryside contained creditors as well as debtors.[2]

There were three major sources of capital in colonial
Pennsylvania: older householders, who apparently preferred to

liquidate their real assets rather than hold on to them after the household had broken up; legacies and dowries of orphans, widows, and wealthy women intent upon preserving their inheritance despite marriage; and intergenerational transfers within families. While householders in other categories tended to lend out a lesser proportion of their total financial assets, they still could be counted among the creditors in the colony.

The attitude displayed in wills, orphans' accounts, and marriage contracts in Chester County indicates that Pennsylvanians believed it wasteful to allow money to sit unused. Just as land should be put into productive use, legacies were expected to "be carefully improved by putting out to Interest for the use of" the children. Of course, just as in the cases where the widow "rented" land from the estate, a tradeoff frequently occurred. Often the interest of the legacies was considered to balance exactly the cost of raising the children. But the account of the interest and the account of the cost of maintaining the children were kept separate in the estate records. Executors understood that they were performing a service to the estate by raising the children, but they also understood that the use of the children's legacies over time had value.[3]

A large source of funds for potential borrowers thus could be found in the dowries of wealthy widows and legacies of the children of the fairly well-to-do. In these cases, executors or trustees were not given the option to diversify the portfolio into other types of investments; the marriage contract or will stipulated that the money be loaned out. Artisan John Parker willed £15 in 1716 to Sarah Blunston, "to be put out at interest until she be at the age of twenty one years or marriage which shall first happen and then she to have the whole both principal and interest." Edward Riley willed £45 to his grandson, to be put to interest until he turned 21, during which time the boy was to be bound apprentice. James Woodward gave his real estate to his sons and £30 each to his two daughters, "to be put to Interest and the said thirty pounds to each of them with the Interest to be paid them at the Age of Eighteen years."[4]

Another large source of loans was those people whose

savings exceeded their own plans for investment. The largest group fitting this category consisted of older residents who had either sold their real estate and livestock or were still bringing in a sizable income but no longer had a young family to establish or support (see tables 1.2–1.4). Much of this money was loaned out on a will-call basis. A typical obligation of this sort, or "bond" as they were called at the time, legally "bound" the borrower to pay the lender double the amount borrowed if the loan was not repaid, with the legal interest incurred, by a given date. Most bonds were held beyond the inscribed due date, however. As long as the interest payments were regularly made, the lender did not call in the loan until he had a need for it. In practice, most were paid off on a timetable determined by the borrower; the most common reason for calling a loan in early was death of the lender. Once the bond had passed the listed due date, however, the lender was legally permitted to charge not only interest but "interest on interest" (compound interest) as well as a penalty for collection if the borrower was forced to go to court.[5]

As in the case of land disputes, however, the community generally stepped in to smooth over debt cases that reached the courts. If the court determined through an evaluation of the borrower's property that the loan could reasonably be expected to be paid back within a given period of time, generally about three years, then the lender was not permitted to attach the borrower's property. Depending on whether the court felt the borrower was trying to defraud the lender or merely caught in awkward, but transitory, circumstances, the court might or might not permit the lender to add on the "interest upon interest"; the borrower always had to pay the court fees.[6]

Bonds seldom exceeded £10 Pennsylvania currency; most lenders held several of these small obligations and most borrowers gave out more than one bond. Apparently both sides felt it was better to spread the risk—the risk of a default, from the lender's point of view, and the risk of premature collection, from the borrower's standpoint. Notes were also issued for an indeterminate period. These were not interest-earning, and generally stemmed from a book debt which could not be paid in the usual six- to twelve-month period. They were negotiable, although it was rare in Pennsylvania to see a note pass through more than two or three hands before being collected. Bonds made up the greatest percentage of debt held in this manner, however—three-fourths of all bonds, bills, and notes in the inventories. For that matter, even in the countryside, where by traditional accounts a great amount of credit would be expected to be given out from the tradesmen and storekeepers to the farmers, book debts represented a very small proportion of total financial assets found in the inventories and accounts. No tradesman could keep at his business for long without extending some short-term credit, but the bills were expected to be paid within a few months. If a colonist wished to borrow money, the arrangement and the interest were made explicit.[7]

Some of the bonds were in fact mortgage arrangements, where the parties to the agreement preferred not to include the land in the written contract explicitly. These bonds could and often did exceed the £10 limit followed by the general borrowers, although they seldom went over £50, or about one-half to one-fourth the value of a typical farm. Another group of bonds appear to have been family loans, normally from father to son. Many loans to children were probably not made that explicit, and several of the wills excuse a son's or son-in-law's debt. Nevertheless, it remains revealing of the personality of the Pennsylvania colonial that so many of these fathers insisted that their sons sign a legal obligation, protecting the other family members from possible default.[8]

Colonists with savings exceeding their investments had other options besides the personal bonds and, of course, real estate. A wide variety of investment opportunities existed in colonial Pennsylvania in the 1700s, as a result of the high degree of diversity the Pennsylvania economy enjoyed. Mines, mills, ships, shipping ventures, and even urban development projects were all available to the interested investor. An investor typically joined with partners on any project. Six seems to have been a common number for ventures; two or three for mills and ships.

For example, Strode's mill, built in 1723 (see figure 2.1), was originally owned by three partners "in company." Unless he was just beginning to get involved in commercial ventures, the typical investor employed his capital in a variety of directions. Putting a little money into a lot of different projects spread the risk for the investor, although it probably also lessened the returns.[9]

Investment projects came and went as fads in the eighteenth century. Two that stand out are the town-development projects and the practice of using a lottery to raise funds. The rapid development of Philadelphia, with the concurrent rise in the value of city lots, was not lost on colonists who had arrived too late to participate in Philadelphia's earliest boom. Throughout the eighteenth century, one town after another was target of a developer's boosterism. Some worked better than others. Bristol Town in Bucks County never returned a profit to its promotors, as it was overshadowed by Philadelphia through its entire development. Newport replaced New Castle, and Wilmington then replaced Newport as the "hot" investment site in Chester and New Castle Counties. Pennsylvanians even bought into the development of Charlestown in Maryland. Lancaster Town was probably the most successful of these projects, and much of the profits from the town's boom fell to the Hamilton family, the town's promotors. While investors in town development generally just bought up lots, Wilmington investors also participated in a joint development of the city's riverbank. Several of the Chester County inventories include "Wilmington bank bills," referring not to a financial institution but to the development of the city's waterfront. Philadelphia "bank bills" had similarly been sold at the beginning of the century.[10]

Lotteries appeared throughout the century but blossomed in the late 1740s. Anyone with a potential project to finance could sell tickets to a lottery; as long as the tickets outsold the prize he could make money. While lotteries were outlawed in some colonies as soon as they appeared, they were permitted to run their course in Pennsylvania. The lotteries finally ran afoul of the legislature, however, when a series of church lotteries collapsed and had to be rescued by the provincial government.[11]

There was thus a lively capital market in colonial Pennsylvania, and the mortgages issued by the General Loan Office of Pennsylvania were only one aspect of this development. The Loan Office stood out from the rest of the economy, however, in that its size and government backing permitted an efficiency of operation that resulted in loans for a greater length of time than were offered in the private sector. Apparently the office also provided capital to people who would have been normally denied loans through the private sector because of potential risk. Much of the lending in the private sector took place between people who knew each other, although lawyers functioned as professional brokers for the estate and dowry accounts. The Loan Office, however, was required by law to lend to anyone with a deed; people who might not have acquired capital privately thus found it available through the government.

The effects of the mortgages fall into three major categories. First, there were changes in the distribution of actual and potential income and wealth as a result of the direct and indirect effects of the subsidy represented by the difference between the 5 percent government interest rate and the market interest rate. Second, the issuing of inexpensive long-term loans could have been expected to change individual behavior regarding capital formation: marginal investments that would not have been undertaken with market interest rates now appeared more attractive. Finally, there was a general perception that the presence of the loans had encouraged the economic growth and development of the colonial economy as a whole. The accuracy of these contemporary assessments needs to be analyzed.

Records of 3,111 loans issued by the General Loan Office from 1724 to 1756 have been located, probably about four-fifths of the total issued; of these, 2,685 were new loans and 426, or about one-sixth, were rollovers. The office could issue loans at one-half the value of land or one-third the value of buildings offered as collateral. The average mortgagor borrowed £65.13*s.*, and 98 percent of the loans were for less than £100 (see tables 5.1 through 5.4).[12]

The subsidy represented by the difference between

Table 5.1. Distribution of Loans

Size of Loan (£)	Number	Percent
10–20	39	1.3
20–30	169	5.4
30–40	334	10.7
40–50	407	13.1
50–60	502	16.1
60–70	377	12.1
70–80	530	17.0
80–90	221	7.1
90–100	477	15.3
Over 100	55	1.8

Average Loan: £65.64

SOURCE: Register of the General Loan Office, Historical Society of Pennsylvania, Philadelphia; Registers of the Pennsylvania General Loan Office, Philadelphia City Archives, City Hall Annex, Philadelphia.

Table 5.2. Size of Loan by Number of Acres

Number of Acres	Number of Loans	Percent of All Loans	Average Size of Loan[a]
0–50	163	6.0	45.77
51–100	584	21.6	55.10
101–150	651	24.1	61.32
151–200	620	23.0	69.09
201–250	339	12.6	71.35
251–300	168	6.2	77.15
301–350	64	2.4	80.11
351–400	34	1.3	96.76
401–450	20	0.7	84.10
451–500	38	1.4	105.00
Over 500 acres	19	0.7	77.21
Missing	411	(13.2)	
Total in acres	2703	(86.9)	64.89
Total with lots	408	(13.1)	70.63

Average acreage: 167 acres

SOURCE: See table 5.1.

[a] Pounds Pennsylvania currency.

Table **5.3.** Loan Amount by Year of Issue

Year	Number	Percent	Loan[a]
1724	1	0.0	56.25
1725	7	0.2	78.07
1726	68	2.2	62.12
1727	47	1.5	58.49
1728	108	3.5	60.19
1729	61	2.0	55.72
1730	175	5.6	66.39
1731	1	0.0	68.75
(1732–1735 are missing)	—	—	—
1736	55	1.8	65.54
1737	97	3.1	62.33
1738	44	1.4	58.27
1739	259	8.3	75.29
1740	264	8.5	72.37
1741	114	3.7	59.77
1742	112	3.6	63.15
1743	80	2.6	61.76
1744	68	2.2	62.34
1745	169	5.4	66.12
1746	173	5.6	61.25
1747	143	4.6	61.89
1748	128	4.1	63.38
1749	142	4.6	64.58
1750	173	5.6	64.77
1751	191	6.1	66.64
1752	126	4.1	68.65
1753	97	3.1	66.02
1754	125	4.0	69.92
1755	68	2.2	68.42
1756	14	0.5	58.89

SOURCE: See table 5.1.
[a] Pounds Pennsylvania currency.

the effective market rate of interest and the 5 percent charged by the government is difficult to calculate because the market rate for long-term loans during the period is not known. Usury laws limited interest to a maximum of 6 percent. There is evidence, however, that borrowers and lenders found ways around the usury law. Franklin quoted 8 to 10 percent, despite the ceiling, in "A Modest Enquiry into the Nature and Necessity of a

Table 5.4. Size of Loan by County of Residence

County	Number	Percent	Average Amount of Loan[a]
Berks	22	0.7	70.36
Bucks	800	25.9	64.19
Chester	826	26.7	66.39
Cumberland	4	0.1	83.00
Lancaster	370	12.0	63.82
Northampton	21	0.7	63.38
Philadelphia City	289	9.3	73.10
Philadelphia County	735	23.8	64.17
York	9	0.3	79.33
New Castle Co., Del.	6	0.2	58.46
West New Jersey	10	0.3	57.97
Missing	19	(0.6)	

SOURCE: See table 5.1.
[a] Pounds Pennsylvania currency.

Paper-Currency" in 1729: "he that wants Money will find out Ways to give *10 per Cent* when he cannot have it for less, altho' the Law forbids to take more than *6 per Cent.*"[13]

One way to charge an effective interest rate higher than the usury ceiling was to give the loan recipient a different sum that the amount printed on the face of the loan. Another method to avoid the usury ceiling was to deal in sterling instead of Pennsylvania currency and offer an exchange rate different from the going market rate. Finally, there is evidence that the German immigrants, who conducted all their transactions in their native language rather than in English, did not even bother with the legal ceiling but used other rates and enforced the contracts privately. Assuming a market rate of 8 to 10 percent, then, the amount of the subsidy would be 3 to 5 percent of the principal remaining in any given year, about £2 to £3½ in the first year of an average loan.[14]

This is not to say that the usury ceiling had no impact on the market. There is also evidence that indicates it was effective in curtailing some loans at higher interest rates. None of the loans in the Chester County Estate Inventories drew more than 6 percent interest. A delinquent loan obviously could not be collected in court at a rate higher than 6 percent, although again there were ways around that restriction as well. There were cases where compound interest, "interest upon interest," was permitted on loans that ran past a due date; there were also a variety of fees and fines that could be added to the collected payment that would raise the effective interest rate. But most of the loans on record either in account books or in the court records were restricted to the "lawful interest" of 6 percent.[15]

An interest rate that remains at the usury ceiling at most times and for most people can be considered fairly good evidence that credit rationing was taking place. The number of loans actually made were in that case less than the potential because of the prohibition against higher interest, and loans that were made went out only to preferred customers and relatives. As noted above, quite a number of loans were made in the countryside in this manner, with well-off countrymen loaning money to their neighbors and relatives. The fact that the loans were only to their neighbors, however, would indicate that the usury ceiling had curtailed a possible province-wide loan market. Unless potential lenders were completely unresponsive to interest rates—which is belied by the evidence—it must be concluded that loans which could have been made were not. Thus not only did the Loan Office offer capital at lower than market interest rates, it offered capital where none at all might have been available. It is easy to see why there were a thousand landholders on a waiting list for mortgages through the Loan Office.

The Loan Office, while small by contemporary standards, was an unusually large financial institution for the market conditions that existed in Pennsylvania at the time. It extended three loans a week on average while it was operating regularly. Furthermore, the Loan Office was not permitted to discriminate on the basis of personal friendship. As long as a potential borrower could produce clear title, he had to be given a loan. Advantages of scale had effects beyond enabling loans to be offered to a greater proportion of the populace. The size of the Loan Office and the number of loans issued also enabled a greater internal efficiency of operation. The office was able to balance its portfolio as a smaller merchant house could not, compensating for bad loans and foreclosures with other loans elsewhere. While the government could have backed the Loan Office, it never had to in any way other than enforcing Loan Office decisions. The office operated as a profitable institution that returned money to the government, providing half the operating revenue for Pennsylvania throughout the period of its operation and enabling the Pennsylvania government to avoid direct taxation until the beginning of the Seven Years War.

LOAN RECIPIENTS

Who received the loans? As Franklin noted, the loans enabled some tenants to make their first purchases of land. It is not immediately apparent from Loan Office regulations, however, just how this took place. To apply for a loan, the potential mortgagor had to appear before the Loan Office trustees with a clear title in his possession. Thus, unless the seller was willing to give title before he received his money, which sometimes happened, a first-time buyer could not receive a mortgage. Land purchased through sheriffs' sales could be mortgaged immediately. There were some cases where family holdings were apparently mortgaged to pay for a son's purchase of new land. For example, John McMichel, Jr., of New Providence in Chester County appeared as a landholder in the tax records the year after John McMichel, Sr., took out a loan on his only farm. John David willed his son Joshua the land "where he [Joshua] dwells," provided he paid the Loan Office mortgage. Furthermore, a seller could loan a purchaser the price of the land until he received his mortgage money from the government.[16]

The John Swift Letterbook contains an interesting example of government loans being used to help tenants purchase the land on which they resided. As noted above, in chapter 3, Swift had been sent from London to sell land owned by

Figure 5.1. Gilpin House (headquarters of Lafayette), Brandywine Battlefield Park, Delaware County, Pennsylvania. The wood portion of the house was built in 1695 and the stone added in 1745. Joseph Gilpin took out a Loan Office mortgage, probably on this property, for £71.5*s.* in 1727. His son Joseph, who inherited the house in 1739, received a Loan Office mortgage, perhaps on the same property, for £71.10*s.* in 1730. Reproduced with permission of the Chester County Historical Society, Chester County, Pennsylvania.

his uncle, John White, who had purchased the land some time before from William Penn. Swift was warned by neighboring landowners that he would have to offer the land to the tenants first. Swift offered four-year mortgages at 6 percent, and the majority of the 31 tenants had no trouble making payments and purchasing the land. Worried about the ability of the rest to finish making payments, Swift decided to offer them title after they had paid half the purchase price of the land, explicitly to enable them to take out mortgages from the Loan Office. "I told them . . . to pay one half of what their Land comes to . . . and when they have done that, I have promised to make them a title, which they design to Mortgage in the Loan Office, and so pay the whole." In fact, thirteen of the 31 tenants did precisely that, including one, a "horse jockey," whom Swift had been sure would be a complete loss. Swift sold the land for £40 to £50 per hundred acres, but the Loan Office valued it at rates from double to triple the amount Swift asked. Apparently, many of the tenants had made substantial improvements on the property. Both Swift and the Loan Office considered those improvements to belong to the tenants, not the original landowner.[17]

Cases where the loans were used to garner large amounts of property do not seem to be typical. The Loan Office was very careful about exceeding the £100 limit to any one mortgagor, no matter who he was. This perhaps is a case where the Quaker foundations of the Pennsylvania government had a palpable effect on the way policy was carried out; even William Fishbourne, prosecuted for illicitly borrowing large sums of money from the Loan Office while trustee, could not find formal ways to borrow more than the legal limit (see chapter 7). One hundred pounds was a very small sum of money for the types of land speculation that went on at the highest levels. The majority of the mortgagors, in fact, appear to have owned only one homestead, which they were mortgaging. Place of residence and location of mortgaged land were generally the same in the mortgages, and a sample of mortgagors compared with land purchase records do not show any extra purchases being made around the time they received their Loan Office money.[18]

While the loans thus tended to be restricted to landholders, they appear to have been fairly evenly distributed within that group. Omitting the 426 re-emitted mortgages, 2,685 individuals took out mortgages during a period when the number of households rose from approximately 8,000 to 30,000. Between 1739 and 1755, 698 Chester County residents took out mortgages, about one-fifth of all Chester County householders in 1754. Both the Chester County mortgagors from the 1720s and those from the 1750s appear to have been assessed for wealthholdings higher than those of the average Chester County resident, not a surprising finding, given the assumption that most mortgagors already owned land (see tables 5.5 and 5.6). Half of the mortgagors fell in the upper one-fourth of the tax distribution; one-fourth in the upper 10 percent.[19]

The main distinction thus appeared to be whether one was eligible for the loans or not; Franklin's observations notwithstanding, the dividing line was prior ownership of land. Loans were fairly evenly distributed among the original counties, with little difference as to the average amount; the newer counties (Berks, York, Cumberland, and Northampton) had far fewer mortgages, although it must be remembered they were part of older counties for most of the loan period. City dwellers with lots received a higher average loan, but not appreciably so

Table 5.5. Chester County Tax Payments, 1729

Tax Paid[a]	All Householders		Loan Recipients	
	Number	*Percent*	*Number*	*Percent*
Less than 0/10	9	0.6	0	0.0
0/10–1/8	145	9.7	0	0.0
1/8–2/6	294	19.6	4	5.2
2/6–3/4	145	9.7	4	5.2
3/4–4/2	161	10.7	9	11.7
4/2–5/0	192	12.8	10	13.0
5/0–5/10	46	3.1	4	5.2
5/10–6/8	118	7.9	11	14.3
6/8–7/6	108	7.2	8	10.4
7/6–8/4	31	2.1	2	2.6
8/4–9/2	43	2.9	4	5.2
9/2–10/0	51	3.4	7	9.1
Over 10/0	155	10.4	14	18.2
Missing	—	—	16	(17.2)
Total	1,498	100.0	93	100.0
Average tax paid:	*All Householders*		*Loan Recipients*	
	5s. 5d.		*7s. 6d.*	

SOURCE: Chester County tax lists, Chester County Archives.

Note: The freeman's tax of nine shillings per head was not included, although inmates and the poor were included as possessing no wealth. The tax was ordered at a rate of 3 pence per pound assessed wealth in improved real estate and livestock. However, the rates seriously underrepresent wealth holdings.

[a] Shillings/pence Pennsylvania currency.

Table 5.6. Chester County Tax Payments, 1754

	All Householders		Loan Recipients	
Tax Paid[a]	*Number*	*Percent*	*Number*	*Percent*
Less than 0/10	125	3.5	1	1.0
0/10–1/8	956	26.7	8	7.8
1/8–2/6	714	19.9	15	14.6
2/6–3/4	545	15.2	20	19.4
3/4–4/2	444	12.4	14	13.6
4/2–5/0	284	7.9	16	15.5
5/0–5/10	149	4.2	4	3.9
5/10–6/8	130	3.6	6	5.8
6/8–7/6	87	2.4	6	5.8
7/6–8/4	37	1.0	4	3.9
8/4–9/2	32	0.9	1	1.0
9/2–10/0	40	1.1	6	5.8
Over 10/0	41	1.3	2	1.9
Missing	—	—	23	(18.3)
Total	3,584	100.0	126	100.0
Average tax paid:	*All Householders* 3s. 1d.		*Loan Recipients* 4s. 7d.	

SOURCE: Chester County tax lists, Chester County Archives.

Note: The freeman's tax of six shillings per head was not included, although inmates and the poor were included as possessing no wealth. The tax was ordered at a rate of 2 pence per pound assessed wealth in improved real estate and livestock. However, the rates seriously underrepresent wealth holdings.

[a] Shillings/pence Pennsylvania currency.

(see tables 5.2 and 5.4). Obvious distinctions were made in the size of loan according to occupation; a merchant or gentleman could expect to receive near the maximum of £100 but rarely more. One-fourth of the mortgagors referred to themselves as artisans of various sorts, and three-fourths of these lived outside Philadelphia City. The sixty-nine widows and spinsters, it might be noted in passing, received almost precisely the average amount (see tables 5.7 and 5.8).

Approximately half of the Assemblymen between 1729 and 1754 held a mortgage at some time during those years. Among the more well-known mortgagors were Joseph and Edward Shippen, Isaac and Debby Norris, James Hamilton (a borrower in 1740), Charles Brockden, Samuel Carpenter, Joseph

Table 5.7. Size of Loan by Occupation

Occupation	Number	Percent	Average Loan[a]
Selected Occupations			
Yeoman	2033	66.9	64.78
Widow/spinster	69	2.3	65.39
Merchant	47	1.5	87.58
Gentleman	59	1.9	91.11
Miller	47	1.5	74.04
Shipwright	22	0.7	77.85
Total "Artisan"[b]	(737)	(24.2)	(63.55)
Professional			
Clerk	4	0.1	69.00
Lawyer ("esquire")	5	0.2	93.80
Physician	5	0.2	76.00
Schoolmaster	1	0.0	72.00
Surveyor	1	0.0	91.25
Cloth/Apparel			
"Blew dyer"	1	0.0	82.50
"Brass button maker"	1	0.0	42.00
Clothier	1	0.0	55.00
Clothworker	1	0.0	56.00
Collarmaker	1	0.0	52.50
Feltmonger	4	0.1	48.56
Fuller	10	0.3	63.60
Glover	1	0.0	97.50
Hatter	2	0.1	73.75
Shoemaker	1	0.0	59.00
"Silk dyer"	1	0.0	54.00
Staymaker	1	0.0	100.00
Taylor	60	2.0	54.51
Weaver	87	2.9	58.66
Woolcomber	2	0.1	69.00
Woolmaker	1	0.0	26.25
Metals			
Blacksmith/smith	84	2.8	65.70
Blockmaker	1	0.0	38.50
Boltmaker	2	0.1	31.13
Cutler	2	0.1	66.75
Gunsmith	5	0.2	87.00
Hammerman	1	0.0	70.00
Ironmonger	2	0.1	201.25
Locksmith	2	0.1	73.00
Stonecutter	2	0.1	38.00
"Tine-plate worker"	1	0.0	28.00

Table 5.7. Size of Loan by Occupation (*cont.*)

Occupation	Number	Percent	Average Loan[a]
General Trade			
Carter	4	0.1	42.88
Cooper	44	1.4	73.52
Wagon maker	1	0.0	70.00
Wheelwright	9	0.3	48.75
Retail			
Barber	1	0.0	65.00
Haberdasher	1	0.0	96.00
Innkeeper	17	0.6	63.88
Shopkeeper	8	0.3	74.13
Tavernkeeper	1	0.0	48.00
Tobaconnist	2	0.1	78.75
Construction			
Bricklayer	6	0.2	61.15
Brickmaker	1	0.0	59.50
Carpenter	91	3.0	65.82
Glazier	3	0.1	46.50
Mason	43	1.4	61.92
Plasterer	2	0.1	24.25
Food			
Baker	2	0.1	68.50
Butcher	10	0.3	64.73
Victualer	4	0.1	45.63
Wood			
Chairmaker	1	0.0	50.00
Joyner	20	0.7	61.53
Sawyer	5	0.2	60.80
Turner	14	0.5	59.88
Leather			
Cordwainter	89	2.9	64.27
Sadler	21	0.7	74.11
Skinner	12	0.4	55.98
Tanner	25	0.8	62.07
Liquor			
Brewer	8	0.3	79.46
Vintner	1	0.0	158.75
Miscellaneous			
Clockmaker	1	0.0	60.75
Collier	1	0.0	66.00
Gardiner	3	0.1	54.00

Table 5.7. Size of Loan by Occupation (*cont.*)

Occupation	Number	Percent	Average Loan[a]
Laborer	5	0.2	53.00
Mariner	7	0.2	73.14
Painter	3	0.1	69.83
Potter	2	0.1	70.00
Ropemaker	1	0.0	78.00
Soap boiler	1	0.0	60.00

SOURCE: See table 5.1.

[a] Pounds Pennsylvania currency.

[b] All trades except yeoman, widow, merchant, gentleman, miller, shipwright, lawyer, doctor, and clerk.

Table 5.8. County by Occupation

County	Yeoman	Artisan	Widow	Merchant	Gentleman	Miller	Total
Berk	20	0	0	0	0	0	21
	95.2	0.0	0.0	0.0	0.0	0.0	0.7
	1.0	0.0	0.0	0.0	0.0	0.0	
	0.7	0.0	0.0	0.0	0.0	0.0	
Bucks	589	164	11	3	11	8	791
	74.5	20.7	1.4	0.4	1.4	1.0	26.0
	29.0	22.3	15.9	6.4	18.6	17.0	
	19.4	5.4	0.4	0.1	0.4	0.3	
Chester	609	151	16	5	4	22	814
	74.8	18.6	2.0	0.6	0.5	2.7	26.8
	30.0	20.5	23.3	10.6	6.8	46.8	
	20.0	5.0	0.5	0.2	0.1	0.7	
Cumberland	4	0	0	0	0	0	4
	100.0	0.0	0.0	0.0	0.0	0.0	0.1
	0.2	0.0	0.0	0.0	0.0	0.0	
	0.0	0.0	0.0	0.0	0.0	0.0	
Lancaster	294	41	6	2	10	5	359
	81.9	11.4	1.7	0.6	2.8	1.4	11.8
	14.5	5.6	8.7	4.3	16.9	10.6	
	9.7	1.3	0.2	0.1	0.3	0.2	
Northampton	18	1	0	0	0	0	20
	90.0	5.0	0.0	0.0	0.0	0.0	0.7
	0.9	0.1	0.0	0.0	0.0	0.0	
	0.6	0.0	0.0	0.0	0.0	0.0	

160   *Loan Office and Capital Formation*

Table 5.8. County by Occupation (*cont.*)

County	Yeoman	Artisan	Widow	Merchant	Gentleman	Miller	Total
Philadelphia	7	186	20	34	17	3	289
City	2.4	64.4	6.9	11.8	5.9	1.0	9.5
	0.3	25.2	29.0	72.3	28.8	6.4	
	0.2	6.1	0.7	1.1	0.6	0.1	
Philadelphia	479	185	16	3	16	9	718
County	66.7	25.8	2.2	0.4	2.2	1.3	23.6
	23.6	25.1	23.3	6.4	27.1	19.1	
	15.8	6.1	0.5	0.1	0.5	0.3	
York	6	1	0	0	1	0	8
	75.0	12.5	0.0	0.0	12.5	0.0	0.3
	0.3	0.1	0.0	0.0	1.7	0.0	
	0.2	0.0	0.0	0.0	0.0	0.0	
New Castle Co.,	3	3	0	0	0	0	6
Del.	50.0	50.0	0.0	0.0	0.0	0.0	0.2
	0.1	0.4	0.0	0.0	0.0	0.0	
	0.1	0.1	0.0	0.0	0.0	0.0	
West New	4	5	0	0	0	0	10
Jersey	40.0	50.0	0.0	0.0	0.0	0.0	0.3
	0.2	0.7	0.0	0.0	0.0	0.0	
	0.1	0.2	0.0	0.0	0.0	0.0	
Total	2033	737	69	47	59	47	3040
	66.9	24.2	2.3	1.5	1.9	1.5	

SOURCE: See Table 5.1.

Kirkbride, Joseph Wharton, Nicholas Scull, and Francis Alison. Names of wealthy eighteenth-century Philadelphians, however, do not in general correlate well with the list of mortgagors: only eleven could be found, for example, in Bridenbaugh's early description of Philadelphia, and fewer in Tolles' history of Quaker merchants. The very wealthy, one presumes, had access to other sources of long-run capital.[20]

Thus the typical mortgagor took out one loan in the 1740s in the amount of £65.13*s*. He classified himself a yeoman with 167 acres of land in Bucks, Chester, or Philadelphia County; after 1745 he was as likely to be in Lancaster County. He used his homestead for collateral. If he lived in Chester County, he was taxed at a rate commensurate with the fact that he was among the upper one-fifth of wealth holders. While some were officeholders or otherwise well-known contemporary figures, by far most were not. Because he already had land when he took out the loan and continued to hold only the one homestead, it is open to question what he did with the loan.

CAPITAL FORMATION AND THE LOANS

While the loans were not generally used to buy land, they were apparently not used merely for consumption. Considerable investment—that is, production of capital goods that could be used in turn to produce future goods and services—took place in Pennsylvania during the period of the loans. Grist mills, fulling mills, and sawmills were built and improved, iron foundries established, ships built. On farms, typical improvements included "good English meadow," orchards, fences, outbuildings, stone houses, stone barns. Well before the start of the Seven Years War, as described in chapter 2, a mixed economy of agriculture and manufacturing flourished and contributed to both international and domestic trade.

The diversity of the economy was reflected in the data on the loans. To return to the distribution of occupations in table 5.7, it is interesting to note the number of mortgagors (one-third) who gave their occupation as something other than yeoman. This is a lower bound; anyone with landholdings was entitled to call himself a yeoman, even if he practiced another occupation as well, and the mortgagors obviously were landholders. Samuel Nutt, for example, founder of Coventry Forge and Redding Iron Works, labeled himself a "yeoman."

The merchants and gentlemen who took out loans had access to many other sources of funding. Indeed, they regularly loaned amounts in excess of the £100 ceiling. The £99 Joseph Wharton borrowed in 1736 (as a cooper) and the £60 in 1754 (as a gentleman) seem to disappear in the complex records of his finances. Wharton annually borrowed sums triple the amount of the Loan Office mortgage in the short-term money markets of Philadelphia; mortgages for up to seven years were also available for much larger sums at the time. For those with reliable credit and access to Philadelphia, the Loan Office provided sums that were only a small part of their financial needs.[21]

Within that context it is interesting that seventeen of the earliest iron masters in Pennsylvania borrowed money from the Loan Office at some point. "Iron monger" William Branson borrowed the unusual (and ostensibly illegal) sum of £350 pounds in 1745; two years later he opened a new set of iron works. Samuel Nutt borrowed £99 in 1736, the year Redding Number Two was opened in partnership with Branson, and a year before the opening of Warwick. His widow Anna, who continued to run his foundries after his death, borrowed £49.10s. to make improvements in 1751. Several of the partners in the first iron works in the Manatawny region took out mortgages when the foundries were being built, and by the Revolution Manatawny was a major manufacturing center in the colonies. Thomas Potts took out loans to construct Colebrookdale and Mount Pleasant furnaces; Thomas Rutter borrowed money while developing Colebrookdale, Rutter's Forge, and Pine Forge. Thomas Mayberry borrowed £70 on Green Lane Forge while building Hereford Furnace in 1745; the former was then abandoned for lack of wood and transportation. Another unusually large loan of £460 to John Taylor in May 1745 certainly contributed to the opening of Pennsylvania's first slitting mill in 1746.[22]

Other, less prosaic, occupations received funding from the Loan Office. James Gillingham, creator of "masterpieces in mahogany," received £60 in 1745. The naturalist John Bartram borrowed £80 in 1738, while studying Latin, writing his first treatise, and shipping plant specimens to England. Surveyor Nicholas Scull borrowed money in 1740 and in 1753; Francis Alison took out loans while establishing the New London School and later while a trustee of the Academy of Pennsylvania. James Claypoole, who labeled himself a "painter" in his application for a loan in 1745, operated a paint supply shop, painted portraits, and assisted young painters in establishing careers.[23]

By far the majority of the mortgagors, however, were "yeomen" or independent farmers. Investment in agriculture was never clearcut in the records because it was so direct. An increase in investment often represented a change not in purchasing but in time allocation. The farmer cleared land; planted fruit trees and vines; built, repaired, and improved homes, barns, outbuildings, and fences; made and repaired farming implements and other tools. In addition, the farmer could buy livestock; he might also purchase "capitalized labor" in the form of slaves or indentured servants, or he might purchase human capital in the form of an apprenticeship for his son.

EFFECTS OF THE LOANS

The manner in which the paper money was distributed had almost as great an effect on the economy as the money itself. Loans encouraged investment, rather than consumption, and the size of the financial institution created to issue the loans led to economies of scale and a more efficient allocation of capital. These changes in turn could have promoted changes in equity (that is, distribution of income and wealth), changes in the rate of growth of the economy as a whole, and changes in the rate of growth of income per person.[24]

The Loan Office seems not to have affected the distribution of income and wealth to a very great extent. Had the economy been functioning at full employment of all resources, then the issuing of paper money (as noted in the previous chapter) would have resulted in inflation and the loans would have been financed through a hidden tax on all purchasers of goods and services. Alternatively, had the government borrowed money privately to finance the Loan Office then it could be said that loans made through the Loan Office merely replaced those that would have been made elsewhere, with greater or lesser efficiency depending on circumstances. But the Loan Office was not financed through either inflation or government borrowing. The Loan Office paid for itself, and the money which was loaned cannot be considered to have been taken from private sources.

To the extent that the loans represented a government subsidy in terms of the difference between the effective market interest rate and the government interest rate of 5 percent, then the loans did have an effect on the distribution of income. If loan recipients were limited to those who possessed clear title, the government transfer was available only to one segment of society. Landholders who had cleared their title before the Loan Office Act went into effect were in a position to benefit (although the definition of "clear title" seemed to change during the three decades the Loan Office was in operation). After the law went into effect, all land with clear title became more valuable as a purchase than land without. Far more land transactions were recorded as a result. Finally, landholders as a class benefited because the availability of the loans raised the value of mortgageable land. With loan money available, purchasers were able to offer more for the same amounts of land than previously.

Tenants did try to use long-term leaseholds as collateral for Loan Office mortgages. After a long debate by the Assembly in 1726, the office was ordered only to consider ownership of land or buildings on ground rent. Tenants were therefore not able to participate in the government subsidy program available through the Loan Office. At least some people were able to use Loan Office mortgages to make a first purchase of land, however, and to the extent that that was so, then the subsidy was available to most householders in the province. Furthermore, a tenant who purchased land on which he had placed improvements was able to receive money for the value of the improvements (which he owned) as well as the land he was purchasing.[25]

Finally, to the extent that the Loan Office functioned in a more efficient manner than the private money market because of its size and the governmental presence as guarantor, loans were made available to householders who did not have the right family, religious, or business connections to receive money under the conditions of credit rationing. Loans which would have been high-risk for a Philadelphia merchant or artisan or a Chester County miller or large landholder were less risky for the government-run Loan Office, in part because of its size and in part because of the greater ease with which a government loan could be prosecuted. Without credit rationing, loans to higher-risk householders would have perhaps been made at an interest rate so high as to close out the majority of potential borrowers; with credit rationing there was no opportunity at all for those outside the operating networks to acquire capital.

No one in the private market in Pennsylvania in the middle of the eighteenth century had the resources to operate a financial institution the size of the Loan Office. Corporations required a legislative charter, and hence formal approval from the Board of Trade. The South Sea Bubble had soured the royal bureaucracy on corporations, and as a result approval could not be obtained. An attempt to operate a private land bank in New England was ended by the British government for that reason.[26] Borrowers who would have represented high risks to private lenders in Philadelphia or in the countryside presented lower risks to the Loan Office. These people would not have been able to borrow money for investment; they were forced to finance all investment out of their own savings. In other words, a farmer who could not borrow money for the purposes of improving his land had two choices: go into debt with a local shopkeeper or merchant at high implicit interest rates or forego current consumption because he had to spend time working on improvements on the farm rather than on a cash crop.

The Loan Office thus made below-market loans available in Pennsylvania, and seems to have distributed those loans in a more efficient and equitable manner than the private market. When both these factors were combined, the result was a reduction—at times a remarkable reduction—in the cost of capital and a resulting increase in the amount of investment taking place in the economy. As the available capital stock on a farm grew, the amount a household was able to produce with available labor increased considerably.

As individual farms increased in productivity, the economy as a whole also developed greater capacity to produce in the aggregate and in the amount available per person. The population increased dramatically during this period, from approximately 31,000 in 1720 to 184,000 in 1760. The proportion of colonists residing in Pennsylvania almost doubled from 6.64 percent in 1720 to 11.53 percent forty years later. Despite the intervening war years, there seems to have been no *major* period of economic decline from 1725 to 1755. In his study of southeastern Pennsylvania, historical geographer James Lemon found the rate of growth higher between 1730 and 1760 than at any other time in the eighteenth century. Population increased at an annual rate of 4 to 5 percent during those thirty years, declining to an average of 1.9 percent a year for the rest of the century. Philadelphia grew so rapidly that it quickly surpassed Boston as the largest city in British North America. Soon Philadelphia was the second or third largest city in the British Empire after London. And, as noted in chapter 2, the economy grew at a rate of 0.6 to 1.65 percent per person a year.[27]

With this growth in population came increases in diversification. The Pennsylvania economy had never been solely agricultural (see chapter 2). From the beginning Pennsylvanians practiced a mixed economy with a fair amount of manufacturing. Increases in productivity on the farm led to increased demand for manufactured items; farm families in turn chose to produce more of the goods they already found valuable and they also chose to participate in the market for manufactured goods. Household members practiced occupations other than farming, in particular the young women, who turned to dairying and textiles.

The amount of investment over this period was notable. As described in chapter 2, major industries were firmly entrenched in Pennsylvania by the time of the Revolution. Labor poured into Pennsylvania, but labor alone could not produce income. Land was plentiful, but it could produce little except fur until cleared and readied for agriculture; metals were available, but not without equipment and labor; knowledge about trades abounded, but tools and inventory were necessary to make use of it. Before land, labor, or technology could be used in production, capital was necessary to invest in land clearing, tools, and equipment. As historian John McCusker wrote in his study of Philadelphia shipbuilding, "While Pennsylvania's rate of economic growth is considerable, the ability of the colony's economy to generate increasing amounts of investment capital is even more striking."[28] Attributed variously to entrepreneurship or Quaker thrift, surely some credit must be given as well to the Pennsylvania government for making capital available at inexpensive rates during the formative period of the regional economy.

CHAPTER SIX

Government and Trade in Colonial Pennsylvania

Explicit economic policy concerning trade in Pennsylvania consisted mostly of setting up rules by which trade could proceed. The dominant economic theory of the time, mercantilism, dictated that trade should be actively promoted by legislation. By rewarding some occupations and discouraging others, and by setting up a system of colonies to supply the correct products to the home country, the mercantilist politician believed he could produce advantageous trading relationships within and without the nation. While there were politicians in Pennsylvania influenced by such philosophies, the colony was in no position to play such an active game with regard to trade. Furthermore, the general populace frowned on such interference and resisted any attempts to encroach on their economic independence.[1]

Nor was there a desire to return to those premercantilist economic policies devoted to the protection of a barricaded city-state. Despite the concentration of political power on the township rather than provincial level, there was no clamor for barriers between localities. The sole institution in the colonies with even mildly medievalist leanings was the City Corporation of Philadelphia, which proved so incompetent in its half-hearted promotional endeavors that it bothered no one.[2]

Virtually all trade regulation as developed in Pennsylvania in the first half of the eighteenth century was concerned with reduction of the costs of acquiring information about the market. The classical model of economic relationships generally assumes that there are no impediments to trade such as costs of acquiring information or transportation costs required to move a good physically from the producer to the consumer. When describing economies in history, however, such easy assumptions cannot be made. In fact, changes in transportation and transactions costs have historically accounted for many of the changes in the structure and output of an economy. Long-run reductions in transportation costs over the course of the nineteenth century, for example, had an important impact on the growth of the American economy.[3]

According to economic theory, information costs imply that a buyer cannot tell all he needs to know about the options available in the market place, sometimes about the price and quantity of the goods available, but more generally about the quality of those goods. The buyer must spend more money to find out about the products he wishes to purchase; as a result, he has less money to spend on the product itself. The result will be fewer quantities of the product actually purchased, and, depending on the relative price elasticities of supply and demand, greater costs for the consumer and less income for the producer. Some of these costs will be transferred to others in the economy in the process of acquiring the information. In many cases, information "brokers," or specialists in acquiring information, will surface, and they will receive much of the transfer of income. Some of the transfer will result only in a redistribution of income within the population. Some of it will be felt in the economy as a reduction in efficiency because the consumer will not be able to acquire the product at its lowest potential cost of production; the consumer will purchase some other product, but one for which the economy is perhaps less suited or one which the consumer desired less. Part of the absolute reduction in trade which will result because of the extra costs for the consumer will be lost to the economy without replacement. Economists call this loss the "deadweight loss."[4]

A reduction in information costs reverses the process. Consumers receive more of the good at lower cost. Producers experience increased total revenue while supplying a greater amount of the good. And the economy as a whole experiences an increase in available goods because of the increased efficiency and reduction in deadweight loss. If there is a short-run loser when information costs are reduced, it would perhaps be the information broker, whose services would no longer be necessary. In colonial Pennsylvania, however, the merchants who played that role enjoyed too much flexibility within the economy to have been greatly hurt by the loss of one relatively minor function.[5]

The first aspect of trade in Pennsylvania to be regulated was the standardization of weights and measures. An inspector was appointed to check weights and measures of shopkeepers, packers, and overseas merchants, and was paid a fee by the trader at the time of inspection. From the beginning of the century, the provincial and local governments in Pennsylvania regulated markets and fairs as well. Such regulations served three major functions. The first was that of reducing information costs. With market locations and fair days well established and publicized in advance, buyers and sellers could plan to make the journey confident that a market would exist when they arrived. Time was not wasted waiting for others to appear; spoilable commodities were not ruined. Furthermore, the greater the number of people appearing at a specific location, the greater the choices for both producers and consumers, and the greater the likelihood that prices would approach a level corresponding to the needs and income of consumers and the costs of producers.[6]

A second goal in the establishment of public markets and fair days was the prevention of fraud. Clearly this was an important factor in the regulation of "vendues," the large open auctions at which many goods imported into Philadelphia were sold. Government officers could better supervise the operation of such vendues if they limited the place and time of operation; a fraudulent seller could be better traced if he had been required to be licensed beforehand. Fraud, of course, would have increased information costs associated with operating in the market—not only would a prospective consumer have to seek information actively, he would have to beware of deliberately disseminated dis-information.[7]

Fears of fraud in the market place, the probability of a bit of graft on the part of Philadelphia officials, and the desires of retailers for greater access to the Philadelphia market resulted in a major uproar over the establishment of a second market in the city. The efficiency of the Philadelphia officials in controlling the market was placed in doubt by their apparent fear of some of the stall operators, particularly the butchers. Moreover, the honesty of the Philadelphia Common Council had long been questioned. Actually, there was probably no need any longer for either market. Philadelphia had developed beyond the point that it needed a legally established market. Buyers and sellers were available every day and could doubtless find their own spot in which to transact business without assistance from the government.[8]

Nevertheless, such regulations were preserved. Another purpose in formally establishing market and fair days was the desire to bring trade to a region by formally announcing when it would be possible. Such schemes worked only where trade was already passing through the area anyway. A final reason some traders were regulated actually had less to do with trade than with peacekeeping. Peddlers in particular were licensed more out of the general fear of property owners toward transients than for any other reason.[9]

Virtually all of the regulations concerning trade in colonial Pennsylvania, then, were efforts to reduce the costs of information associated with participating in the market place. There were, however, three exceptions. Through the entire colonial period, the Pennsylvania legislature continued to re-enact laws establishing an assize of bread. It regulated the liquor trade extensively. And it granted permission for the operation of ferries across rivers within the province.

Regulation of the assize of bread was probably the only major piece of legislation with medieval roots continually passed by the Pennsylvania legislature. The regulations described the varieties of bread which could be offered for sale by bakers in the city of Philadelphia and gave the maximum legal prices for each. The price was fixed to the price of wheat; that is, the bakers were permitted a standard markup. The relationship to the price of wheat allowed the bakers a sufficient loophole that their prices were never severely restricted by the law. In fact, the bakers complained to the legislature about the law only once. In 1727, the bakers petitioned that the clerk of the Philadelphia market was "not justifying the Weight according to the Price they [the bakers] give for wheat." The bakers were sent back to the City Council to have the difficulty cleared up and appeared to have had no more problems with the assize.[10]

Both the importing and retailing of liquor were taxed in Pennsylvania, although the purpose was mostly to generate revenue for the government. Liquor taxes provided half the operating budget of the Pennsylvania provincial government during the middle of the eighteenth century; funds provided by the General Loan Office made up the other half. The ability of colonial Pennsylvanians to consume liquor did not seem much affected by the tax. At any rate, it was difficult to mount a moral argument against it. To enforce the tax, retailers in liquor were required to take out a license. Both refusal to pay the tax and the selling of liquor without a license were fineable offenses. Innkeepers were also licensed as a check against their committing a variety of possible offenses, including selling liquor to minors and servants. An innkeeper wishing to set up operations within two (later five) miles of an iron foundry was required to obtain permission from the owners; essentially the owners bound the innkeeper to a promise not to "entertain" the employees of the foundry. In this case, when free trade clashed with the manufacture of an "important" product, the "important" product won, as it would a century later, when manufacturers piled restrictions on the behavior of workers in the name of social stability and increased productivity. But as noted in chapter 2, the iron foundries were the exception to the normal mode of operations in the colony.[11]

The final activity extensively regulated by the colonial legislature was the practice of operating a ferry across a waterway. Technically, the proprietor owned all waterways in the province, and as such only he could grant the privilege of keeping a ferry. This privilege had been acquired by the legislature early in the century, however, during the period when Penn was incapable of running his own affairs. In England, ferries were regulated both as a source of revenue for the regulator and as a way of keeping the service predictable. In Pennsylvania the legislature apparently intended only the latter purpose, although Penn had clearly expected to derive revenue from this service. His heirs would later try to retrieve the privilege.[12]

From the legislature's point of view, ferry regulation was necessary to establish reliable service in a predictable location, reducing the costs of trade by keeping transportation costs down. A single ferrykeeper could charge monopoly prices and segment the market into users with varying needs, charging each the maximum they would pay. A traveler needing an emergency crossing at two in the morning might thus be charged much more than the third member of a neighbor's party crossing at noon. With an unregulated ferryman, there would be no guarantee on price; there would also be no assurance that on any given day he would be at home. From the ferryman's standpoint, regulation protected him from competition: anyone with a raft could send his prices plummeting, with the interloper bearing none of the burden. Both consumers and ferrymen were generally satisfied with the compromise. The legislature designated an official ferryman with monopoly rights (usually two miles up and down the river) to a well-traveled route in return for agreeing to prices set in the enabling act. These rights continued for a set number of years, frequently seven, and they extended to the ferryman and his heirs.[13]

One of the proprietary rights Thomas Penn intended to recapture on his sojourn in Pennsylvania was the privilege of being the sole grantor of ferry routes in the province. Penn was not really interested in trade; he wished to receive the income that would come from ferrymen willing to pay for the privilege. The legislature, on the other hand, wished to retain control over where ferries would be placed. The two compromised on a solution whereby the legislature proposed the location but Penn named the ferryman; the legislature thus retained control over the trade route but Penn kept the income from the payments by these placemen.[14]

REGULATION OF STAPLE EXPORTS

All these aspects of the regulation of trade were taken for granted by the residents of colonial Pennsylvania. Faced with a depression perhaps caused in part by problems in the trade of its export staple, the Pennsylvania legislature took an active role in adding a new form of trade regulation, again in the interests of reducing information costs. In the process, however, the distance Pennsylvania had traveled from the mercantilist outlook of British and other colonial politicians was clearly established.

When Quaker merchant Francis Rawle offered his agenda for Pennsylvania economic policy in a pamphlet in 1721, the establishment of a loan office to issue paper money was only the second order of business; the first was to establish an inspection system for export flour:

> It is a necessary and primary Maxim in every Trading Country That the Credit of the Country must be preserved: in doing of which two things are needful:
> I. The Produce and Manufactory most be good in their Kinds, and not wanting in Weight or Measure
> II. The Pay of the Country ought to be ready and punctual.[15]

Inspection of export staples had for some time been seen as accomplishing two economic goals for a state. First, it raised the price of a valuable export, which was always desirable for a mercantilist; second, it increased the power of the metropolis over the countryside. In Pennsylvania, however, inspection was used for one purpose alone—to establish a signal by which West Indian purchasers of Pennsylvania foodstuffs could properly evaluate the quality of a purchase.

Flour inspection had been enforced in New York in the seventeenth century, but for purely mercantilist purposes.[16] The first charter of privileges to the city of New York in 1665 granted the city the monopoly of bolting and packing all flour and ship bread intended for export from the province. In their petition to Governor Thomas Dongan for a new charter in 1683, the Mayor and Common Council of New York wrote that, according to the old charter which they wished to have renewed:

> No Flower was to be bolted or packed or biskett made for Exportacon butt in the Citty of New York being for the encouragemnt of trade and keepeing up the Reputacon of New York Flour which is in greater request in the West Indies and the only support and maintenance of the Inhabitants of this Citty and if not confirmed to them will ruine and depopulate the same.[17]

Dongan approved the charter with the bolting restriction, complying with instructions from the Duke of York's secretary in England:

> As to w[ha]t you write of Bolting Flower or Biskett, and transporting it, the Com[issione]rs thinke you are to act prudentially herein and upon well weighing the mattr with your Counsell you may determine this there, but soe as by all means chiefly to encourage the City of N. Yorke, . . . alwayes [take] care of the interest and advantages of your City of N. Yorke, that being the Staple of your trade and indeed the key of your Country.[18]

New York City's monopoly of flour bolting, which led to a virtual monopoly of flour milling for export, met with increased resistance in the countryside as the West Indian flour trade grew. Finally, with the cooperation of Governor Benjamin Fletcher, the Albany and country representatives in the Assembly, who far outnumbered New York City's, passed the "Bolting Act" of 1694, revoking New York City's flour monopoly:

The People of the City of *New-York* under colour and pretext of
their Charter or Custom, . . . [have enacted regulations to] forbid the bringing of any Flower or Bread, for Exportation, to *New-
York*, under the Penalty of Forfeiture of the same, which said City
being the principle Port of this Province for the sending forth the
Produce and Manufacturage thereof, and the chief Market within
the same, they thereby not only prohibit the importation and selling
such Flower and Bread at the same City, and obstruct and hinder
all Bolting of Flower and Baking of Bread for Exportation, . . .
in all other Parts of the Province, but also arrogate to themselves
the sole Bolting, [etc.] all such Flower and Bread, raised or to be
produced within the Province, and under colour and pretence of
the said Orders, [etc.] have taken, condemned, and converted to
their own Uses, divers Quantities of Flower belonging to several
of their Majesties good Subjects of this Province. . . . [Therefore]
the said pretended By-Laws, Orders, Ordinances or Regulations
of the People of *New-York* aforesaid, . . . or concerning or relating to the Prohibition, Obstruction, or Hinderance of the using,
practicing, or enjoying of any other lawful Trade, Mystery, or Occupation, or against the Importing in or to, or Exportation from
the City of *New-York*, or any other lawful Port in this Province,
any Wine, Corn, Flower, Bread, Flesh, Fish, Victuals, Wares,
Merchandizes, and all other things vendible, and not by the common Law or Statutes of the Realm prohibited; . . . are hereby
declared void and null.[19]

New York City responded with a double campaign.
First, it attempted to have the Bolting Act rescinded by the Privy
Council. James Graham, Collector of the Port, wrote to William
Blathwayt of the Board of Trade in 1698:

The humour now running amongst the most eminent
of our people and which hath overspread our whole Province, is,
that nothing can be more advantagious for the Province then that
the revenue were abolished; assigning for their pretences the
hardship this Province lyes under when all the adjacent Provinces
are free. This doctrine is very taking with the people in regard to
the great advantages that have attended some of them since the
bolting of flower hath been taken from the Citty of new Yorke,

and the market thereof placed at every Planter's doore through
out the Province; they therefore inferr that if the revenue were
extinguished there would be no need of a Port at New York; and
so every Creek and Bay in the Province would be a port and by
that means manage their unlawfull trade without controule and
thereby reduce the government unto an annarchy.[20]

The passage of the Bolting Act was also included in the list of
grievances against Governor Fletcher by Thomas Weaver, the
province's agent in London.[21] The City then established a tax of
three shillings per half-barrel on all flour brought into the city
from outside for re-export. Governor Bellomont wrote back home
that country members of the Assembly refused to vote him money
for the support of the government until New York City lifted the
tax on country flour. Bellomont had to remove the City Recorder and replace him with someone who would vote against
the ordinance. New York City did agree to lift the tax on country
flour, and the assembly finally voted money for the government.[22] There the matter ended, although as late as 1708 Governor Cornbury recommended to the Board of Trade that the
regulation be reinstated:

> The trade of this Province is much decayed of late years, I mean
> for these ten years past, or more, for in the year 1693/94 it re-
> ceived its most fatal blow by this means; 'Till that time nobody
> was permitted to bolt, but the Citizens of New York, then the
> Bolters were under rule, proper Officers being appointed to view
> all the flower that was Exported, so that no bad commodity was
> suffered to go out; But in that year an Act of Assembly was passed
> whereby all persons in the Country as well as the City were per-
> mitted to Bolt; By which means two great Inconveniencies have
> hapned, one (which is the greatest) is, that the commodity is vi-
> tiated; for the Country Bolter being under no rule or Check, does
> not care what the commodity is, so it pass out of his hands; so
> that he very often mingles Indian Corn flower with his Wheat
> flower; this being discovered in the West Indies has so cried down
> our flower that the Pennsylvania flower sels for three shillings the
> hundred more than ours; . . . And this I look upon as the great-
> est Inconveniency that has hapned by that Act; The other is that

the Country Bolter ingrosses all the Corn of the County where he lives, And there being Bolters in almost every county, it is very difficult for the City Bolters to get corn to carry on their Trade; the Consequence of which is, that the Bolters remove into the Country; If they remove the Coopers must remove too, for they will find no work in the City; That this will be the case we see by experience Already, several having removed themselves, by which means the City will in some years be unpeopled; These two Inconveniencies have hapned by the above mentioned Act, which I take to be the greatest cause of the Decay of our trade.[23]

While New York City's monopoly in the flour trade had been broken and inspection thus made no longer mandatory for the province as a whole, the city apparently did continue to inspect its own flour for export on a voluntary basis. Flour thus stamped with the seal of New York continued to receive higher prices in the West Indies than Pennsylvania flour.

Pennsylvania's legislature had shown no interest in a flour inspection law such as New York's. During this early period the system was associated with the establishment of the bolting monopoly for New York City, and after the failure of the Society of Free Traders, an early attempt at a Philadelphia trading monopoly by William Penn, no one in Pennsylvania showed any inclination to grant mercantilist privileges for the "metropolis" (see chapter 7 following). As long as inspection was associated with the idea of restricting trade to one city, it could never be attractive to the Pennsylvania legislature.

Changes in the market for flour in the West Indies in the second decade of the eighteenth century convinced Pennsylvanians, however, that inspection might be useful not as a mercantilist tool to enhance the metropolis but as a means to enable the increasingly competitive flour trade to continue at all. At the end of the seventeenth century, West Indian sugar planters began to realize that it was to their advantage to concentrate on the production of sugar for export and import much of the necessary foodstuffs to feed their labor force. Increasing demand for food products in the West Indies over the next several decades resulted in a boom in prices for those products in the nearest area that could produce them for export: the British North American colonies. Not only flour but also ship bread, called "biscuit," and meat products were soon being sent from New England and New York to the islands.[24]

Pennsylvania, settled in the middle of the boom, immediately began to take advantage of the situation. As more producers entered the West Indies food market, however, and as that market began to level off, prices began to level off as well. Entrepreneurial profits available in the first decades of the West Indies food market declined. To the extent that falling prices in the 1710s reflected the end of the gain to the first entrants into the market, they were felt equally in New England, New York, and Pennsylvania.[25]

But much to the dismay of Pennsylvania, while prices for flour fell in the West Indies for all producers, New York flour retained a higher price. The discrepancy was attributed to New York's inspection law, apparently still in force voluntarily in the city. As Francis Rawle wrote in 1721:

> We are informed by late Advice from *Jamaica,* That *New-York* Flour is sold for *40 s. per Barrel, Pennsylvania*-Flour at 30 s. The Reason for this Difference in the Sales is undoubtedly the Badness of our Flour. Our Bolters pack up what they please, but in *New-York* all their Flour is weighed and examined, at an Office appointed for that Purpose.[26]

There were several possible solutions to the problem of low flour prices. The first was to establish for Pennsylvania an inspection system that would increase both the quality of flour and the recognition of that quality on the part of potential buyers. Another solution would be to enlarge the market. As Rawle suggested in 1725, the colony through a bounty could encourage merchants to ship flour to southern Europe rather than to the West Indies. "By this Means Encouragement will be given to find out new Markets . . . there will less Quantities be sent to the Islands, this will abate the Glut, and consequently what goes, will fetch the better Price."[27] The Pennsylvania government was hardly in a position to pay such a bounty, however, and the

Assembly never even considered the idea. Rawle himself discarded as impracticable what he thought would be best solution: establishing a monopoly for North American flour in the West Indies.

> For we cannot do as the *Dutch* are said to do, after they extorted from *England* the whole Spice Trade of the *Indies*, were careful to send no more home than they knew would supply *Europe*, so kept up the Price to a vast Profit of their *India*-Trade. Or should we attempt to enhance the Price of Wheat by the method the *Virginians* did to enhance the Price of their Tobacco, the Success would not answer, for the same Reason it had not the desired Effect with them, which was the Restricting the planting of Tobacco to less Quantity, thereby to make it scarce and of greater Value; For *Maryland* not concurring in the Project, it gave them the Advantage of a better Price to the Cost of *Virginia*. And this is the Inconveniency attending contiguous Governments that are distinct, and independent, where if one Government make a Law, tho' never so much for the public Utility, the other frustrates these good Designs from their private Uses, tho' it might be to their mutual Benefit to have concurr'd therein.[28]

Legislated monopolies and bounties proved neither popular nor possible in Pennsylvania, but the idea of inspection caught on quickly. The Assembly received a series of petitions recommending flour inspection, along with increases in the money supply; it passed an inspection law easily in 1722 and gave it top priority when it had to be renewed in 1734.[29]

Inspection, which had been seen as part of the whole system of mercantilist restrictions suggested in New York in the previous century, had taken on a new meaning in Pennsylvania by 1722. Rather than a means to control an unruly market to permit the development of a privileged group within the state, inspection had come to be seen as a way to develop the market itself to its full potential. Through inspection, more would be produced, of better quality, and more would be consumed, of better quality. Both the producers in Pennsylvania and the consumers in the West Indies would benefit.

The reason flour inspection would benefit trade was

because of the reduced costs of information. Historians have long recognized that property rights are a prerequisite to the workings of a market economy. As important as property rights, however, but relatively neglected in economic history, is the free flow of information among buyers and sellers. As noted above, the establishment of uniform weights and measures answered this need for free flows of information. When the seller claimed that his product weighed a certain amount, the buyer was assured that the claim was likely to be true. Otherwise, substantial productive capabilities of an economy would have been wasted in the search for information; economists call these "information costs." When information costs are reduced, the economy benefits in the same manner as when transportation costs are reduced: that is, suppliers receive higher prices at the same time consumers pay lower prices. More is produced, more is consumed, and yet there is still more income left over for other goods and services. Reduction of information costs thus promotes economic growth, an increase in the amount of goods and services available per person.[30]

One way that information costs are reduced in the market is by a process called "signaling." Prices are considered the most important "signals" in the economy; they should "signal," or communicate, the cost of producing a good, the aggregate desire on the part of consumers for the good, and the ability of consumers to pay for the good, given their current incomes and the costs of other goods in the economy. Prices do not always work well as "signals," however. One documented case where prices will not communicate the quality of a product is in the case where the product is marketed in bulk, with no means of separating one producer's output from another's. Under these circumstances, the temptation is very strong to cheat, to include poor quality output in the shipment in the hopes that it will be disguised in the rest. Consumers can be expected to respond to the average quality of the product as a whole, offering a price higher than the value of the poor quality output included in the shipment, but lower than the value of the high quality shipment. Producers of low quality goods are thus encouraged to produce more; producers of high quality goods to produce less. The overall quality deteriorates even further as poor quality producers increase their share of the total, and the price again falls. Hypothetically, a downward spiral could ensue whereby the market for the commodity would completely disintegrate.[31]

In practice, informal "signaling" arrangements usually take the place of prices before the market completely dies. Buyers and sellers find ways to communicate quality on the side, thus enabling the market to continue in operation. These informal communication networks, however, are not without costs: to be precise, they generate information costs which reduce the ability of the economy to operate efficiently. The government or some other agency with authority can at this point step in and create a formal "signaling" system which can communicate the quality of the goods to the buyer and dispense with the need for a separate communications system. The flour inspection system of Pennsylvania operated in precisely this manner: by assuring buyers of a certain quality, sellers in turn were assured of a certain price. Awkward and expensive informal "signaling" networks could be avoided. The concurrent reduction in information costs undoubtedly increased income per capita in the province and in the West Indies as well, where higher quality flour could be procured at a lower price.[32]

When Pennsylvanians first entered the West Indian market they did so on a highly personal level, making use of merchants and planters who were either relatives or, literally, Friends. The network of Quakers proved helpful in their endeavors, as the local Friends meetings could be relied upon to enforce contracts made between Quakers. Jonathan Dickinson, for example, left the West Indies to begin a career as a merchant in Philadelphia; his relatives, who remained in the West Indies, became customers for the flour he bought in Pennsylvania. Generally he received an order for a certain amount of flour, which he purchased and shipped to the West Indies on consignment for his customer. Under this system, his word was the only signal necessary to communicate the true value of a shipment of flour. His relatives could trust that any accidents that Dickinson felt were his fault would be made good to them, and they also knew that they bore some of the risk in the venture themselves. Shipping to known merchants on their risk in the West Indies, Cadwallader Colden also had no trouble communicating the quality of his flour. As long as merchants in Philadelphia were able to fill orders from specific customers in the West Indies, they knew they had to be careful in specifying the quality of the shipment or they would lose their customers. Trust in a merchant's word was an important part of the busines world in the eighteenth century.[33]

Such was not the case when the "glut" appeared in the West Indies market for flour at the beginning of the century. Working with a known customer, while safe, was also slow and cumbersome. As flour prices continued to fall, West Indies purchasers showed a reluctance to agree on a price far in advance of shipment. It was impossible to act quickly on a change in market conditions in a specific port. Information about market conditions from the West Indies had to arrive by ship, which took six weeks. Most merchants then had to locate a shipment and load it, which in itself wasted at least two weeks; the return trip took another six weeks. Thus it would take over three months for suppliers to respond to a change in prices in the West Indies, and by that time the market could have changed dramatically.

Merchants found it increasingly necessary to buy flour at the best price in Pennsylvania, load it on a ship, and send it to the islands in the care of a factor, usually the ship captain, although occasionally a son in training to become a merchant. The merchant's agent on shipboard would order the ship from port to port until the best price was found, frequently a price specified beforehand by the merchant in Philadelphia. As the agent received a portion of the shipment in pay, there was no reason to doubt he would act in the best interests of the other owners of the shipment. However, once the merchants left the network of known buyers to send ships tramping about the West Indies, they found they had lost the ability to communicate ("signal") the value of their shipment to a potential buyer of a particular shipment. Not only did it become difficult to communicate the quality of the flour vis-à-vis other Pennsylvania flour, but the number of ships bearing the name "Pennsylvania" perhaps attested to the increasing difficulty of convincing a strange buyer that the produce came from Pennsylvania at all.[34]

The result of this uncertainty was that buyers paid a price commensurate only with the average quality of flour in the port. Thus the seller of high quality flour received a price lower than the true value of his product; the seller of low quality flour, on the other hand, received a price higher than his flour was worth. As producers in Pennsylvania began to respond to the lack of a price differential for quality flour, the producer of high quality flour was less inclined to continue incurring costs that would not be met in the price; the producer of low quality flour, however, was encouraged to produce even more. The inevitable result was a lower average quality of flour, a lower average price, and another shift in the type of flour produced back in Pennsylvania when the lower prices were communicated to producers. Unless the downward drift of prices could be stopped, there might soon be no market at all for Pennsylvania flour in the West Indies.

The solution was to come up with a "signal" that could be used by any seller in the West Indies, whether or not he knew the buyer. A brand name that would be trusted abroad would qualify as such a signal; hence the perception of government inspection as a reasonable solution. The situation was aptly described in a petition from seven Jamaican merchant houses, sent to the Pennsylvania Assembly in the summer of 1722 and published in the *American Weekly Mercury* one year later:

> The Badness of most of the Flour, imported here from *Pennsylvania* for some time past, has been so evident, that not only curious housekeepers, but also the common Bakers, have entertained such a general Disesteem of all Flour whatever coming from thence, that they are with Difficulty persuaded at any time to look upon *Pennsylvania* Flour; And at this Day the best of that country is sold at 20 s. per *Barrel* in Parcel, and 25 s. Retail, while Choice *New-York* Flour sells daily at 10 s. per *Barrel* more. Thus the Reputation of a Place once famed for the

Best Flour in *America*, is perfectly lost: Which, what sad Effects it must have on the Trade of that Place, as well as the Necessity of Redressing the Grievance, and restoring Credit to that important Province; we offer to the Consideration of the Legislators thereof.[35]

The response of the Pennsylvania legislature to this and other petitions was the enactment of an inspection act in the summer of 1722. At first inspection was voluntary; as the law was finally reformulated in 1725 and remained until the end of the colonial period, inspection was required for all flour and ship bread exported from the province. Unlike the system in New York three decades earlier, Pennsylvania's did not require exported flour to pass through the port of Philadelphia; inspectors were appointed for all three counties. In practice, however, virtually all flour was exported through Philadelphia, and the Philadelphia inspector and his deputies essentially ran the system. All bolters and bakers were required to register a "brand-mark" with the inspection office, and that brand was placed on all casks for export. An inspector or one of his deputies inspected each cask by boring a hole in random spots and testing the quality of the flour (or ship bread). The flour had to "be and be made Merchantable, and of due Fineness, without any Mixture of coarser or other Flour, and honestly and well packed, in well seasoned Cask, with the Tare thereof thereupon marked." If the flour passed inspection, the inspector placed the brand of the Province of Pennsylvania on the outside of the cask. The inspector received one pence per cask for his troubles, which added up to quite a tidy sum, exceeding at times the salary of the Pennsylvania governor. The price was low, however, compared to the value of the brand in the West Indies market. Merchants' accounts books for the time consistently show that the flour was indeed inspected before export—or, at least, the inspector was paid. The act was continued in force throughout the colonial period, although later revisions of the law added grades, eventually four in all, from coarse to "super-fine," reflecting the practice apparently already being followed in the inspection office.[36]

An analysis of price movements related to the enactment of the law are made difficult by the simultaneous enactment of the first paper money bill in Pennsylvania. By adjusting Anne Bezanson's price series for flour to sterling on the basis of John McCusker's exchange rates, however, I have identified a turning point of sorts for flour prices in the second quarter of 1723, one year after the enactment of the law. This development seems consistent with a change in attitude in the West Indies toward Pennsylvania flour (see table 6.1). Flour prices changed erratically, however—as did prices for any agricultural commodity.

A comparison of Pennsylvania flour prices to those of rival New York suggests that the new law had a positive effect. This comparison eliminates price movements due to weather or war, because both colonies faced similar constraints. Although New York flour prices are more difficult to obtain than those of Pennsylvania, observations available through newspaper price currents series offer some information. Twelve observations from the *American Weekly Mercury* (printed in Philadelphia by Andrew Bradford) from January 1720 to November 1721 show Pennsylvania flour prices averaging only 83.7 percent of New York's (see table 6.2). New York prices do not appear again, in the *Mercury* or any other colonial newspaper, until January 1725, when the *Mercury* printed a series of eight observations to July 1729. This time, after the inspection law was in force, the relationship had reversed, with New York prices only 85.9 percent of Pennsylvania's. Curiously, a slightly different pattern emerges from the price currents series of the *New York Gazette*, printed by William Bradford, brother of the *Mercury*'s printer. Here New York prices appear closer to Pennsylvania's—93.1 percent, with a rising trend showing New York closing the gap. Prices from the 1730s in the *Pennsylvania Gazette* (printed by Benjamin Franklin and Hugh Meredith) and the *New York Gazette* are equally inconclusive: Franklin has Pennsylvania with slightly higher prices; Bradford gives New York the edge.[37]

Virtually all the contemporary testimony, however, sides with the Pennsylvanians. Contemporaries from New York,

Government and Trade

Table 6.1. Pennsylvania Flour Prices, 1720–1727

Quarter	Pennsylvania Currency[a]	British Sterling[a]
First, 1720	9.56	7.03
Second, 1720	9.00	6.49
Third, 1720	9.39	6.71
Fourth, 1720	9.08	6.60
First, 1721	8.50	6.18
Second, 1721	8.50	6.18
Third, 1721	9.25	6.73
Fourth, 1721	9.09	6.61
First, 1722	8.88	6.59
Second, 1722	8.92	6.59
Third, 1722	9.48	7.11
Fourth, 1722	8.44	6.17
First, 1723	8.38	6.09
Second, 1723	8.67	6.31
Third, 1723	9.05	6.35
Fourth, 1723	9.12	6.39
First, 1724	9.59	7.19
Second, 1724	10.71	7.75
Third, 1724	11.42	7.91
Fourth, 1724	12.08	7.97
First, 1725	12.25	8.59
Second, 1725	11.42	8.01
Third, 1725	11.98	8.60
Fourth, 1725	12.83	8.79
First, 1726	11.93	8.18
Second, 1726	12.17	8.34
Third, 1726	13.00	8.91
Fourth, 1726	12.92	8.86
First, 1727	12.32	8.44
Second, 1727	11.81	8.09
Third, 1727	11.38	7.76
Fourth, 1727	10.33	6.77

SOURCE: Anne Bezanson et al., *Prices in Colonial Pennsylvania.* Prices in Pennsylvania current money were converted to British sterling using the exchange rates in John J. McCusker, *Money and Exchange in Europe and America, 1600–1775*, pp. 183–85.
  [a] Pounds per hundredweight.

the West Indies, and Maryland all claimed that Pennsylvania flour was valued more highly. The change in relative positions of New York and Pennsylvania after Pennsylvania's inspection law went into effect led for the first time to petitions in the New

Table 6.2. Prices of Pennsylvania and New York Flour, 1720–1740

Date	Pennsylvania Currency	Pennsylvania Sterling	PA price/ NY price	New York Currency	New York Sterling	NY price/ PA price
American Weekly Mercury						
Jan. 1720	9.50	7.04	80.1%	14.50	8.79	124.9%
March 1720	9.50	7.04	88.1%	13.50	7.99	113.5%
April 1720	8.75	6.29	79.1%	13.13	7.95	126.4%
May 1720	8.75	6.29	83.0%	12.50	7.58	120.5%
June 1720	9.50	6.83	83.5%	13.50	8.18	119.8%
July 1720	9.50	6.83	83.5%	13.50	8.18	119.8%
Aug. 1720	9.25	6.65	81.3%	13.50	8.18	123.0%
Sept. 1720	9.50	6.79	83.0%	13.50	8.18	120.5%
Oct. 1720	9.50	6.79	83.0%	13.50	8.18	120.5%
March 1721	8.25	5.98	79.7%	12.25	7.50	125.4%
Sept. 1721	9.50	6.91	101.3%	11.25	6.82	98.7%
Nov. 1721	8.87	6.45	81.1%	13.13	7.95	123.3%
Jan. 1725	12.25	8.79	120.7%	12.75	7.28	82.8%
Sept. 1725	12.00	8.27	113.8%	12.00	7.27	87.9%
Dec. 1725	13.00	9.33	123.1%	12.00	7.58	81.2%
April 1726	12.00	8.28	120.2%	11.38	6.89	83.2%
March 1727	12.13	8.11	121.6%	11.00	6.67	82.2%
May 1728	9.63	6.42	100.9%	10.50	6.36	99.1%
May 1729	9.00	6.06	105.2%	9.50	5.76	105.2%
July 1729	11.00	7.40	131.9%	9.25	5.61	75.8%
New York Gazette						
April 1726	12.00	8.28	121.4%	11.25	6.82	82.4%
May 1726	12.00	8.28	111.6%	12.25	7.42	89.6%
June 1726	12.00	8.28	111.6%	12.25	7.42	89.6%
July 1726	13.00	8.97	116.0%	12.75	7.73	86.2%
Sept. 1726	13.00	8.97	103.8%	14.25	8.64	96.3%
Oct. 1726	13.13	9.06	104.9%	14.13	8.64	95.4%
Feb. 1727	12.52	8.37	102.3%	13.50	8.18	97.7%
March 1727	12.13	8.11	99.1%	13.50	8.18	100.9%
March 1728	9.88	6.59	103.6%	10.50	6.36	97.5%
May 1728	9.63	6.42	100.9%	10.50	6.36	99.1%
Pennsylvania Gazette						
April 1730	12.00	7.89	102.2%	12.87	7.72	97.8%
May 1731	7.75	5.08	101.6%	8.25	5.00	98.4%
July 1731	6.75	4.50	90.0%	8.25	5.00	111.1%
Oct. 1731	10.00	6.45	115.0%	9.25	5.61	87.0%
June 1732	7.75	4.79	98.8%	8.00	4.85	98.8%
New York Gazette						
Sept. 1733	9.0–12.0	5.4–7.2	70–93%	11.5–14.0	7.73	107–143%
March 1734	9.75–10.0	5.7–5.9	95–97%	10.00	6.06	103–106%

Table 6.2. Prices of Pennsylvania and New York Flour, 1720–1740 (cont.)

Date	Pennsylvania		PA price/ NY price	New York		NY price/ PA price
	Currency	Sterling		Currency	Sterling	
Aug. 1734	10.7–11.0	6.3–6.5	94–97%	11.00	6.67	103–106%
March 1736	9.00	5.39	93.1%	8.83	5.25	106.9%
Sept. 1739	8.25	4.92	93.7%	8.83	5.25	106.7%
Oct. 1739	8.50	5.07	96.6%	8.83	5.25	103.6%
Nov. 1739	7.88	4.67	89.0%	8.83	5.25	112.4%
March 1740	7.50	4.47	85.1%	8.83	5.25	117.4%

Note: Pounds currency per hundredweight flour.

York legislature to reinstate mandatory inspection in that colony. But memories of the old system kept the legislature from passing any laws inspecting flour until 1750.[38]

The success of Pennsylvania's flour inspection influenced other colonies to enact similar laws. Virginia and Maryland enacted tobacco inspection laws in 1730 and 1747, respectively; New York finally acquiesced to flour inspection; and several colonies established inspection of packed meat. By the Seven Years War, packed meat and lumber were added to flour and ship bread as exports requiring inspection in Pennsylvania.[39]

Pennsylvania's flour inspection set up the framework within which the wheat economy could expand as the colony grew. Technological changes in the middle of the century—for instance, the introduction of the "French burr-stone," which improved the quality of the flour produced—could be reflected in the price of the product when the miller branded it and the province assured the buyer that such a mark was indeed valid. Since they were receiving higher prices for Pennsylvania flour, millers were able to reach far down into Maryland and Virginia for sources of wheat, expanding Philadelphia's hinterland as far south as the Shenandoah and Georgetown as well as to the portions of New Jersey which had always used Philadelphia as a port.[40]

The major trade regulations in colonial Pennsylvania were thus mainly rule-setting laws, providing a framework within which information about the market could be provided to all participants on a relatively costless basis. The willingness of merchants to participate in the inspection of export flour demonstrated that they found the system useful to their export trade. Flour inspection provided a case where the Pennsylvania colonists, usually reluctant to enact laws concerning the economy, passed active legislation because they thought it would lead to increased income for most households in the colony.

CHAPTER SEVEN

Public Finance:
The Government
as Economic Agent

The Pennsylvania government served more functions
in the economy than merely that of setting the standards and
arbitrating trade. The government itself formed a sector of the
economy, providing public goods through the imposition of taxes
and a complex schedule of fees for services rendered. Through
most of the colonial period, local and county government proved
much more effective at providing services than the provincial or
royal government. The growth of internal transportation
throughout the period led to an increase in the ability of a cen-
tralized government to exercise control over the hinterland. The
Seven Years War would bring this increased potential to the attention of both Philadelphia and London.

While the provision of public goods and services could
be viewed as a positive contribution of the government sector to
the Pennsylvania economy, colonists were also well aware of
the potential dangers inherent in a strong government. Experience had taught colonists to fear the role of monopolists and
placemen who would use the government's power to acquire
economic privileges. Throughout the colonial period, there would
always be those on both sides of the Atlantic only too willing to
use government in this fashion. As long as the provincial government remained weak, however, and as long as the powers of
monopoly and political appointment remained in the hands of

the legislature, the acquisition and enforcement of privilege would prove too expensive for the reward.

THE PROVISION OF PUBLIC GOODS AND SERVICES

From 1711 to 1755, the provincial government of Pennsylvania collected neither property nor head taxes from the populace. As a result, the few government services perceived as necessary by the colony had to be financed by directly taxing those most concerned, generally by imposing a system of fees and fines on the use of government services. The unwillingness of the general population to provide government funds on a provincial level also limited the potential for public improvements. Little apparently impeded development within townships and counties, where the governments had much more moral authority with the public to collect taxes or services. It was not until the Seven Years War, however, that projects encompassing Pennsylvania as a whole could be financed, either through the government or private investors.

For nearly 40 years the provincial government in Pennsylvania did not collect taxes because the last attempt to do so, in 1711, had proved a dismal failure. Every year after 1711 another law appeared on the books trying a different method for obtaining the tax money. But even when the collectors themselves were personally charged with their districts' tax money, they flatly refused to collect. The legislature itself, perhaps in sympathy with local resistance to taxes, imposed a one-year limit on each of the tax collection laws, hindering whatever attempts were made at enforcing them. Efforts at collecting the tax finally ended in 1717 and were not renewed until 1755.[1]

The provincial government was able to provide sufficient funding for the little that was asked of it through the liquor taxes and the operations of the General Loan Office. All liquor imported into the colony, as well as liquor sold by the drink, was taxed. The purpose of the General Loan Office was to introduce paper money into circulation to ease a perceived currency shortage; the Loan Office was expected to provide cheap capital for farmers as well. The Loan Office operations proved so efficient, however, that the profits were able to supplement the liquor tax to the extent that no other taxes were needed.[2]

While no provincial taxes were levied during this period, local taxes were collected almost annually in each county. County governments usually charged about one to three pence per pound of assessed wealth, with the definition of wealth including improved land and livestock. Later in the century a trade tax would also be added. Freemen without families to support were charged an extra fee, usually six shillings per head. Inmates, as defined in chapter 2, were taxed separately, seldom above one or two shillings. The poor, usually listed in the township's tax return, were not taxed at all. County officials appear to have had virtually no difficulty assessing and collecting these local taxes, in part because the local governments exercised much greater control over the community than the provincial government.[3]

Local taxes were small because the local governments did not need much money to run their affairs. Tax money was used in a large part to finance locally run poor relief programs and workhouses; the special importance of these programs to Quakers may have accounted for the willingness of the public to finance them. The other major destination of tax money was paying for overruns of county programs when those responsible for the fees would not or could not come through with them. Tax money was also used in part to pay back loans borrowed from the Loan Office, which in turn were used by the counties to support the building of courthouses and workhouses.[4]

It is difficult to say how long direct taxation might have remained the sole jurisdiction of local government in Pennsylvania. When the province entered the Seven Years War, however (amidst a great deal of quarreling among pacifists, the frontier settlers, and the British government), the provincial government was pushed by London and opinion in other colonies to levy taxes to pay for the war effort. Taxes jumped from one or two pence per pound assessed wealth to eighteen pence, or a shilling and a half, in 1755. At the war's end, the success of collecting such a large tax from a previously recalcitrant population was lost on no one. The sudden increase in perceived ability by the provincial government to finance its activities exposed an equally sudden increase in the real power of that government and a fall in the relative power of the localities. The governor and the proprietors quarreled with the legislature over the disposition of the money so collected, and it would just be a matter of time before London would show interest in the funds as well.[5]

By and large, most government activities in Pennsylvania during the colonial period were not financed directly through the government budget. Pennsylvania followed the standard contemporary practice in Europe of assigning commissions to the agents in charge of performing government services, making it incumbent upon the agents to collect for themselves. An efficient government agent presumably could collect more money than an inefficient one, and the community was always ready to defend itself against an overzealous agent who tried to use his powers to collect more than was perceived to be his fair share.[6]

Government functions financed in this direct manner involved three general areas: the keeping of the peace, land transactions, and regulation of trade. The entire court and jail system was run on a fee basis. When the government itself brought the indictment, as in felonies or charges of disturbing the public peace, the defendant almost always had to pay charges, even when found innocent. Charges for a private suit were determined by the disposition of that suit, with the loser generally paying the fees, though sometimes they were split. The jailer charged his guests for food and drink, as well as his time and trouble in caring for them, whether or not they were found guilty or innocent. The county only stepped in to pay the fees when the system failed: when the defendant ran away to a different colony without paying, or was indigent but could not be sold as a servant to pay costs.[7]

Government services involving land transactions were also supported by direct fees for services rendered. By law, all mortgages, leases, deeds, and transfers were supposed to be recorded with the county Recorder of Deeds. Furthermore, land transactions involving the Land Office—the purchase of a warrant or patent and the formal return of a survey or a resurvey—involved payments to all of the Land Office agents directly concerned. Acquiring a mortgage from the General Loan Office cost application fees and fees to the clerk upon receiving the money and registering the mortgage in the Loan Office.[8]

All the agencies established by the provincial government to regulate trade were also financed by a fee system. Liquor licenses were required in part to keep track of those in the trade so they could be taxed, and in part to pay for the administration of the tax. A fee was required when weights and measures were tested; fees were charged for every barrel of flour, ship bread, or meat inspected for export. In each case, the tax collector or inspector was not paid a direct salary from the government; he received a pre-agreed percentage of the fees he himself collected for the government.[9]

Direct fees worked best when those standing to benefit the most from the government service shared the cost of it. The fee system thus proved an efficient method for executing the laws governing inspection of certain exports. Every exporter of flour had to pay the inspectors a price proportional to the amount of flour exported. Since the system of inspection worked, they benefited in the same proportion. That they believed it was in their interests can be demonstrated from their willingness to have their shipments branded and to pay the fines. In contrast, the sole beneficiaries of the Navigation Acts tariffs on various articles lived in Britain. As a result, when agents of the British government could not force compliance, which was often, Pennsylvania merchants simply refused to pay. Furthermore, to the extent that most merchants approved of the inspection law and willingly paid the fines, the inspector was provided with sufficient funds to track down the few who did not wish to go along. In contrast, the British customs collector in Philadelphia constantly complained of insufficient funds with which to perform his duties. The flour inspector's income was higher than the port collector's, even though the flour inspector's search costs were lower. The system thus made it easier to enforce a popular law, and more difficult to enforce an unpopular one.[10]

The system worked poorly when the benefits from the government service were spread over a larger group of people than those who paid the direct fees. Probably the least efficient manifestation of the fee system could be found in the court and jail system of requiring defendants to pay costs when they were found innocent. The keeping of the peace benefited the entire populace, whether they were involved in a particular case or not; wrongfully accused defendants bore a grossly disproportional share of that burden. The plight of an acquitted defendant charged with court and jail costs seems, nevertheless, to have aroused little sympathy in the general populace.

When the accused was found guilty, an argument could be made supporting the equity of having the defendant rather than the public pay for the charges of his confinement and prosecution. The problem here was that such a "tax" proved exceedingly regressive in terms of the equity of its burden among different wealth groups. Courts charged standard fees for various crimes without taking into account the relative wealth of the criminal; in effect, conviction was proportionately far less expensive for the wealthier defendant. If a defendant could not pay his fees, he was left in jail, accruing a debt to the jailer to add to his debt to the court. His goods were attached, and if that did not pay off his fines and debts, he could be sold as an indentured servant. If he was already a servant, his master was charged court costs, jail costs, and fees, and his length of servitude was increased to pay off the debt thus incurred to his master.[11]

In the case of land transactions, it could be argued that the benefit to the whole community of recording all land transactions (to prevent fraud) exceeded the benefit to any particular person (who presumably did not feel that he would be either the victim or perpetrator of such fraud). More to the point, however, the Land Office and the proprietors seemed to have been the primary beneficiaries of the registration of land transactions, with the risks involved in formally registering land to be balanced against the benefits. Whether influenced by the prospect of being charged quitrents or the costs of formalizing a deed for registration, virtually half of the population apparently did not find the costs of the fees and travel time worth the benefits. Neither was the population as a whole sufficiently concerned about fraud to insist upon registration when the landowner saw no personal benefit to be gained. As long as disputes involving land could be settled in or out of court on the testimony of neighbors, the registration of deeds was an added piece of security that most settlers believed unnecessary. It was not until after the Seven Years War, when increases in the division of already settled land would make the surveys and formal deeds more important than the word of neighbors in determining the disposition of suits, that deed registration would become an important part of a land transaction for most colonists in the province. In the land case, as in the tariff case, support of a standing government agency by government-levied taxation to register all land transactions would have resulted in more transactions registered than the public apparently wished. The fee system can be said to have worked well in this case.[12]

One final difficulty which has historically arisen when a consignment or fee system has been used to support government activity is the threat that the government agent might use his power to levy the "tax" unequally. That is, the agent might charge a higher, illegal fee to some occupants and ignore the fee, for a kickback, for others. In colonial Pennsylvania, the community was small and strong enough, and the provincial government weak enough, that graft on the part of government agents does not seem to have posed much of a problem. In this highly vocal, complaining society, petitions were cheap; yet few complained of unequal treatment by inspectors or collectors. This situation, too, would change after the Seven Years War.

PUBLIC IMPROVEMENTS

In a developing economy such as that of colonial Pennsylvania, perhaps the most important role for the government was in the building of a public capital stock to reduce trading costs and increase current income and the rate at which the economy diversified. The creation of such public improvements posed serious problems for a government which ran almost entirely on a system of specific fees for specific services rendered. Almost any public improvement would benefit a greater segment of the population than could be induced to pay for it directly. As a result, public investment in colonial Pennsylvania was confined mostly to areas where a strong local government could induce the public to pay. A commitment to public improvements for the colony as a whole had to await a stronger provincial government after 1755.

All of the colonies faced the difficulty of promoting public improvements on a province-wide basis. One prominent remnant of mercantilist theory in the colonies was the belief that government action could create a strong metropolis. Mercantilist theorists understood that a large central city encouraged specialization of various functions, enabling increased gains from trade which benefited the surrounding region. Cities encouraged the development of craft specializations, as well as the growth of financial markets and specialists in trade, both local (shopkeepers) and international (merchants). Areas without a metropolis complained of the income lost when they had to use facilities in ports elsewhere. Maryland in particular would devote many laws to attempts to create a metropolis by force where none existed.[13]

It was with this understanding that William Penn established the city of Philadelphia concurrently with his first grants of land in the province. The city was almost immediately granted a charter, and the city corporation was expected to defend its position as provincial "metropolis." Within the space of half a century, Philadelphia had grown so rapidly that it had become one of the largest cities in the British Empire, surpassing all other British North American colonial cities in size by 1750.

Despite Penn's clear intentions to make Philadelphia a strong metropolis, however, the city's spectacular growth cannot be attributed to explicit policies adopted by the proprietary government. In choosing Philadelphia as the seat of government, Penn guaranteed that the city on the Delaware that would develop would be Philadelphia rather than Chester, New Castle, or Bristol, but designating a provincial capital alone would not have been sufficient to guarantee success. It was not sufficient to make Annapolis a powerful city and would not be enough to defend Annapolis from encroachment in trade by Baltimore when that city mushroomed in size after 1750. In the absence of restraints against trade passing through Philadelphia, the city grew solely in response to the equally stunning growth of its hinterland economy. Philadelphia's ideal location, the rapid growth of and mixed nature of its hinterland economy, and the early presence of skilled craftsmen in the city all proved more important than the presence of the government in determining Philadelphia's eventual importance in the colonies. In fact, the one major piece of legislation which did influence trade in Philadelphia did so in a negative fashion. Restrictions on imported servants led to their disembarking in New Castle when they would otherwise probably have gone to Philadelphia. Even with the inspection laws, however, trade was at no time forced by law to pass through the city. Inspectors were always appointed for other points of departure. The city grew in response to trade, not to government policy.[14]

Ironically, the city government itself proved completely incompetent in the performance of its mercantilist duties as protector of the metropolis. Granted a charter in 1705, the city was governed by a closed corporation. The original members were nominated by Penn; later members were nominated by the original members; all members served for life. As time went on the corporation became more and more disaffected from the city as a whole. Behaving more like a club than a city government, the corporation increasingly lost jurisdiction over its original functions, until its only real activity was to serve as court of the justices of the peace.[15]

The city had originally enacted the usual regulations restricting trade within and outside its boundaries. It permitted trade only in shops or a designated marketplace; it forbade tradesmen and artisans to operate their businesses without purchasing the "freedom of the city"; it designated public wharfs; it laid out roads and made plans to keep them repaired; it licensed and regulated peddlers, woodsellers, and teamsters. But few of these regulations, if any, were ever enforced. The members of the corporation were all successful tradesmen and merchants with little time for city affairs and without sufficient government funds with which to hire deputies. In an effort to add to the city treasury, and in response to complaints by tradesmen and artisans, the city sold "freedoms" in 1717, announcing that in the future only registered freemen would be permitted to practice a trade. For a year city dwellers purchased their freedom only to discover over the next five years that the city still would not prosecute newcomers who did not pay. Market regulations were not enforced, particularly with regard to butchers, who as a group apparently intimidated even the members of the Common Council. Petitioners complained to the provincial legislature that roads were not repaired and that the public wharfs were a shambles. Worst of all, however, was the sloppy fashion with which the corporation handled public finances.[16]

Whenever someone was owed money by the city government for some service, he presented a bill to the city treasurer and was reimbursed; whenever someone had to pay a fine or fee, he paid the treasurer. The treasurer kept all the books and the money, and for his services received 5 percent of all incoming money and 5 percent of all outgoing money—in other words, 10 percent of the city budget. In the first 25 years the city corporation was in operation, not once did the city treasurer present an account of the city money. The situation became embarrassing in 1730 when William Fishbourne was convicted by the legislature of embezzling money from the General Loan Office, for William Fishbourne had been city treasurer for the last two decades. While Fishbourne was never accused by the city government of any misdeeds—indeed, there is no mention in the city records of the impeachment proceedings in the legislature—the legislature itself specifically barred him from continuing to hold any office in the province, obviously with his role as city treasurer in mind.[17]

The corporation's complacency in the Fishbourne case along with its apparent inability to keep the city in good repair led to a separation of city functions by the provincial legislature. The legislature effectively took away the city's ability both to tax and to decide on public improvements by establishing an elected board of commissioners similar to the commissioners elected for the same purpose in each of the three original counties. Legislation approving street repair, lights, wharfs, and the improvement of Dock Creek (the city sewer) all came from the provincial legislature rather than from the city corporation. Well aware of the importance of the city to the rest of the colony, the colonial legislature took charge of improvements within the city, leaving the financing and execution of those improvements to the commissioners, and the enforcement of laws to the corporation in its role as city court. While the legislature did not create the city itself, the members did act to keep the city functioning and in good repair.[18]

Except for the assistance given to Philadelphia in legislating approval for improvement projects, the legislature was not responsible for much in the way of developing the physical capital of the colony. The legislature built the Pennsylvania State House, financing it by subscription and paying the investors back with money earned by the Loan Office. The purpose of the State House, however, was not economic development but civic pride (and greater comfort to the legislators). The Council was technically in charge of laying out and keeping in repair the "King's Highways," main thoroughfares throughout the colony. But in practice the Council was impotent to create or repair roads without the cooperation of the township through which a road passed. The Council had substantial control over the placement of bridges, but the specific townships themselves usually requested the bridges in the first place and exercised judgment on the benefits derived from keeping them repaired.[19]

Of all public improvements developed in Pennsylvania during the eighteenth century, the most important was the network of roads upon which goods traveled to market (see map, p. 19). While transportation in the Chesapeake depended heavily on waterways, roads were more important to trade in colonial Pennsylvania. Both wheat and flour, respectively the major crop and export of Pennsylvania, were packed in smaller barrels which were never directly rolled on the ground. Sometimes they traveled on the water in shallops. More frequently they were carried in carts overland, the wheat to the miller, the flour from the miller to the Philadelphia wharfs. Manufactured imports from Europe traveled back to the countryside in carts, and locally crafted products were either directly picked up by horse or cart, or shipped by cart to a market town and picked up there to be returned to the countryside in another cart. Even iron was transported by cart.[20]

The importance of the network of roads to the Pennsylvania trade can be seen in the road petitions in the county courts. A typical petition requested a "good cart road" leading to the main highway to Philadelphia, or a "passage to mill and market." Petitioners seldom asked for a road to the nearest river; if the route requested was not to the Philadelphia high road, then it was to a highway connecting two major market towns such as Concord and Chichester.[21]

Some of the earliest roads developed without official permission. An Indian trail widened by the passage of settlers to new lands might become the de facto path by which most people traveled from one point to another. Such roads were always in danger of being cut off when someone purchased property through which the road passed and erected fences. Nottingham petitioners asked that a road be cut from Limestone Ridge to Nottingham, as the old road (originally an Indian trail) had been blocked by new settlers. Travelers from a section of Tredifryn had a good road to the Great Road for fourteen years, but petitioned the legislature in 1719 that "this Road now is Like to be stopd" by a planter putting new improvements on his land. A formally laid out road, however, was protected against encroachments by property owners on the route. "Inhabitants of Springfield and Marple [petitioned] the court against one Job Yarnall for Stoping the Road formerly laid out from Springfield to the Navagable Water at Amos Land and Corneill," Yarnall having "suffered to hang gates where the same passes through the improved part of his Land." Yarnall was ordered to clear the obstructions.[22]

A person who needed a road to connect his plantation through another's to a main market road began with a petition to the county court of quarter sessions. Six people would be designated to view the prospective route of the road and return a description to the court, at which time orders would be sent out to have the road cleared. If the court felt the road would benefit others besides the petitioner, or if the road went between two undeveloped pieces of property, then the petitioner usually cut the road himself and the township later shared responsibility for keeping it repaired. In some cases, however, if it was necessary to build fences along the road to protect property already improved or if the road was seen to benefit only the petitioner, then the petitioner was also required to compensate the landowner(s) through whose land the road cut for the loss of land and building the fences. The petitioner was also charged with the costs of keeping the road repaired. Such petitions were relatively rare, however; in most cases neighbors must have assisted in offering inoffensive routes to market roads where someone's land was blocked.[23]

The most common type of petition requested a road for an entire community that felt cut off from the market. Similarly, a group would petition for a road leading to or from a mill, presumably with the encouragement of the mill owner. Petitions requested roads to churches or meeting houses as well. In these cases it was up to the discretion of the Commissioner of Roads in the concerned township to designate those who would clear and repair the roads, although one presumes that the petitioners who signed in favor of the road were most often tapped.[24]

Responsibility for repair of roads fell to the township through which they passed. A Commissioner of the Roads was appointed for each township to assign people to work on the roads or to pay a fee with which a substitute could be hired. Failure by a township to keep a road in repair resulted in a petition to the county court, but such incidents were sufficiently rare as to suggest that members of the community generally accepted their responsibility in such matters.[25]

The Provincial Council appears to have encountered greater difficulties keeping its roads repaired than the counties or townships. Roads west in particular posed a constant problem for the Council. They sometimes had to pass through undeveloped land, and the beneficiaries could be far away from the townships which were told to maintain the road. As Speaker of the House and developer of the town of Lancaster, Andrew Hamilton was able in 1734 to push through the Lancaster Road (in competition with Logan's Conestoga Road), which may account in large part for the town's success. The road had still not been cut by 1737, however; inhabitants of Whiteland, Caln, and other townships through which it was to pass complained to the County that "to Clear the said Road would be altogether Impracticable by Reason the Courses and Distances therein are in many places exceeding Irregular." Another example of the Council's problems with townships appeared in Jacob Vernon's petition to the Chester County Court in 1740: the townships of Caln and Bradford had defined their boundaries so that the portion of the Great Road to Philadelphia passing between them lay within the legal limits of neither—thus, they argued, they could not be responsible for repairing the road.[26]

Intercolonial roads appear to have been used more for communication links than for transporting goods. Flour or wheat destined for the Philadelphia area from the Lower Counties or the Eastern Shore traveled briefly overland to a point of departure on the water for the Delaware Bay, and then most likely by shallop to the city. But a gentleman planning to visit the city for business or pleasure, or a packet rider with mail, would go by horse overland. Coastal ships carried the trade between New York and Boston and Philadelphia; only travelers on horseback could be found on the major King's Highways between those points. There was thus less reason to keep those roads in the type of repair which was absolutely necessary for the market roads in the hinterland, and contemporary complaints suggest that they did indeed suffer by comparison.

Bridges formed the final type of capital improvement erected by the government to improve transportation. Unless they crossed an insignificant creek (in which case there was less likelihood of a bridge than a ford), bridges almost always drew the attention of the provincial government. Road transportation and water transportation came into direct conflict when a bridge was built, for it cost much more money to build a bridge sturdy enough to enable a cart to cross a river safely, yet high enough to permit boats to pass through. Even when the bridge was wholly contained within a county or township, the legislature could get involved because the rivers belonged to the province and the proprietor.[27]

The period in Pennsylvania before 1755 saw much local activity in the way of public improvements. Community government appears to have been much stronger in Pennsylvania than the provincial government. Counties and townships seemed to have had no difficulty meeting the needs of inhabitants for passable roads between markets, mills, and manufacturing centers. Provincial roads, on the other hand, were much more difficult both to build and to maintain. As long as groups settled in a contiguous fashion, with new townships developed along the relatively settled areas of old ones, it was apparently relatively easy to link up to major marketing centers through small roads leading to already established thoroughfares. In the cases where Palatines or Ulster Scots settled far away from already established areas, however, it was very difficult to force the townships farther in to support a new road. This was perhaps the one case where the outlanders were better off remaining in an old county; it was easier for the county to force compliance with an order to build or cut a road than for the province. The system of requiring localities to keep roads in repair led to

the development of a usable and evidently efficient network of
local roads within the original counties leading to Philadelphia
and the Delaware. The system would not prove so efficient when
a series of larger roads would be required fanning out through
the Philadelphia hinterland into the frontier areas.[28]

Such a casual approach to the development of roads
west could not meet the needs of the militia in defending the
frontier as the Seven Years War approached. As a result, the first
major western roads built in Pennsylvania were cut to carry troops
and supplies to the frontier forts. The success of this venture in
western roadbuilding demonstrated both that such roads could
prove extremely useful to landowners along the route (the Shippens, with land in Lancaster, were instrumental in the building
of the military roads), and that such roads could not be built by
the townships. Plans made during the 1750s for a private road
to Lancaster eventually led to the building of America's first
turnpike four decades later.[29]

Whether the economy had reached a threshold that
led promotors away from the local approach toward a broader
vision, or whether the experience of the Seven Years War demonstrated that such provincial-wide plans could be accomplished, there was after the war a sudden spurt of developmental plans that looked to the colony as a whole, not to a few
localities. Planners for meadowland dikes (to grow hay to feed
cattle) turned to the legislature for authority to form corporations. The first plans were made for the Lancaster Pike, as well
as the Chesapeake and Delaware Canal. The purpose was still
the prosperity of the locality, but for some, the definition of locality had changed. As we can see, the developmental spirit described by Louis Hartz existed in Pennsylvania one hundred years
earlier than he imagined. The only difference was in the size of
the region one considered his locality.[30]

PRIVILEGE-SEEKING BEHAVIOR IN PENNSYLVANIA

While the tax farming system seemed a relatively efficient means of producing government goods and services, it was not without its hazards. In Europe the practice had produced a class of government placemen who made a living from buying and selling the rights to act as the government's agent. These same bureaucrats also profited from the sale of monopoly rights to a variety of industries within the economy. The game of looking for profits from government-granted privileges rather than through production of goods and services for the market, can be called privilege-seeking behavior, to contrast it with the profit-seeking activities of the entrepreneur. English privilege seekers do not seem to have been nearly as successful as their counterparts in France, but in England as well as France the business of government was growing into a little side economy separate from that which traded in goods and services through the market.[31]

Standard mercantile theory dictated that it was useful to grant a monopoly to some enterprising soul who wished to develop an industry that could reduce the nation's dependency on external trade. In the sixteenth century the English government granted a variety of monopolies, all in the name of enhancing national power. While mercantilist theory languished after the 1500s, the practice of granting monopolies continued into the eighteenth century.[32]

In practice, monopolies often proved easier to grant than to enforce. Similarly, a profit could not be realized on tax collection until after the taxes had been collected. It was the problem of the monopolist to enforce his monopoly, and the placeman to bring in the revenue due his position. Furthermore, to acquire either a monopoly or a lucrative government position, it was necessary to pay off those with the right to grant the privilege. That cost increased along with the number of palms to be crossed with coin. Costs of enforcement and acquisition thus cut into the expected returns to privilege seeking.[33]

Throughout the colonial period, Pennsylvania could

not provide much in the way of subsidy or support for those who hoped to use government influence to earn their living. As the power of the legislature increased, the costs of acquiring a privilege increased as well. In this period before well-organized political parties, there were simply too many people who would have to be paid off to obtain a privilege from the Pennsylvania legislature. At the same time, the costs of enforcement were high. The population of Pennsylvania was too scattered to make enforcement easy, as more than one customs inspector was to learn. Costs were too high, and rewards too low, for many Pennsylvanians to become involved in the Continental game of privilege seeking.

Most of the experience Pennsylvanians had with privilege seeking thus came not from within the colony, but from Pennsylvania's position as a colony at the end of the line of the British bureacracy. After all, Pennsylvania's very existence was the product of privilege-seeking behavior on the part of William Penn, a talented courtier whose father had loaned money to the king. When Charles II gave Penn the territory to cancel the debt, Penn acquired not only a very large area of land, to sell as he chose, but also monopoly rights and the rights of government in his new property. As Penn and his descendants were soon to find out, however, privileges granted in England proved difficult if not impossible to enforce in Pennsylvania.[34]

The case of quitrents proved instructive in demonstrating the difference between privileges granted on paper and privileges possessed in fact. William Penn, a newcomer to court life, clearly thought it would be interesting to pursue the role of lord of the manor in his New World colony, and he took a great deal of interest in the possibility of erecting a perfect government to rule his fiefdom. However, he was also in need of a steady source of income to support his life-style in England and was counting on Pennsylvania to provide it. It might have seemed that ownership of so much land would have been enough, but Penn apparently did not believe that he should be asked to sell *his* land to provide himself an income. As proprietor, Penn believed that he was owed a competency from his tenants, the

Pennsylvania colonists; indeed, he evidently believed that they would gladly pay such a benevolent and enlightened lord an annual sum so he could live in the dignity his station deserved.[35]

The colonists themselves, of course, saw the matter in a wholly different light. Quitrents were a major—if not *the* major—source of disagreement between the colonists and the proprietary family throughout much of the colonial period. For their part, the colonists did not think the returns offered by the proprietors in terms of service were worth such high personal taxes, and the unwillingness of the Penns to live off revenues from land sales only contributed to the colonists' disillusionment with the proprietors. Penn never got over his disappointment that neither the land nor the proprietary powers could provide him with a sizable income. By his death he had been forced to mortgage the land to keep up with the debts he had incurred both through colonization and his life-style in London. Penn's failure demonstrated that whatever the possibilities were for income from Pennsylvania, they could not be realized in England.[36]

For this reason, after the death of Penn's widow Hannah, Penn's son Thomas came to the colony to live. He diligently pursued his interests, combating Baltimore's challenge to his territory in person and pursuing the quitrent battle in court. No agent could have spent this much effort on the problem. If the Penns were going to collect on their father's privileges, at least one of them had to remain in Pennsylvania himself. And as long as he remained in the colony, Penn was successful, slowly breaking down the impediments to collection of his rental payments and his quitrents.[37]

If the Penns could not collect all the quitrents they felt they were owed, and did not choose to sell off all their land, they still had a potential source of income through the sale of monopolies and public offices in Pennsylvania. The Land Office, controlled by the Penns, proved the one spot in Pennsylvania from which a prospective privilege seeker might be successful. Profits from the Land Office came from insider information rather than the fees, however. Not only the chief officers, but also the

surveyors employed by the Land Office speculated in the purchase of new lands as they came on the market, using their position to acquire some of the more choice pieces before the public realized they were available. Nicholas Scull made his fortune
in this manner. There were not very many people employed by
the Land Office, however, and at least two of them were already
in Penn's employment as general agents (James Logan and Richard Peters). While Peters, Logan, and the surveyors made money
off of their positions in the Land Office, it is not clear that the
Penns did.

Penn himself possessed a monopoly to the Indian fur
trade, which he shared with his agent James Logan. Logan in
turn shared the trade with his business partner and, later, relative through marriage, Isaac Norris. Logan's rights to the fur trade,
which stemmed from his position as Indian agent, came not from
direct payments to the Penns but rather as payment for his services as the Penn family agent in the colony.[38]

William Penn was successful in acquiring income
through the sale of monopoly rights to trade, a privilege he possessed on paper, as the case of the Free Society of Traders demonstrated. Ostensibly backed by the most powerful individual in
Pennsylvania, proprietor and lord William Penn, the society received nearly exclusive trading privileges in the city of Philadelphia and the province as a whole. As Gary Nash has shown,
however, the society could not maintain its monopoly status in
the face of fierce opposition from other merchants. The failure
of the society did not bode well for the possibility of a future
career in privilege seeking in Pennsylvania. If Penn could not
grant a trading monopoly, it is difficult to see who could have.[39]

Nowhere was the difference between American and
British practices regarding privilege seeking more noticeable than
in the case of the provincial governors. Pennsylvania was only
one of many colonies and dependent territories that included
Ireland, and governorships were only one of several kinds of
colonial appointments. Before coming to Pennsylvania, for example, William Keith held the position of collector-general for
the southern district of the American colonies. Governors lob-

bied for their position with favors and money and expected to receive benefits commensurate with the amount they had expended. In both ways they were frequently disappointed. The efforts of former Governor Charles Gookin, Keith's predecessor, to have himself appointed governor of the Lower Counties (now Delaware), with the latter seceding from Pennsylvania, only served to waste both his time and his money. Keith was similarly unsuccessful in his efforts to be nominated governor of New York or New Jersey.[40]

Once in place as governor, most appointees soon discovered that the best way to reap the rewards granted by Penn was to switch allegiance to the nearest award-granting body— the legislature. But the governors were required to perform a service for their fee: they had to rubber-stamp legislation passed during the session. Aside from the salary earned by catering to the legislature, there were few rewards available to colonial governors, as more than one bitterly complained.

The potential privilege seeker in Pennsylvania was thus frustrated. On the one hand, monopoly privileges once received were extremely difficult to enforce, as the Free Society of Traders found out. On the other, it was unclear just who wielded what power in Pennsylvania. To the extent that the power resided in the legislature, there were simply too many payments that would have had to have been made. While the number of petitions suggests that colonists lobbied for various posts granting incomes within the government, including ferry monopolies, collectorships of impost, or inspectorships of flour, there is little evidence to suggest that payments to individuals were required to acquire those posts. In fact, it was to prevent such practices that the legislature carefully guarded its right to make appointments. Aware that the governor would sell appointments that he had full right to, the legislature refused to allow that right to slip from its fingers.

The seriousness with which the legislature took its duty to prevent the English practice of privilege seeking from invading the province can be seen in the way the William Fishbourne incident was handled in 1730. Fishbourne, a wealthy merchant, was a highly respected member of the Quaker community in the early 1700s. Treasurer of the Common Council of the City of Philadelphia and representative of the City and County in the Assembly, Fishbourne was one of the first trustees of the General Loan Office in 1723. As the trustee residing in Philadelphia and as a person with long-term experience as treasurer of the city, Fishbourne had responsibility for keeping the books and the money in his house; in practice, he oversaw the clerks and virtually ran the office on his own. As treasurer of the city of Philadelphia, Fishbourne kept the accounts, again at his own house, and received and disbursed funds in the name of the city, keeping the standard 5 percent fee for services rendered. During his fifteen years as treasurer of the city, Fishbourne was never asked to account to the city or subjected to an audit. As noted above, the city government was notoriously lax in its attention to monetary matters.[41]

Fishbourne's troubles began when he married a young girl in 1727. Apparently persuaded to live beyond his means, he began to make up the difference by "borrowing" sums from the Loan Office funds he kept in his house. This sort of personal use of government funds, however, was not unusual for a government agent. It was a familiar part of the system of tax farming. As long as Fishbourne could account for the money when it was requested, there was nothing in the practice of the city government or the habits of the local sheriffs to forbid his actions. However, the province, unlike the city, wished to audit the actions of the Loan Office carefully. The legislature apparently took seriously its stated design to keep loan money in circulation and not allow it to be hoarded by a few wealthy borrowers. When the legislature asked Fishbourne for the money and he could not come up with it, he committed an unforgivable sin in the eyes of the Quaker community: he accused a vagrant of having stolen the money. When, on inspection, it was learned that the lock on the chest had been tampered with *after,* not before, it had been opened, it was apparent that Fishbourne was lying. Members of the government, from the governor to the council to the legislature, switched from defender of Fishbourne to accuser. After an impeachment trial in the Pennsylvania legislature in 1730, Fishbourne was found guilty and a law enacted to prevent him from ever holding office in any form again.

Interestingly, the city government had nothing to say on the matter. Fishbourne's name simply disappeared from the minutes. The amount Fishbourne "borrowed" was not small: £1,800. Clearly, the legislature intended to keep the Loan Office free from this sort of behavior. Later on, other trustees would be accused of careless use of the funds in their possession, although none to the extent of Fishbourne. In a matter as important to trade and the economy as paper money and loans, the legislature was not going to permit privilege-seeking behavior to affect the impact of its policies.[42]

In both cases, the case of the placemen and the case of the government-granted monopoly, there were always people ready and willing to use the government to further their own interests. And there were always those who opposed such privilege-seeking behavior. However, the costs of privilege seeking had to be computed against the returns. During most of Pennsylvania's colonial history, the costs of privilege seeking outweighed the benefits. Only the Penn family and their personal agents were able to reap monopoly benefits from their privileged position with regard to Pennsylvania's government. And both the Penns and the Logan-Norris clan acquired their privileges early in the history of the colony, before the Charter of Privileges gave the legislature control over further granting of economic privileges.

As long as settlements were relatively scattered and interior modes of transportation slow and inefficient, enforcement of privileges would be that much more costly, and government structure would have to be that much stronger. Expenditures to enforce paper benefits would eat away at the actual gains to be reaped from such benefits. At the same time, the more people actively involved in appointments and monopoly legislation, the more expensive it would be to obtain such privilege. When only one or two ministers or a governor were responsible for appointing positions, then it would be easy to grease a palm and acquire a spot. When, however, there were large numbers of legislators to be convinced, a lot more money would have to be spent to pay enough to acquire a vote.

At the end of the colonial period, Pennsylvania's population density had increased dramatically. The same internal improvements that so greatly enhanced trade also made it that much easier for a privilege seeker to enforce his monopoly. Privilege seeking became a more lucrative activity as a result. It is thus no coincidence that more attention came to be paid to the problem of privilege seekers and fears that British placemen would corrupt American politics.

Government in Pennsylvania could be used to provide public goods and services that by definition would not be forthcoming from a private economy, but colonists early developed a determination to avoid the British practice of privilege seeking through the government. The attitudes of colonial Pennsylvanians toward government were summarized in 1739 by Andrew Hamilton, in his last speech to the House after ten years as Speaker:

> It is not to the Fertility of our Soil, and the Commodiousness of our Rivers, that we ought chiefly to attribute the great Progress this Province has made, within so small a Compass of Years, in improvements, Wealth, Trade and Navigation, and the extraordinary Increases of People, who have been drawn hither from almost every Country in Europe; a Progress which much more ancient Settlements on the Main of America cannot at present boast of; No, it is principally and almost wholly owing to the Excellency of our Constitution, under which we enjoy a greater Share both of Civil and of religious Liberty than any of our Neighbours. . . .
>
> We have no Officers, but what are necessary, none but what earn their Salaries, and those, generally are either elected by the People, or appointed by their Representatives. . . .
>
> The Taxes which we pay for carrying on the Publick Service are inconsiderable; for the sole Power of raising and disposing of the Publick Money for the Support of Government is lodged in the Assembly, who appoint their own Treasurer, and to them alone he is accountable.[43]

Conclusion

The period 1725 to 1755 was characterized by phenomenal economic growth in Pennsylvania. Natural increase and high immigration rates combined to cause rapid population growth, spilling over the political borders of the colony into Virginia and the Carolinas. Traditional family and community networks coexisted with a thriving, diversified market economy in the Pennsylvania countryside as well as in the city of Philadelphia. While further development of the economy would be interrupted by political strife and two wars, the economic transition to the nineteenth century was well under way in the colonial Pennsylvania countryside.

Economic growth in Pennsylvania in the 1700s was strongly affected by economic policies chosen by the colonists themselves. For most of the period before the Seven Years War, Pennsylvania's chief policymaking body was the General Assembly. Lawmakers in Britain had to be taken into consideration, but the impetus to policy itself came from within the colony. The Assembly seemed remarkably unified and appears to have served the interests of the colony as a whole, although the legislature itself was far from representative. The economic policies developed by the Assembly during this period of relative autonomy concentrated on three issues: money, capital formation, and the regulation of a cumbersome international market in flour. Explicit Pennsylvania economic policy appears to have been successful: the colony grew dramatically, emerging by the end of the century as a leader in politics and economics, and one of the first regions to experience the beginnings of industrialization.

A look at the economic policies developed by a virtually independent legislature in colonial Pennsylvania makes it clear that the critical period for explicit policy came during the economic depression of the early 1720s. Not only did the city and countryside put pressure on the legislature to ease the economic crisis, but the Penn family, under the control of William Penn's widow and faced by a major series of court battles back in Britain, was in no position to interfere with any of the legislature's activities.

While the legislature clearly would have preferred another paper money issue some time in the mid-1740s, it is otherwise unlikely that it would have demonstrated any greater propensity to establish new policies during these years. For most of its existence, in fact, the Pennsylvania legislature seems to have preferred inactivity to direct intervention. Economic policy in the first two decades of the colony's existence concerned establishing the colony's independence from Penn's control over economic matters and setting up the rules enabling a market system to function properly. Gary Nash and James Lemon, in separate works, have described the success of the colony in overcoming Penn's attempts to force settlement patterns into a township grid and to restrict Philadelphia's overseas trade to the privileged Free Society of Traders. Nash has also described the early success of the colony in avoiding quitrents or taxes. Rule-setting by the legislature has not attracted much attention, however—and with good reason, because it was done matter-of-factly with little overt controversy.[1]

Historians from the turn-of-the-century constitutional historian William Shepherd to recent economic historians J. R. T. Hughes and Douglass North have concentrated extensively on the establishment of rules regarding land ownership in the colonies early in their existence. For Pennsylvania, however, there was never any question on the part of the settlers about property rights or land ownership. A belief in strong property rights had been carried over from Europe; the colonists took them for granted. Furthermore, the colonists used both written contracts and the force of custom to enforce those property rights. Consequently, more interesting than landownership per se is the variety of categories colonists used to designate ownership of improvements according to custom. The clear distinction we might make between landownership and tenancy was not at all as rigid in the eighteenth century. Even intangible improvements such as landclearing could be owned by a tenant. Thus Pennsylvanians made significant technical distinctions in some kinds of property holding, encouraging capital formation by enabling a tenant to own the capital improvements without having to own the land.[2]

 With property rights well established a century before the Constitution was written—and with never a question that they should not be—the other remaining laws necessary for a market economy involved the establishment of rules, specifically allowing for contract enforcement and for assurance that weights and measures were correct. It did take a while for some of the issues surrounding contract enforcement to be settled, not because there was ever any question that contracts would be enforced, but because during the periods when money was scarce laws had to be reworked to be fair to both parties as the payment mechanism changed. Thus, there were several laws involving the problems of payment of debt under duress, problems such as what items could be used to pay debts off, at what rates, and when property could be confiscated for nonpayment of debt. The Assembly, the courts, and the general populace made a distinction between nonpayment of debts because of poor management decisions or bad luck, and nonpayment of debts because of the lack of a medium of exchange. There also seems to have been some feeling that producing units should not be broken up. If a farm could be shown to be capable of paying a debt off within a reasonable amount of time, then the creditor was not permitted to attach the property for auction. On the other hand, the legislature worried about the creation of loopholes which would enable debtors *never* to pay their creditors. Such loopholes would destroy the credit market by making it far too expensive to lend due to the increased risk involved. The series of laws involving debtors, therefore, can be seen as a series of oscillations between an attempt to protect debtors and to keep producers from having to sell off assets under their true value and an attempt to prevent irresponsible debtors from cheating their creditors.[3]

One of the first laws passed in Pennsylvania regulated weights and measures and provided for an inspector to gauge scales and casks by a standard guaranteed by the government. As the century progressed, the laws were amended to include more efficient mechanisms for measuring the volume of casks and greater varieties of containers measured. The object of such laws, which were quite similar to laws passed later regulating quality of export staples, was to provide assurance that the product sold was the product delivered, thus ensuring that prices of the items in question would reflect the item itself and not uncertainty regarding the true amount.

Once these basic laws were passed, the Pennsylvania legislature generally avoided measures concerning the economy. In contrast to neighboring New York, Pennsylvania never went through a period of experimentation with mercantilist laws, perhaps because of the later founding of the colony or perhaps because of a general Quaker dislike for government. With the exception of William Penn, few were able to use the government as a tool for increasing private income. Those who did earn their living through the government, such as sheriffs, collectors of duties, and inspectors, received their income for the performance of specific duties. They were not using the government to assist them in restraining trade in their favor. Indeed, in the case of inspectors, the job they performed actually increased the volume of trade taking place.

Not only was mercantilism avoided on an individual level, but policies generally associated with mercantilism were shunned by the Pennsylvania government as well. At no time in the colony's history did the legislature pass laws granting Philadelphia special metropolitan privileges to encourage the city's growth vis-à-vis other towns in the region. Despite the complaints of New Castle, Philadelphia's preeminence came not from government restrictions but through its ideal situation for trade. Philadelphia funneled agricultural products from the countryside in Pennsylvania and New Jersey to the West Indies and in turn sent manufactured goods back. The government was situated in Philadelphia, but the presence of government alone would have been insufficient to develop a city of Philadelphia's size. The Maryland government, after all, could not make Annapolis an important port.

To say that through much of its history the legislature of colonial Pennsylvania did not enact much legislation of any sort is not, however, to say that policy governing Pennsylvania was formulated in London. Colonists regularly ignored whatever legislation or regulations emerged from Britain specifically applying to the colonies. Despite laws to the contrary, iron and woolen products were manufactured in Pennsylvania and sold in the domestic market as early as the second decade of the 1700s. Smuggling of forbidden items to and from forbidden ports was openly practiced, even during wars. It is not that Pennsylvanians were content having policy determined abroad. Their inactivity was itself a statement of policy: they simply did not choose to enact a wide spectrum of laws regulating economic practices.

Faced with a severe depression and a downward spiraling of demand in the market for the colony's major export, however, the legislature was pushed to respond to the demands of a suddenly active countryside. Political historians have highlighted the political strife surrounding the Keith-Lloyd-Logan controversies in Pennsylvania around 1720: the central issue of the conflict was whether or not to print paper money and issue it on long-term loans. Legislators were voted in and out of the Assembly over that issue. Later, when the question of reissuing the money as loans and printing £30,000 more came up, near riots ensued in the countryside at election time. When the ability of the province to participate in the market at all appeared to be in question, the government could no longer remain passive.[4]

The results of the sudden activity of the government

in the years 1722 and 1723 included two acts which would be steadfastly defended through the next thirty years: the flour inspection act of 1722, requiring inspection of export flour and ship bread; and the paper money emission act of 1723, establishing the General Loan Office of Pennsylvania. Through the next six years of political turmoil, a total of £75,000 Pennsylvania paper currency was printed and made legal tender, virtually the entire amount that would be in circulation until the Seven Years War. The General Loan Office was established and was soon functioning smoothly. The system of flour inspection was developed in the form it would keep for the next six decades, with branding of casks of export flour and ship bread made mandatory and inspection legally required by law before wheat products could be exported.

After the paper money, loan office, and flour inspection laws were put into effect and began to have a positive impact on the economy, political turmoil subsided as quickly as it had begun. William Keith's attempt in late 1727 to continue the infighting as Speaker of the House, after having been removed by the Penns as governor, met with failure. All basis for disagreement, except personal vendettas or desire for power, were removed when the economy turned around. Prior to the Seven Years War, the legislature's major battles with Thomas Penn and the Board of Trade would be over the reenactment of these laws and unsuccessful attempts to issue more money.

The economic policies of the legislatures of 1722–1723 were considered successful by later observers. It has usually been assumed that the effect of issuing paper money was to increase aggregate demand during a period when it was ineffectual for the purposes of maintaining a desirable level of income. The argument proceeds in the following manner: with demand below a level which would create full employment of resources, an injection of government deficit spending would result in an increase in demand without increasing prices. As demand increased, more resources would be employed until full employment had been attained. Government revenues from a booming economy would take care of the deficit created during the depression, and further injections of deficit spending would only result in inflation.[5]

On the face of it, Pennsylvania's experience in the 1720s would appear to fit this pattern, as a series of economic historians noticed in the 1930s and 1940s. The government printed paper money and issued it to the public without causing a great deal of inflation; one must therefore conclude that the economy was indeed underemployed and that deficit spending worked for Pennsylvania insofar as it helped to end the depression. But such an interpretation of the effects of the paper money issues ignores a basic fact: the economy of colonial Pennsylvania bore little resemblance to the institutionally complex economy John Maynard Keynes had in mind when he developed this mode of analysis in the *General Theory*. There were few institutional barriers to the clearing of markets through price mechanisms, and thus the cause of the depression of the 1710s–1720s was not likely to have been insufficient demand.[6]

If the economic problem facing the Pennsylvania colonists in 1722 was not insufficient demand, then why did the printing of paper money not result in inflation? The answer can be found in the arguments the Pennsylvanian proponents of paper money made: the money was desired not to increase an existing money supply but to create a new form of money itself. Paper money was desired as a medium of exchange, because as such it operated far more efficiently than any other option available in domestic trade at the time. When paper money entered circulation, it replaced more cumbersome mechanisms—the use of flour, wheat, or other agricultural products, and complicated bookkeeping systems by which accounts were transferred from one creditor to another. The resulting efficiencies decreased the costs of trading in Pennsylvania, having the same effect as the building of roads or canals would a century later.

The result of a reduction in the costs of trading was to increase the effective prices offered producers and decrease the effective prices offered consumers, with the result that production could be increased with the same number of resources. The resulting economic growth required a greater stock of money to service the increased number of transactions. Thus, the increase in the money supply resulting from the issuing of paper money did not lead to inflation. The early block of paper money issues first went to replace more inefficient forms of money; later issues of paper money supplemented the earlier issues to meet increases in trade. But the later issues did not have to be nearly as large as the first. In fact, not until the end of the period did demand again increase in the countryside for new, large issues of paper money, and the legislature responded by calling for a new major increase in the mid-1740s. It is as a financial innovation, then, that the paper money issues functioned to alleviate in part the depression of the early 1720s in Pennsylvania—not solely as a Keynesian injection of deficit spending to offset inadequate demand.

The effects of the paper money issues in Pennsylvania exceeded their purely monetary implications, however: the manner in which Pennsylvania distributed the paper money had an impact that was equally important. Unlike previous issues in the colonies, the paper money in Pennsylvania was distributed through a "land bank": paper money was loaned at amounts between £12.15s. and £100 at 5 percent interest to residents with land worth double the amount of the loan or housing worth treble. Loans were repaid in equal installments at simple interest, the interest was used to run the government, and the principal was reloaned to new mortgagors. In effect, Pennsylvania had formed a government bank (in imitation of the country banks in England which loaned money on land and personal wealth) on which it issued notes. This situation was different from those in other colonies, where the issues were backed by the promise of future tax money to the government.

The size of the General Loan Office, which issued about three loans a week when in full operation, enabled it to operate on a much more efficient level than individuals making private loans. Loans could be made to anyone who possessed clear title to land—as opposed to the private market, where lenders released money only to people they knew. With many more loans outstanding than even the largest private moneylender in the colony at the time, the Loan Office was able to spread the risk of the loans and thus could afford to take higher-risk loans than the general public. While the interest rate appears to have been far below the effective market rate in the private sector, the Loan Office was immensely successful for the government, turning over the original loans quickly while bringing in half the operating revenue for the entire provincial government.

The effects of the loans on the economy seem generally to have been positive. To the extent that some residents were denied access to the loans through lack of real estate to present as collateral, the Loan Office represented a mild form of income and wealth redistribution. However, this redistribution was greatly offset by the benefits accruing to the entire population, whether mortgagors or not, from the growth in the economy spurred by the capital formation that the Loan Office encouraged. To the extent that mortgagors had not previously owned land, the establishment of the Loan Office resulted in a more equitable redistribution of wealth; to the extent that previous landholders took out loans to improve their property, the presence of the Loan Office encouraged economic growth through capital formation, thus raising provincial incomes for all producers as the colony realized economies of scale in trade.

Most of the mortgage recipients, it would appear, were previous landholders, but available evidence shows that they did not own more than one piece of property and that they did not use the loans to buy another. The loans were used either to replace loans made through local merchants at a much higher effective interest or to replace borrowing upon a mortgagor's own savings—the only other option for those outside the personal network within which the private mortgage market operated. The loans thus seem to have enabled farmers to build barns, outbuildings, fences, meadows, and orchards, without greatly lowering their level of consumption, thus keeping aggregate demand high for the colony as a whole. While the great majority of the loans went to "yeomen" farmers, artisans also had access to funds either through landownership in the countryside (where many artisans resided) or through the houses they owned on ground rent in the city. The ultimate result of the loans was to encourage economic development and to increase the speed with which Pennsylvania was transformed from an undeveloped economy into a more diversified trading system, with internal trade increasing in proportion to external trade throughout he century. Increases in trade resulted in increases in productivity, as producers were able to concentrate on products for which they possessed a greater comparative advantage. The result was, it seems, more goods available per person in the economy—in other words, economic growth.

The final product of the active legislatures of 1722–1723 was the flour inspection act of 1722. Participation in a very cumbersome overseas market for flour depended on the flow of information about the quality of Pennsylvania's product in general, as increasing competition led to greater uncertainty on the part of purchasers as to the product they were receiving. Observing that in the West Indies New York's inspected flour received higher prices than Pennsylvania's uninspected product, the legislature followed the urging of pamphlets from the countryside and enacted a law enabling inspection to take place in Philadelphia. Within a few years inspection was made mandatory; although three inspectors were set up in the three counties, the Philadelphia inspector remained the major official in the colony, as most of the flour exported went through that port.

The result of compulsory flour inspection, requiring a brand name on all casks of flour exported from Pennsylvania, was an increase in Pennsylvania flour prices relative to New York's. Furthermore, once the inspection system was in place, it enabled the grading of flour to take place with assurance to the buyers that the grade noted on the outside was indeed the quality of the flour inside. Assured of the quality of the flour, the purchasers were willing to pay a price commensurate with that quality, and producers were encouraged to produce a high quality staple. Thus the actual quality of Pennsylvania flour, as well as the perception of that quality, increased throughout the century.

Pennsylvania's flour inspection was perceived as a success throughout the colonies, with other assemblies enacting inspection laws in imitation of Pennsylvania later in the century. Higher prices for Pennsylvania flour enabled the colony's millers to reach far into Virginia and Maryland, as well as into the New Jersey and Pennsylvania countryside, for sources of flour for their mills. Pennsylvania flour, produced from Virginia and Maryland wheat, was exported through Philadelphia, thus increasing that port's preeminence as the economic leader of the colonies. Higher incomes in the Pennsylvania hinterland encouraged tradesmen and artisans to settle in the area, increasing the economy's diversification, and setting the stage for industrialization in the next century.

These explicit policies were successful, but they represented only half of the effective economic policy of Pennsylvania in the mid-eighteenth century. At least as important was the role of the community in the name of custom. By selectively enforcing only those laws the community desired, and in the manner the community found appropriate, government at the township and county level proved as decisive as the provincial legislature in the establishment of policy. Custom as interpreted in colonial Pennsylvania was intended to promote the prosperity of the individual household.

Land policy was only one of the areas in which the effective practice in the countryside answered the wishes of the populace rather than those of proprietors or legislature. The export inspection system worked only so long as it was supported by the colonists, who were well practiced in the art of smuggling to avoid unpopular trade restrictions. Only those public improvements which directly affected the townships charged with their cost were built or maintained.

Both the economic and political conditions leading to the enactment and enforcement of these successful economic policies were, however, coming to an end by the beginning of the 1750s. The Board of Trade had already shown signs of increasing interest in the mainland colonies; prohibition of paper money in Massachusetts was the beginning of a trend which would continue until the Revolution. The only way for the Pennsylvania legislature to receive permission for new issues of

paper money in the 1750s was to abandon the use of the currency for economic development through the land bank and
designate the money for the uses of the king in fighting the Seven
Years War; when the war was over, London intimated that
Pennsylvania had no more need for paper money. Although the
legislature was, after a battle, permitted to reissue the war money,
the precedent of London's involvement in Pennsylvania's money
supply had been set.[7]

The Seven Years War brought an end to political unity
within the legislature as well. Although some less rigorous
Quakers remained, the legislature no longer remained so thor-
oughly under Quaker control. Immigrants who had settled in
the back counties began to complain about underrepresentation;
artisans in the cities would soon begin to demand the rights that
went along with a metropolis. Interests in the countryside would
compete with interests in the city, interests in the east compete
with interests in the west, and participants in the international
trade with those beginning to depend on internal trade.

Ultimately, too, interests in Pennsylvania would
compete with those of the British empire. By the 1760s, the colony could no longer be ignored by London. The needs of the
British empire would increasingly clash with those of the pro-
moters of internal developments and manufactures in Pennsylvania. Economic matters which would have passed by the Board
of Trade a generation earlier had to be avoided. Continued economic growth was threatened by the Board's policies—notably,
the Board's dislike of manufactures in general and banks and
corporations in particular. The ability to collect provincial taxes
was put to the use of the home government, not just to Pennsylvania. If Pennsylvania was to prove profitable as a colony,
Britain would have to find ways to skim off provincial income
from a vigorous economy which increasingly was the mother
country's competitor. Pennsylvania could offer no product to
enhance the metropolis except tax money.

Pennsylvania's period of semi-independence in economic policymaking thus came to an end in 1755. More and
more, the economy of Pennsylvania was beginning to look like

England's: mixed farming and artisanal manufactures; production of iron and woolen products for sale; a well-developed mercantile community in Pennsylvania searching for greater opportunities for investment in the hinterland. Unless the Board of Trade was successful in changing the major products of the Pennsylvania economy, these products increasingly would compete with products of the mother country not only within Pennsylvania itself, but in the West Indies, in the Chesapeake and the Carolinas, and in Europe. This pattern of vigorous growth was largely a product of the colony's natural endowment combined with the economic custom of the countryside. To some considerably extent, however, it was also a tribute to the successful policies implemented by the Pennsylvania General Assembly in the period before 1755. Public perceptions of the success of Pennsylvania economic policy would be remembered when the power to create those policies would be endangered in the coming decades.

Notes

Introduction

1. *Maryland Gazette* (Annapolis), May 31, 1753.
2. [Francis Rawle], "Ways and Means for the Inhabitants of the Delaware to become Rich wherein the several *Growths* and *Products* of these COUNTRIES are demonstrated to be a sufficient Fund for a flourishing TRADE," p. 16. The "countries" referred to are New Jersey, Pennsylvania, and the "Three Lower Counties," now the state of Delaware.
3. Jack P. Greene, *The Quest for Power: The Lower Houses of Assembly in the Southern Royal Colonies, 1689–1776;* Bernard Bailyn, *The New England Merchants in the Seventeenth Century;* Mary Alice Hanna, *The Trade of the Delaware District Before the Revolution;* Victor L. Johnson, "Fair Traders and Smugglers in Philadelphia, 1754–1763"; Peter D. McClelland, "The Cost to America of British Imperial Policy"; Roger L. Ransom, "British Policy and Colonial Growth: Some Implications of the Burden from the Navigation Acts"; Robert Paul Thomas, "A Quantitative Approach to the Study of the Effects of British Imperial Policy upon Colonial Welfare: Some Preliminary Findings"; Gary M. Walton, "The New Economic History and the Burdens of the Navigation Acts."
4. Joan Thirsk, *Economic Policy and Projects: The Development of a Consumer Society in Early Modern England;* Joyce Oldham Appleby, *Economic Thought and Ideology in Seventeenth-Century England;* Joyce Oldham Appleby, "The Social Origins of American Revolutionary Ideology."
5. Louis Hartz, *Economic Policy and Democratic Thought: Pennsylvania, 1776–1860.*
6. Diane Lindstrom, *Economic Development in the Philadelphia Region, 1810–1850.*
7. Douglass C. North, *Structure and Change in Economic History;* Douglass C. North, *The Economic Growth of the United States.*
8. Gary B. Nash, *Quakers and Politics: Pennsylvania, 1681–1726;* Alan Tully, *William Penn's Legacy: Politics and Social Structure in Provincial Pennsylvania, 1726–1755;* Frederick B. Tolles, *Meeting House and Counting House: The Quaker Merchants of Colonial Philadelphia, 1682–1763;* Carl and Jessica Bridenbaugh, *Cities in the Wilderness: The First Century of Urban Life in America, 1652–1742;* James T. Lemon, *The Best Poor Man's Country;* Joseph E. Illick, *Colonial Pennsylvania: A History.*
9. Barry Baysinger, Robert B. Ekelund, Jr., and Robert D. Tollison, "Mercantilism as a Rent-Seeking Society," in James M. Buchanan, Robert D. Tollison, and Gordon Tullock, eds., *Toward a Theory of the Rent-Seeking Society,* pp. 235–268; James M.

Buchanan, "Rent Seeking and Profit Seeking," in Buchanan et al., *Rent-Seeking Society*, pp. 3–15; Anne O. Krueger, "The Political Economy of the Rent-Seeking Society"; George A. Akerlof, "The Market for 'Lemons': Quality Uncertainty and the Market Mechanism"; Hayne E. Leland, "Quacks, Lemons, and Licensing: A Theory of Minimum Quality Standards"; Michael Spence, "Job Market Signaling"; Richard A. Posner, "Taxation by Regulation"; George J. Stigler, "The Theory of Economic Regulation"; Jacob Mincer, "Labor Force Participation of Married Women: A Study of Labor Supply"; Gary Becker, "A Theory of the Allocation of Time"; Gary S. Becker, *A Treatise on the Family.*

10. For a summary of British regulations pertaining to colonial trade, see the introduction to Jack P. Greene, ed., *Great Britain and the American Colonies*, pp. xi–xlvii. See also Albert Anthony Giesecke, *American Commercial Legislation Before 1789*; Winfred T. Root, *The Relations of Pennsylvania with the British Government, 1696–1765*; William R. Shepherd, *History of Proprietary Government in Pennsylvania*; Arthur Cecil Bining, *British Regulation of the Colonial Iron Industry*, p. 3; Eleanor L. Lord, *Industrial Experiments in the British Colonies of North America.* For the hiring of a lobbyist to prevent the passage of the Molasses Act, see *Votes and Proceedings of the House of Representatives of the Province of Pennsylvania, Pennsylvania Archives*, 3:2120–21, 2127–34 (hereafter cited as *Votes*). For the Penn-Baltimore disputes, see Gary B. Nash, *Quakers and Politics: Pennsylvania, 1681–1726*; and Alan Tully, *William Penn's Legacy: Politics and Social Structure in Provincial Pennsylvania, 1726–1755.*

11. Greene, *American Colonies*, pp. xi–xlvii; *Votes*, 2:1091–99, 1107, 1177, 1323; Shepherd, *Proprietary Government*, pp. 495–539, 351–434; Root, *Relations of Pennsylvania*, pp. 129–157.

12. *Votes*, 2:1091, 1346–47, 1392; Shepherd, *Proprietary Government*, pp. 495–539; Root, *Relations of Pennsylvania*, pp. 129–157; Jack P. Greene and Richard M. Jellison, "The Currency Act of 1764 in Imperial-Colonial Relations, 1764–1776"; Paton Wesley Yoder, "Paper Currency in Colonial Pennsylvania," p. 86; for examples of tariff laws see chs. 214, 220, 240, 308, 341 of *Laws of the Province of Pennsylvania, 1700–1740.*

13. Nash, *Quakers and Politics*, pp. 10, 89–114, 198–199, 226–236.

14. Shepherd, *Proprietary Government*, pp. 67–76; Nash, *Quakers and Politics*, pp. 92–97, 216–217, 251–55, 316; Tully, *William Penn's Legacy*, pp. 14–15, 44–45; General Loan Office Books F-L, Norris of Fairhill Manuscripts, Historical Society of Pennsylvania (hereafter cited as HSP).

15. Nash, *Quakers and Politics*, pp. 226–236; James Steel Letterbook, 1730–1741, Logan Papers; James Logan Letterbooks, 1714–1745, Logan Papers, HSP; Tully, *William Penn's Legacy*, pp. 11–15.

16. The governor in Pennsylvania was formally termed the "lieutenant governor"; one of the Penns was always "governor."

17. Nash, *Quakers and Politics*, pp. 227–32; Shepherd, *Proprietary Government*, p. 435.

18. Nash, *Quakers and Politics*, pp. 251–73, 314–19. See, for example, *Votes*, 1:437–41, 478–81, 503–5, 768–81; 2:1146–48, 1176–80.

19. *Votes*, 2:1223; Thomas H. Wendell, "The Life and Writings of Sir William Keith, Lieutenant-Governor of Pennsylvania and the Three Lower Counties, 1717–1726," pp. 11–44.

20. *An Historical Review of the Constitution and Government of Pennsylvania* (this work has been attributed to Benjamin Franklin, but he denied having written it), p. 73.

21. James Logan to Robert Hunter, governor of New York, February 1718, James Logan Letterbook, 1715–1720, vol. 2.

22. *Votes,* 2:1767–69, 1771; Tully, *William Penn's Legacy,* pp. 3–22.
23. Sister Joan de Lourdes Leonard, CSJ, "The Organization and Procedure of the Pennsylvania Assembly, 1682–1776," pp. 403–405.
24. *Votes,* 3:2484.
25. Tully, *William Penn's Legacy,* pp. 23–43.
26. Nash, *Quakers and Politics,* pp. 200–205, 227–232; Shepherd, *Proprietary Government,* pp. 225–232.
27. Nash, *Quakers and Politics,* pp. 332–335; Tully, *William Penn's Legacy,* pp. 44–50; Thomas Wendell, "The Keith-Lloyd Alliance: Factional and Coalition Politics in Colonial Pennsylvania"; Tully, pp. 103–106.
28. Chs. 34, 55, 153, 158, 159, 176, 187, 213, 259, *Laws of the Province of Pennsylvania, 1700–1740.*
29. *Ibid.,*, Frederick B. Tolles, *Meeting House and Counting House: The Quaker Merchants of Colonial Philadelphia, 1682–1763,* pp. 75–78, 251–252; Book of Discipline of the Yearly Meeting 1719 belonging to the monthly meeting of Chesterfield, New Jersey, "From our Yearly Meeting held at Philadelphia for Pensilvania and the Jerseys," Friends Historical Library, Swarthmore College. "Conductor Generalis."; Lucy Simler, "The Township: The Community of the Rural Pennsylvanian."
30. Philadelphia, Pennsylvania, *Minutes of the Common Council of the City of Philadelphia;* Judith M. Diamondstone, "Philadelphia's Municipal Corporation, 1701–1776."
31. Tully, *William Penn's Legacy,* pp. 15–17, 23–37, 135–140; Wendell, "The Keith-Lloyd Alliance."
32. *Votes;* James Hamilton Letterbook, 1749–1783; Penn-Hamilton Correspondence, 1748–1770, Penn Papers, HSP; James H. Hutson, "Benjamin Franklin and Pennsylvania Politics, 1751–1755"; James H. Hutson, *Pennsylvania Politics, 1746–1770: The Movement for Royal Government and its Consequences.*
33. James T. Lemon, *The Best Poor Man's Country,* pp. 13–23; Tully, *William Penn's Legacy,* pp. 53–78; Ralph L. Ketcham, "Conscience, War, and Politics in Pennsylvania, 1755–1757"; Hutson, *Pennsylvania Politics;* Nash, *Urban Crucible.*
34. See ch. 1 on the role of youth in the economy; chs. 2, 101, 118, 119, 120, 164, 289, 309, and 339, *Laws of the Province of Pennsylvania, 1700–1740; Votes,* 3:2227, 2239, 2245, 2251, 2259, 2299, 2332–35.
35. *Votes,* 3:2334–35.
36. Tully, *William Penn's Legacy,* pp. 8–15, 20–29, 127–133; Shepherd, *Proprietary Government,* pp. 36–53, 435–473.
37. Shepherd, *Proprietary Government,* pp. 495–539; Tully, *William Penn's Legacy,* pp. 153–160; Richard Ryerson, *The Revolution Is Now Begun;* Ralph L. Ketcham, "Conscience, War, and Politics in Pennsylvania, 1755–1757"; John J. Zimmerman, "Benjamin Franklin and the Quaker Party, 1755–1756"; Hutson, *Pennsylvania Politics.*

1. The Household Economy of Pennsylvania

1. For relevant discussions regarding production within the unit of the household, see Alan Macfarlane, *The Origins of English Individualism: The Family, Property and Social Transition;* Jacob Mincer, "Labor Force Participation of Married Women: A Study of Labor Supply"; Gary S. Becker, "A Theory of the Allocation of Time," and Gary S. Becker, *A Treatise on the Family.*
2. Much of the discussion of the Pennsylvania economy in this chapter and

the following chapter is based upon an analysis of three samples drawn from the wills and inventories in the Chester County Archives, West Chester, Pennsylvania. The first sample, from 1717–1721, included 83 decedents; the second, 1732–1737, included 185; and the third, 1748–1751, included 304. Values in the inventories were adjusted to control for inflation during the period by using the sterling exchange rate in the tables in John J. McCusker, *Money and Exchange in Europe and America: 1600–1775*, pp. 183–186. A reliable price list is available for the period in Anne Bezanson et al., *Prices in Colonial Pennsylvania*. However, converting the prices into a consumer price index would be extremely difficult as not enough is known about purchasing habits to construct even a remotely accurate "market basket" of the proportions of goods a typical consumer could be expected to buy at different periods of time. Bezanson was aware of the problem, and did not try to weight the major price "index" given in the book. While the index is useful for some purposes, specifically analysis of changes in the price of wheat, it is not very useful in judging whether specific prices changed in response to changes in supply and demand for particular goods or whether they reflected a secular rise in prices caused by inflation. Colonists regularly imported a large quantity of goods from the British Isles, and inflation in Pennsylvania currency on the west side of the Atlantic would be reflected in a change in the exchange rate between colonial money and British sterling. British sterling was probably the most stable form of money in the western world at the time. Furthermore, the colonists themselves were deeply concerned with the relationship between the value of Pennsylvania currency and that of the British pound sterling. I have concluded that the risk of error from using an improperly weighted price index is probably greater than the discrepancy between the true rate of inflation in Pennsylvania and the exchange rate. For these reasons I used the exchange rate in making adjustments to the raw figures in the inventories. The point is probably moot: neither series shows much movement in the value of Pennsylvania currency over the period in question. The years with the greatest discrepencies between the two series, 1731, 1741–1743, and 1746–1748, were not included in the three sample periods. See tables 4.1 and 4.2.

      3. Chester County Wills and Inventories, Chester County Archives (hereafter cited as CCWI); Estate Accounts, Chester County Archives (hereafter cited as CC Estates).

      4. Inheritance laws, chs. 31, 43, 46, 124, 125, 127, *Laws of the Province of Pennsylvania, 1700–1727*.

      5. No. 52, Nicholas Pyle; no. 116, Peter Taylor; no. 121, David Morris; no. 432, James Miller; no. 433, Moses Mendenhall; no. 464, Aaron Harlan; no. 465, Isaac Bayley; no. 522, Jacob Minshall; no. 532, William Pyle; no. 1081, John Hall; no. 1086, Jeremiah Cloud; no. 1119, Thomas Smith; no. 1167, James Woodward; no. 1168, James Willson, CCWI.

      6. No. 15, Edward Bennett; no. 34, Joseph Baker; no. 1310, John Vaughan, CCWI.

      7. No. 12, James Brown; no. 30, John Hendricks; no. 453, James Gibbons; no. 531, David Thomas; no. 1353, Alexander Frazier; no. 1254, John Edwards, CCWI.

      8. No. 437, James Townsend; no. 447, Joseph White; no. 512, Nicholas Pyle, Jr.; no. 516, Philip Yarnall; no. 519, George Peirce; no. 1086, Jeremiah Cloud; no. 1152, John Brinton; no. 1412, Job Harvey, CCWI.

      9. No. 98, Thomas Withers; no. 29, James Whitaker; no. 131, Frances Yarnell; no. 436, Joel Baily; no. 439, Joseph Roades; no. 471, Samuel Sellers; no. 1131,

John Yearsley; no. 516, Philip Yarnall; no. 532, William Pyle; no. 1084, Nicholas Jones; no. 1088, John Townsend, Sr., CCWI.

10. CCWI; Est. H 1745, Josiah Hibberd, CC Estates; and no. 467, Jeremiah Taylor; no. 1174, Edward Riley; no. 1204, Sarah Taylor, CCWI.

11. Est. C 1742, Abel Clayton; Est C 1745, William Craig; Est. B 1748, Thomas Bonsall; Est. E 1743, Evan Evans; Est. H 1741, Evan Howell; Est. H 1745, Josiah Hibberd; Est. H 1753, Thomas Hope; Est. Mc 1750, James McCullough; Est. O 1751, Philip Otley; Est. P 1745, John Pugh, CC Estates.

12. For example, Hugh Pugh's two oldest children were bound out because the entire estate was willed to his youngest, "he having but one hand," to provide for his education. No. 1222, CCWI.

13. Benjamin Franklin ran away from his brother's care in Boston to come to Philadelphia. Benjamin Franklin, *Autobiography.*

14. CCWI; see chapter 2.

15. David Galenson's otherwise excellent study of indentured servitude in America seriously neglects the incidence of binding of youths other than immigrants. The reasons for this omission are twofold: Galenson concentrates his study on the Chesapeake and the West Indies, areas where immigrant labor was much more important to the labor force. Second, Galenson assumes that labor conditions in England applied automatically in the colonies. However, whether or not bound labor was still common in England in the eighteenth century, there is no doubt it was a common practice in the middle and northern colonies throughout the colonial period—not only for immigrants, but also for American-born youths. See David Galenson, *White Servitude in Colonial America: An Economic Analysis.*

16. James Steel Letterbook, May 2, 1738; Logan Papers, Historical Society of Pennsylvania (hereafter referred to as HSP).

17. "A Book of Discipline of the Yearly Meeting 1719 belonging to the monthly meeting of Chesterfield, New Jersey, From our Yearly Meeting held at Philadelphia for Pensilvania and the Jerseys," Friends Historical Library, Swarthmore College (hereafter referred to as Quaker Discipline Book).

18. "Conductor Generalis"; no. 9, Chester County Court of Quarter Sessions, Petitions, Chester County Archives (hereafter cited as CC Quarter Sessions Petitions).

19. See the case of Andrew Campbell, servant to John McGrew, and the Overseers of the Poor in Londonderry Township, No. 182, CC Quarter Sessions Petitions. See also nos. 15, 28, 51, 85, 173, and 231. Joseph Muckleduff wrote in his will "that William McConnall and Sarah McConnall be set free at the age of twelve years and that my brother [Samuel] shall not keep them till they come of age and that the said Samuel shall not suffer them to be bound to anney other parson or parsons what so ever," no. 1332, CCWI. As an example of how the assignability of all bound servants could go awry in the case of a bound family member, see the case of James and Mary Sprole, who according to their petition were persuaded by her sister's husband, one McGinniss, "to let them have one of their Children to live with the said McGinniss and his Wife for Company." They let McGinniss have their nine-year-old daughter, and had her formally indentured for purposes of discipline. Three years later, McGinniss was indicted for the supposed rape of a servant (he pleaded no contest), thrown in jail, and his goods sold—including the young girl. There is no record whether her parents were able to break the indenture.

20. No. 476, Thomas Nixon; no. 1094, Philip David; no. 1230, Elizabeth Freeman; Phillip Tanner, a "Cloath Worker" in East Nottingham, willed that his son James live with his mother until 21, "but if he prove stuborn and disobedient then to be bound out to a sharp master a fuller." No. 1379, CCWI. Examples of fatherless children bound out because of the poverty of the estate can be found in no. 128, Isaac Barton; no. 448, Thomas Jenkin; no. 600, Jane Lewis; no. 1260, Elizabeth Patterson, CCWI; and Est. B 1753, Samuel Black, CC Estates.

21. No. 522, Jacob Minshall, CCWI; "Account of Servants Bound and Assigned Before James Hamilton, Mayor of Philadelphia" (hereafter cited as Servants Bound Before James Hamilton).

22. Servants Bound Before James Hamilton; and no. 91, William Buller; no. 100, Charles Whitaker; no. 1196, William Brown; no. 110, Jacob Trego; no. 1223, Robert Petterson; no. 496, Richard Hughes; no. 1365, John Marshall, CCWI. The wife of Edward Russell, for example, was paid £13 "for Education and Learning Sarah [Coeburn] the Trade art & mystery of a Tayloress," Est. C 1735, Coeburn; John Culen's estate paid Abraham Asheton's wife £6 to teach Margaret Culen the same skills, Est. C 1752, Culin, CC Estates.

23. No. 1286, Joseph Townsend; no. 1358, William Morris; no. 1391, Job Pyle; no. 1412, Job Harvey; no. 15, Edward Bennett; no. 106, George James; no. 1174, Edward Riley; no. 433, Moses Mendenhall; no. 460, John Holston; no. 469, Thomas Townsend; no. 512, Nicholas Pyle, Jr.; no. 532, William Pyle; no. 1119, Thomas Smith; no. 1189, Joseph Mendenhall; no. 1232, William John; no. 1332, David Sheerer; no. 1167, James Woodward, CCWI.

24. Servants Bound Before James Hamilton, 31:203; as an adult, Jacob Grubb had himself apprenticed to learn the mystery of a cooper and be taught to read and write; Servants Bound Before James Hamilton, 31:96; see no. 1244, Abraham Vernon, CCWI, for a servant girl with four years to serve who was not valued in the inventory because her contract was only verbal.

25. For example, see Est. H 1741; Est. P 1747; Est. T 1752, CC Estates.

26. Nos. 14, 76, 92, 108, 122, 126, 127, 129, 131, 147, 149, 154, and 181, CC Quarter Sessions Petitions.

27. All of the servants bound before Hamilton were redemptioners; that is, they gave the captain their bond and then sold themselves as servants in Philadelphia. They had the choice of masters, and the price was negotiated in Pennsylvania. Michael Wooldridge was thus able to bind himself apprentice for seven years and five months service and the paying of a £15 passage in return for being taught the "art or mystery of a cooper." In contrast, John Hacknedy was indentured in Ireland in 1740, as was Robert Doeherty, who signed an indenture agreeing to seven years of servitude wherever the ship sent him and freedom dues "according to the Custom of the Country" wherever he found himself at the end of his indenture. Nos. 191 and 198, CC Quarter Sessions Petitions. As an example of a third type of indentured immigrant, see the petition of Philip McRory, who arrived in New Castle already bound to a Philadelphia merchant, who immediately had him sold to a new owner. No. 183, CC Quarter Sessions Petitions.

28. Marianne S. Wokeck, "A Tide of Alien Tongues: The Flow and Ebb of German Immigration to Pennsylvania, 1683–1776."

29. CC Quarter Sessions Petitions, Servants Bound Before James Hamilton.

30. The runaway petitions are too numerous to list. CC Quarter Sessions Petitions.

31. Nos. 73, 117, 124, 138, 150, 171, 172, 176, 179, 184, 185, 206, 211, 226, and 234, CC Quarter Sessions Petitions.

32. Nos. 26, 31, 91, 96, 136, and 215, CC Quarter Sessions Petitions.

33. The instances of servants suing masters were too numerous to list. CC Quarter Sessions Petitions.

34. CC Quarter Sessions Petitions.

35. Nos. 80, 202, 214, CC Quarter Sessions Petitions.

36. CCWI; Carville Earle, *The Evolution of a Tidewater Settlement System: All Hallow's Parish, Maryland, 1650–1783,* table 8, p. 46; Paul E. G. Clemens, *The Atlantic Economy and Colonial Maryland's Eastern Shore: From Tobacco to Grain.*

37. Gary B. Nash, *Quakers and Politics: Pennsylvania, 1681–1726;* Earle, *All Hallow's Parish,* p. 46. Paul Clemens argues convincingly that planters on Maryland's eastern shore turned to slavery when immigrants began showing a preference for Pennsylvania over Maryland in the early 1700s. Clemens, *Atlantic Economy.*

38. Clemens; David Klingaman, "The Significance of Grain in the Development of the Tobacco Colonies."

39. No. 1212, Christopher Taylor; no. 1389, Deborah Nayle; no. 2430, Negro Bella; no. 426, John Baldwin; no. 507, John Baker; no. 1332, Joseph Muckleduff, CCWI.

40. Quaker Discipline Book. For more on the dilemma slavery presented for Quakers, see Jean Soderlund, *Quakers and Slavery: A Divided Spirit.*

41. Thornbury Tax Return, 1726, Chester County Archives; Henry Mylls, a laborer in Chester County, had three children in Ireland and one in Pennsylvania, no. 1172, CCWI; no. 221, CC Quarter Sessions Petitions.

42. James Lemon, *The Best Poor Man's Country,* pp. 93–95; Lucy Simler, "Tenancy and Economic Development in Eighteenth-Century Chester County, Pennsylvania."

43. Samuel Nutt's widow, Anna Nutt, continued and expanded the foundry "in company with" Robert Grace and her nephew, Samuel Nutt, Jr., who married her daughter Rebecca by her first husband John Savage (also an early ironmaster in Pennsylvania). After the death of Samuel Nutt, Jr., Rebecca married Robert Grace, keeping the company all in the family. Anna Savage Nutt's other daughter, Ruth Savage, married ironworker John Potts. Their son, Thomas, married Anna Nutt's granddaughter, the child of Samuel Nutt, Jr., and Rebecca Savage Nutt Grace. Thus began the Potts iron and steel dynasty in Pennsylvania. I am grateful to Estelle Cremers of the French and Pickering Creeks Conservation Trust in Chester County for explaining this rather complex geneology to me.

The Franklin Stove was cast at Coventry Forge, and the first model occupied the parlor fireplace at Rebecca Nutt's house.

See Stephen Innes, *Labor in a New Land,* for an earlier example of wage labor in western Massachusetts in the 1600s.

44. Coventry Iron Works, Ledgers and Daybooks, Forges and Furnaces Account Books, HSP.

45. *Ibid.*

46. *Ibid.*

47. *Ibid.*

48. *Ibid.*

49. *Ibid.*

50. *Ibid.*
51. *Ibid.* Pine Forge Ledgers, Forges and Furnaces Account Books; Richard Hayes Ledger, HSP.
52. Coventry Iron Works.
53. *Ibid.*
54. *Ibid.*
55. *Ibid.*
56. *Ibid.*
57. *Ibid;* Pine Forge Ledgers; Richard Hayes Ledger. See also Innes, *Labor in a New Land.*
58. The exchange rates from Pennsylvania currency to British sterling were taken from John J. McCusker, *Money and Exchange in Europe and America,* table 3.7, pp. 183–185. The wages in southern England can be found in K. D. M. Snell, *Annals of the Labouring Poor* (New York: Cambridge University Press, 1985), Appendix.
59. Paul Paskoff, *Industrial Evolution: Organization, Structure, and Growth of the Pennsylvania Iron Industry, 1750–1860;* Estelle Cremers, *Reading Furnace, 1736;* Arthur C. Bining, *Pennsylvania's Iron and Steel Industry.*
60. Macfarlane, *The Origins of English Individualism,* ch. 3.

2. Uncertainty, Diversification, and Economic Performance in Colonial Pennsylvania

1. Much of the discussion of the Pennsylvania economy in this chapter is based upon an analysis of three samples drawn from the wills and inventories in the Chester County Archives. See chapter 1, note 2.
2. See, for example, James Henretta, "Families and Farms: *Mentalite* in Pre-Industrial America"; and Alan Macfarlane, *The Origins of English Individualism: The Family, Property, and Social Transition.*
3. Gary B. Nash, *Quakers and Politics: Pennsylvania, 1681–1726.* Lemon suggests that the German sects and the Quakers both benefited from the economic support offered by their close-knit religious communities, James T. Lemon, *The Best Poor Man's Country.*
4. Estate Accounts, Chester County Archives (hereafter cited as CC Estates).
5. "Book of Discipline of the Yearly Meeting 1719 belonging to the monthly meeting of Chesterfield, New Jersey, From our Yearly Meeting held at Philadelphia for Pensilvania and the Jerseys," Friends Historical Library, Swarthmore College (hereafter cited as the Quaker Discipline Book).
6. Quaker Discipline Book; Frederick B. Tolles, *Meeting House and Counting House: The Quaker Merchants of Colonial Philadelphia, 1682–1763,* pp. 38–60.
7. Almanacs were a mainstay of the colonial printing presses. William Bradford published an almanac by Daniel Leeds in New York every year from 1687 to 1713. Daniel Travis produced an almanac annually in New York from 1707 to 1723. In Philadelphia, Jacob Taylor wrote an almanac every year from 1700 to 1746. And, of course, the most famous almanac was Benjamin Franklin's "Poor Richard," which was published from 1733 to 1747 and replaced in 1748 with "Poor Richard Improved." See also Carl and Jessica Bridenbaugh, *Rebels and Gentlemen: Philadelphia in the Age of Franklin.*
8. George Rogers Taylor, "American Economic Growth Before 1840: An Exploratory Essay," p. 432; Marc M. Egnal, "The Pennsylvania Economy, 1748–1762: An Analysis of Short-Run Fluctuations in the Context of Long-Run Changes in the Atlantic

Trading Community"; Stuart Bruchey, *The Roots of American Economic Growth 1607–1861: An Essay in Social Causation*, pp. 18–31; James A. Henretta, *The Evolution of American Society, 1700–1815: An Interdisciplinary Analysis*, pp. 68–81; Douglass C. North, *The Economic Growth of the United States, 1790–1860*, pp. 17–18; James F. Shepherd and Gary M. Walton, *Shipping, Maritime Trade, and the Economic Development of Colonial North America*, pp. 24–25; James T. Lemon, *The Best Poor Man's Country* (Baltimore: Johns Hopkins University Press, 1972; Norton Library, 1975), pp. 27–31.

9. Chester County Wills and Inventories, Chester County Archives (hereafter cited as CCWI). I wish to thank historian Lucy Simler of the Chester County Archives for bringing to my attention the relative prosperity of the weavers.

10. David Klingaman, "The Significance of Grain in the Development of the Tobacco Colonies"; Marc M. Egnal, "The Changing Structure of Philadelphia's Trade with the British West Indies, 1750–1775"; David E. Dauer, "The Expansion of Philadelphia's Business System into the Chesapeake."

11. CCWI.

12. CCWI; Lemon, *The Best Poor Man's Country*.

13. *Ibid.*; Coventry Iron Works, Ledgers and Daybook; Pine Forge Ledgers, Forges and Furnaces Account Books, HSP.

14. CCWI.

15. No. 38, Jane Smith; no. 98, Thomas Withers; no. 129, John Hendrickson; no. 531, David Thomas; no. 1134, John Freeman, CCWI.

16. Philadelphia, *Minutes of the Common Council of the City of Philadelphia*, pp. 118–135; CCWI; Estate Accounts, Chester County Archives (hereafter cited as CC Estates); Coventry Iron Works; Registers of the Pennsylvania General Loan Office, Philadelphia City Archives; Register of the General Loan Office, Historical Society of Pennsylvania (hereafter cited as HSP); Arthur Cecil Bining, *Pennsylvania's Iron and Steel Industry*, pp. 31, 170. For the similarly mixed nature of the contemporary British countryside, see A. E. Musson, *The Growth of British Industry*, pp. 14–18.

17. Dauer, "The Expansion of Philadelphia's Business System into the Chesapeake."

18. *Pennsylvania Gazette*, December 28, 1732.

19. Stephanie G. Wolf, *Urban Village: Population, Community, and Family Structure in Germantown, Pennsylvania, 1683–1800*, pp. 104–107; Coventry Iron Works; Richard Hayes Ledger, HSP; Est. G 1750, Daniel Griffith; Est. M 1752, William Morris, CC Estates; and No. 80, Abraham Scott, CCWI. Note the number of weavers living outside Philadelphia as reported in tables 2.3 and 5.8.

20. Arthur Harrison Cole, *The American Wool Manufacture*, pp. 3–56, particularly pp. 11–13.

21. Est. B 1735, Bunting, Chester County Minors' Estates (hereafter cited as CCME); Est. B 1755, Backhouse, CCME; Est. C 1752, Culin, CCME; Richard Hayes Ledger, HSP; and no. 11, Jacob Trego; no. 571, Daniel Pyle; no. 115, Ann Letart; no. 604, John Camm; no. 20, John Hanes, CCWI; Coventry Iron Works.

22. No. 609, Joseph Hibberd; no. 1321, John Moore; no. 1407, Francis Swaine; no. 1281, John Marshall; no. 1286, Joseph Townsend; no. 1310, John Vaughan; no. 1356, William Mascall, CCWI.

23. CCWI; Registers of the Pennsylvania General Loan Office.

24. See table 2.3; Jacob Roman, a Chester Town smith, owned a "mill anvil" worth £8; perhaps it was connected with a water-powered mill (No. 1209, CCWI); John Plain of Coventry left an "iron dying furnace" in 1748 (No. 1096, CCWI). Cov-

entry Forge put "steal tips" on agricultural implements as early as the 1730s (Coventry Iron Works).

25. Bining, *Iron and Steel*, pp. 31, 50–53, 170; Coventry Iron Works.

26. *An Act for the better Regulating the Retailers of Liquor* (1725), ch. 289, *Laws of the Province of Pennsylvania*, 1700–1727; *An Act for regulating Retailers of Liquors near the Iron-Works* (1736), ch. 339, *Laws of the Province of Pennsylvania*, 1700–1740; William Branson mortgage, May 31, 1745, Register of the Pennsylvania General Loan Office, Philadelphia City Archives; John Taylor mortgage, April 15, 1745, Register of the Pennsylvania General Loan Office.

27. Jacob M. Price, "Economic Function and the Growth of American Port Towns in the Eighteenth Century"; Dauer, "The Expansion of Philadelphia's Business System Into the Chesapeake."

28. CCWI. Gloria Main similarly restricted a sample of inventories to "young fathers" in a study of eighteenth-century wealth patterns. Gloria L. Main, "The Standard of Living in Colonial Massachusetts," *Journal of Economic History* (March 1983), 63:101–8. For a discussion of the life cycle and standards of living, see Jackson Turner Main, "Standards of Living and the Life Cycle in Colonial Connecticut," *Journal of Economic History* (March 1983), 63:159–65, and Jackson Turner Main, *Society and Economy in Colonial Connecticut.*

29. CCWI.

30. *Ibid.*

31. *Ibid.*

32. CCWI. For estimates of economic growth in the nineteenth century, see Robert Gallman, "The Pace and Pattern of American Economic Growth," p. 41. Gallman estimates that income per capita grew at a rate of .3 percent to .5 percent a year during the colonial period. Lemon found a stagnating economy in Pennsylvania during the period 1700–1730 and an expanding economy from 1730 to 1760; Lemon, *The Best Poor Man's Country*, pp. 219–224.

The problem with the tax assessments was highlighted when compiling a list of the taxes paid by recipients of mortgages from the Pennsylvania General Loan Office. The average tax paid by mortgage recipients in Chester County was 7s. 6d. in 1729 and 4s. 7d. in 1754. The 1729 tax was ordered at a rate of 3d. per pound, and the 1754 tax at a rate of 2d. per pound. By that rate, the average mortgage recipient would have owned £30 real estate and livestock in 1729 and £27.10 in 1754. Yet the loan recipients received an average of £65.12s. from the Loan Office based on real estate holdings that were acquired by law to at least *double* the loan in value. See tables 5.5 and 5.6.

The head tax charged freemen was tied by law to the rate at which real estate was assessed. Thus, if the county commissioners wished to charge freemen a nine shilling head tax, they were required to assess the other county residents at a rate of 3d. per pound. By systematically undervaluing the real estate holdings, assessors were able to collect a fairly stiff tax from the freemen and still remain within the technical bounds of the law. While the situation speaks volumes about the attitudes in the community toward unmarried men, it is not particularly helpful to those interested in the value of wealth holdings in colonial Pennsylvania.

33. For a discussion of the effects of the fear of economic disaster upon the willingness of households to become involved in the market, see Joyce Oldham Appleby, *Economic Thought and Ideology in Seventeenth-Century England*, p. 57. See also Ed Perkins, *The Economy of Colonial America*, ch. 1.

34. Chester County Tax Lists, 1729, 1754. See note 32.

35. Lucy Simler, "Tenancy in Colonial Pennsylvania: The Case of Chester County."

36. *Ibid.*, CC Tax Lists 1729, 1754.

37. Owen Hufton, *The Poor of Eighteenth-Century France, 1750–1789.*

3. Land Use in Pennsylvania

1. William R. Shepherd, *History of Proprietary Government in Pennsylvania*, pp. 5–25; Gary B. Nash, *Quakers and Politics: Pennsylvania, 1681–1726*, pp. 89–97, 215–227, 254–255; Alan Tully, *William Penn's Legacy: Politics and Social Structure in Provincial Pennsylvania, 1726–1755*, pp. 11–15; James T. Lemon, *The Best Poor Man's Country*, pp. 49–61.

2. Nash, *Quakers and Politics*, pp. 7–10; Lemon, *Best Poor Man's Country*, pp. 49–57.

3. James Steel wrote to William Penn, 25 March 1731, "your fine mannor of 1600 acres at Conestogoe was lately settled by a gang of Scotch Irish who threatened to hold it by force of Arms . . . ," James Steel Letterbook, Logan Papers, Historical Society of Pennsylvania (hereafter cited as HSP); John Smith Futhey and Gilbert Cope, *History of Chester County, Pennsylvania* (Philadelphia: Everts, 1881), pp. 152–154.

4. West New Jersey Society, Box 30, Phineas Bond Papers, Cadwalader Collection, HSP; Futhey and Cope, *Chester County*, pp. 150, 181, 183, 193. I am grateful to Lucy Simler of the Chester County Archives for explaining about the existence of the manors and some of the distinctions in categories of land ownership.

5. John Swift to John White, July 30, 1747, John Swift Account Book, HSP.

6. James Steel to John Paris, March 17, 1737, James Steel Letterbook, Logan Papers, HSP.

7. West New Jersey Society, Box 30, Phineas Bond Papers, Cadwalader Collection, HSP. I am indebted to Barbara Weir, assistant archivist at the Chester County Archives, for bringing this collection at HSP to my attention.

8. *Ibid.*; Penn Leases, Box 27, Cadwalader Collection, HSP.

9. West New Jersey Society, Box 30, Phineas Bond Papers, Cadwalader Collection, HSP.

10. Nash, *Quakers and Politics*, pp. 77–78, 92–99; Tully, *William Penn's Legacy*, pp. 14–15, 44–45.

11. Nash, *Quakers and Politics*, pp. 216–217, 254–55; Tully, *William Penn's Legacy*, pp. 15, 44; *An Act for the more Easy and Effectual Collecting of the Proprietarys Quit-Rents* (1705), ch. 131, *Laws of the Province of Pennsylvania, 1700–1712*.

12. Tully, *William Penn's Legacy*, p. 15; General Loan Office Books F–L, Norris of Fairhill Manuscripts, HSP; James Steel to Samuel Blunston, March 3, 1735; February 21, 1736; February 25, 1738; February 19, 1739; March 2, 1739; February 26, 1740; James Steel Letterbook, HSP.

13. Richard L. Bushman, *From Puritan to Yankee: Character and the Social Order in Connecticut, 1690–1765*, pp. 79–103; Kenneth A. Lockridge, *A New England Town: The First Hundred Years: Dedham, Masachusetts, 1636–1736*; Lemon, *Best Poor Man's Country*; Thomas Penn to Andrew Hamilton, March 9, 1752, Penn-Hamilton Correspondence, Penn Papers, HSP; Thomas Sergeant, *View of the Land Laws of Pennsylvania*, p. 34.

14. Shepherd, pp. 26–34, 55–76.

15. Formal registration of the deed might in the end result in having to pay

quitrents as well. When the estate of Josiah Hibberd put a portion of his real estate to auction, the executors had to pay £1.0.10 for quitrents when the land was conveyed; they were then charged an identical amount for the land they retained (Est. H 1745, CC Estates); similarly, Joshua Harlan's estate had to pay £7.4.8 in back quitrents (Est. H. 1746, CC Estates); Evan Harry's estate was charged £4.0.3 for thirty-four years quitrents (Est. H 1747, CC Estates); John Henderson's estate paid £10.19.10 in quitrents when the land was conveyed (Est. H 1753, CC Estates); William Pyle's estate paid twenty-two years back quitrents at £4.2.6 (Est. P 1753, CC Estates); and John Wade, Sr.'s estate was charged £31 for lawyers and sheriffs fees "in the Case of the Proprietors Quit Rents" when the executors sold "a piece of land" to George Ashbridge for £69.

16. Shepherd, *Proprietary Government*, pp. 187–198, 119–131; Nash, *Quakers and Politics*, pp. 74–76, 84, 104; Tully, *William Penn's Legacy*, pp. 3–7; Lemon, *Best Poor Man's Country*, pp. 58–61; Sergeant, *Land Laws*, pp. 39–41, 47.

17. After having been involved in one of these disputes, a settler would typically be put under pressure by the Penns' agents to buy the patent. Shepherd, *Proprietary Government*, pp. 54–76; Futhey and Cope, *Chester County*, pp. 209–210; James Steel Letterbook, Logan Papers, HSP.

18. For the law on seven years' quiet possession see ch. 31 (1705), *Laws of the Province of Pennsylvania*, 1700–1712; for common law regarding quiet possession, see "Conductor Generalis," p. 437; CCWI, 1714–1755.

19. For example, when John Farrer sold an unpaid-for warrant right to land near Conestoga in 1731, James Steel wrote that "thou . . . has taken upon thee to settle on the Proprietors Land . . . and afterwards to dispose of the same in a very unjust manner . . . ," James Steel to John Farrer, January 30, 1731, James Steel Letterbook, Logan Papers, HSP; for other examples see letters written to various people by Steel, April 13, 1731; August 2, 1731; October 15, 1731; February 13, 1732; February 21, 1732; November 29, 1732; June 4, 1734; June 22, 1734; October 8, 1736; James Steel Letterbook, Logan Papers, HSP; Sergeant, *Land Laws*, pp. 35–37, 50.

20. A warrent right to 100 acres was valued at £50 in John Kenyan's estate, no. 1367, CCWI; Alexander Moode, a joiner or carpenter in East Fallowfield, paid £14.1.6 for unpatented land just before his death in 1751, no. 1380; the estate of James Mc-Cullough, a Chester Town smith, sold "an improvement of land over Susquehanna," to John Moore in 1754 for £22.12.6, no. 1288; in 1728 Benjamin Taylor and Christian Grabill each owned an "improvement on a pees of unsurve'd Land" in Conestoga, valued at £30 and £45 respectively.

21. CCWI.

22. Tully, *William Penn's Legacy*, pp. 5–6; James Steel treated correspondents with surveys as if they had full title. See letters to various people, June 5, 1731; June 1, 1733; June 7, 1733; June 15, 1733; October 6, 1733; June 4, 1734; December 17, 1734; June 28, 1735; November 6, 1735; James Steel Letterbook, Logan Papers, HSP.

23. "Conductor Generalis," p. 435; Phineas Bond Box 30, West New Jersey Society, Cadwalader Collection, HSP. The practice of leasing the land but not the improvements continues today in the institution of "ground rent" still seen in some American cities.

24. Phineas Bond Box 30, West New Jersey Society, Cadwalader Collection, HSP.

25. Peters Papers, 3:44, August 22, 1751.

26. *Ibid.*

27. *Ibid.*

28. Logan was possibly acting as agent for the Penns, as the land being leased was in Conestoga Manor; however, Logan did own some land there. The Penn Papers contain another short term lease, eleven years in Perkassey Manor. Book of Leases and Mortgages in the Penn Papers, HSP.

29. Chester County Estate Accounts, Chester County Archives (hereafter cited as CC Estates).

30. Lucy Simler, "Tenancy in Colonial Pennsylvania: The Case of Chester County"; Lemon, *The Best Poor Man's Country*, p. 12.

31. Nash, *Quakers and Politics*, pp. 4–10; Futhey and Cope, *Chester County*, pp. 150, 181, 183, 193, 109–110; West New Jersey Society, Box 30, Phineas Bond Papers, Cadwalader Collection, HSP; Jerome H. Wood, Jr., "The Town Proprietors of Lancaster, 1730–1790; Randolph Shipley Klein, *Portrait of an Early American Family: The Shippens of Pennsylvania Across Five Generations*.

32. Marc M. Egnal, "The Changing Structure of Philadelphia's Trade with the British West Indies, 1750–1775," pp. 163–165.

33. Robert D. Mitchell, *Commercialism and Frontier: Perspectives on the Early Shenandoah Valley*, pp. 59–92; Robert P. Swierenga, "Land Speculator 'Profits' Reconsidered: Central Iowa as a Test Case," *Journal of Economic History* (March 1966), 26:1–28.

34. The seminal work on town development in Pennsylvania (and the colonies) is Lemon, *The Best Poor Man's Country*. See also Wood, "Town Proprietors," pp. 346–368; Terry A. McNealy, "Bristol: The Origins of a Pennsylvania Market Town."

35. The Penns did lease some land in the early 1700s. Nottingham lots were leased (frequently without rent) to protect the land from Maryland encroachments; there were some Conestoga leases. But the Penns generally avoided leasing land until later in the century. See James Steel letters to various people wishing to use manor lands, November 30, 1731; October 15, 1731; February 21, 1732; August 17, 1734; October 19, 1734; November 18, 1734; James Steel Letterbook, Logan Papers, HSP.

36. Sung Bok Kim, *Landlord and Tenant in Colonial New York: Manorial Society, 1664–1775*, pp. 179–180, 221–226, 243–244, 251–261.

37. No. 1128, Matthew Reading; no. 1109, Thomas Griffith; no. 1110, Daniel Griffith; no. 1332, Joseph Muckleduff; no. 1313, Peter Highet; no. 1342, William Thomas; no. 1112, William David; no. 1113, William Owen, CCWI.

38. No. 511, Andrew Hayden, CCWI.

39. Lemon, *The Best Poor Man's Country*, p. 95.

40. Business Papers of Joseph Wharton, 1728–1771, Edward Wanton Smith Papers, HSP; Joseph Wharton Ledger, 1736–1793, Wharton Papers, HSP; CCWI.

41. *Votes and Proceedings of the House of Assembly of the Province of Pennsylvania, Pennsylvania Archives*, 3:2253 and 2261.

4. The General Loan Office and Paper Money

1. Complaints about the state of the West Indies flour trade abounded in the first two decades of the eighteenth century. Gary B. Nash, *Quakers and Politics: Pennsylvania, 1681–1726*, pp. 252–254 (although Nash felt the economy picked up significantly in the second decade); *Votes and Proceedings of the House of Representatives of the Province of Pennsylvania, Pennsylvania Archives*, 2:955, 1164, 1237, 1368 (hereafter cited as *Votes*). James Logan wrote in 1712, "Trade, I believe, has scarce ever been known lower here, than at this time, that to Lisbon thou knows has failed, to the W. Indies 'tis equally dull

So that our Commodities are not likely to bear a price speedily . . ." James Logan to Edward Hacket, July 2, 1712, James Logan Letterbook, 1712–1715, Logan Papers, Historical Society of Pennsylvania (hereafter cited as HSP); see also James Logan to Henry Goldney, October 10, 1715, Logan Letterbook, 1712–1715, Logan Papers, HSP. For a brief summary of the South Sea Bubble episode, see Brian Murphy, *A History of the British Economy, 1086–1970*, pp. 280–292.

2. Jonathan Dickinson to Thomas Mayleigh, September 29, 1720, Jonathan Dickinson letterbook, 1714–1721, HSP; Jonathan Dickinson to Caleb Dickinson in London, October 22, 1720, Jonathan Dickinson letterbook, 1714–1721, HSP; Jonathan Dickinson to "Brother," May 10, 1721, Jonathan Dickinson Letterbook, 1714–1721, HSP. The following anonymous poem about the Bubble appears to have been popular in Pennsylvania at the time:

> When Moses and Isr'el had cross'd the red Sea,
> Nor Dangers nor Fears th'Egyptians dismay:
> How rashly they ventur'd, till Waves them surrounded,
> And all the proud Troops in an Instant was drowned.
> Thus thousands of late have pass'd the South-Seas,
> As safe as in Water not up to their Knees;
> Whilst those that came after, without Wit nor Fear,
> Like Pharoah's great Host, are now nick'd in the Rear.

American Weekly Mercury, January 24, 1721.

3. See chapter 7 for the problems with flour prices. Simeon J. Crowther, "The Shipbuilding Industry and the Economic Development of the Delaware Valley 1681–1776," pp. 42–43; Arthur Cecil Bining, *Pennsylvania's Iron and Steel Industry*, p. 170; James T. Lemon, *The Best Poor Man's Country*, pp. 221–222; Gary Nash, *Urban Crucible*, p. 119.

4. Benjamin Franklin, *Autobiography*, p. 124.

5. Chs. 237–261, *Laws of the Province of Pennsylvania*, 1700–1727.

6. *Laws of the Commonwealth of Pennsylvania*, 1700–1781.

7. For nearly a century, historians and economists have been fascinated by Pennsylvania's apparently successful experiment with paper money in an attempt to overcome an economic recession in the late 1710s and early 1720s. C. W. MacFarlane first noted in 1896 the absence of inflation during the period when Pennsylvania issued paper money through the government-operated land bank in the mid-1700s. Price stability in Pennsylvania, he concluded, resulted from the conservative behavior of the Quaker legislature in limiting the amount of the paper money. Economist Richard Lester reopened this subject in 1938. Interested in the contemporary implications of Pennsylvania's experience, Lester focused on the manner in which Pennsylvania used paper money to increase real income; previous experiments with paper money had all been associated with war finance. Despite these favorable studies, general historical works continued for some years to depict Pennsylvania's experience with paper money as inevitably inflationary, favored by debtors and abhorred by creditors. In the early 1950s, however, concurrent specialized articles by E. James Ferguson and Theodore Thayer reintroduced a Keynesian interpretation of the effects of the colony's paper money. In particular, Ferguson attacked the Progressive assumption that paper money always formed a sore point between merchants and farmers. Paper money was not the center of a class struggle, but an important innovation which was favored by nearly all colonial Pennsylvanians and understood to have contributed greatly to the colony's spectacular growth in

the eighteenth century. In overtly comparing the General Loan Office of Pennsylvania, which issued the paper money, to the mammoth Federal Reserve System, however, these scholars were in danger of anachronistic misinterpretation of the importance of paper money to colonial Pennsylvania. Nevertheless, their studies represented a significant advance over the progressive historians in the analysis of this problem. More recently, Marc Egnal and Joseph Ernst have argued that fluctuations in book credit and flows of payments abroad should also be included in any consideration of the colonial money supply. There the debate rests for the moment. C. W. MacFarlane, "Pennsylvania Paper Currency"; Richard A. Lester, "Currency Issues to Overcome Depressions in Pennsylvania, 1723 and 1729"; Leslie Van Horn Brock, "The Currency of the American Colonies 1700–1764: A Study in Colonial Finance and Imperial Relations"; Paton Wesley Yoder, "Paper Currency in Colonial Pennsylvania." James Ferguson, "Currency Finance: An Interpretation of Colonial Monetary Practices"; Theodore Thayer, "The Land-Bank System in the American Colonies"; Marc M. Egnal, "The Pennsylvania Economy, 1748–1762: An Analysis of Short-Run Fluctuations in the Context of Long-Run Changes in the Atlantic Trading Community"; Joseph A. Ernst, *Money and Politics in America, 1755–75;* Jack P. Greene and Richard M. Jellison, "The Currency Act of 1764 in Imperial-Colonial Relations, 1764–76"; Jack M. Sosin, "Imperial Regulation of Colonial Paper Money, 1764–1773."

8. John J. McCusker, *Money and Exchange in Europe and America, 1600–1775,* pp. 116–131; Curtis P. Nettles, *The Money Supply of the American Colonies before 1720,* pp. 202–228; Clarence P. Gould, *Money and Transportation in Maryland, 1720–1765,* pp. 48–73; Leslie Van Horn Brock, "The Currency of the American Colonies 1700–1764: A Study in Colonial Finance and Imperial Relations." Regarding the practice of clipping, see John Blackwell to William Penn, January 25, 1689, Penn papers, HSP.

9. William R. Shepherd, *History of Proprietary Government in Pennsylvania,* p. 401; Curtis P. Nettles, *The Roots of American Civilization,* p. 265; Brock, "Currency of the American Colonies," p. 6; Joseph A. Ernst, *Money and Politics in America, 1755–1775,* pp. 10, 356.

10. Jacob M. Price, *Capital and Credit in British Overseas Trade: The View from the Chesapeake, 1700–1776.*

11. *Ibid.*

12. Business Papers, 1702–1744, Coates, Reynell Papers; Samuel Emlen Daybooks, 1751–1767; Richard Hayes Ledger, 1708–1740; Samuel McCall Journal, 1743–1749; Samuel Neaves Ledger, 1752–1756; Thomas Paschall Day Book, 1724–1737; Thomas Penrose Journals; Samuel Powel Ledgers and Day Books; Business Papers of Joseph Wharton, 1728–1771, Edward Wanton Smith Collection; Joseph Wharton Ledger, 1736–1793, Wharton Papers; Forges and Furnaces Account Books, HSP.

13. *Ibid.*

14. [Francis Rawle], "Some Remedies Proposed for the Restoring the sunk Credit of the Province of Pennsylvania with Some Remarks on its Trade."

15. Mary M. Schweitzer, "Economic Regulation and the Colonial Economy: The Maryland Tobacco Inspection Act of 1747."

16. Ch. 90, *Laws of the Province of Pennsylvania, 1700–1712; Votes,* 2:1244, 1461, 1499, 1513.

17. Rawle, "Some Remedies Proposed."

18. For an example of the use of flour and wheat as money, with the miller as middleman, see Richard Hayes' Ledger, 1708–1740, HSP.

19. See note 12.
20. *Ibid.* See also CCWI.
21. Murphy, *British Economy*, pp. 280–292.
22. Brock, "Currency of the American Colonies," pp. 7–9; McCusker, *Money and Exchange*, pp. 118–119, 126.
23. Brock, pp. 37–43.
24. *Votes*, 2:1463–65; Paton Wesley Yoder, "Paper Currency in Colonial Pennsylvania," pp. 33–35; Joseph Dorfman, *The Economic Mind in American Civilization, 1606–1865*; Frederick B. Tolles, *Meeting House and Counting House: The Quaker Merchants of Colonial Philadelphia, 1782–1763*, p. 103; Robert Proud, *The History of Pennsylvania*, p. 152.
25. Thomas Wendell, "The Keith-Lloyd Alliance: Factional and Coalition Politics in Colonial Pennsylvania."
26. Rawle, "Some Remedies Proposed."
27. Yoder, "Paper Currency," pp. 28–38, 118; Rawle, "Some Remedies Proposed;" Proud, *History of Pennsylvania*, pp. 152–153.
28. *Votes*, 3:1739; *An Act for Reprinting, Exchanging, and Re-emitting all the Bills of Credit of this Province* (1939), ch. 343, *Laws of the Province of Pennsylvania, 1700–1740; An Act for the more effectual preserving the Credit of our Paper-Money, and recovering the Proprietary Quit-Rents* (1739), ch. 344.
29. Rawle, "Some Remedies Proposed;" Benjamin Franklin, "A Modest Inquiry into the Nature and Necessity of a Paper-Currency"; Dorfman, *Economic Mind;* see Richard Bushman, *From Puritan to Yankee*, pp. 124–125, and Nash, *Urban Crucible*.
30. *Votes*, 3:2090–92; chs. 250, 256, 261, 262, *Laws of the Province of Pennsylvania, 1700–1727*; ch. 343, 1700–1740.
31. "Case for Attorney-General's opinion," no. 19, Box 2, James Hamilton Papers; Thomas Penn to James Hamilton July 31, 1749; July 29, 1751; July 13, 1752; Penn-Hamilton Correspondence, Penn Papers, HSP. Penn wrote to Hamilton in 1753, "I shall be very well pleased to give them [the legislators] £20,000 if at the same time we [the proprietors] can appropriate the Interest by Law."Thomas Penn to James Hamilton, January 9, 1753, Penn-Hamilton Correspondence, Penn Papers, HSP; *Votes*, 4:3239–56, 3283–84, 3490–550, 3558–60, 3572–79, 3586–603; 5:3631, 3649–50, 3690–772, 3872, 3875, 3924.
32. See note 30.
33. Ch. 250, *Laws of the Province of Pennsylvania, 1700–1727.*
34. See note 30; Yoder, "Paper Currency," pp. 291–300.
35. Chs. 275, 315, 343, *Laws of the Province of Pennsylvania, 1700–1740*; ch. 413, *Laws of the Province of Pennsylvania, 1700–1781.*
36. See note 31; ch. 374, *Laws of the Province of Pennsylvania, 1700–1781.*
37. Harry D. Hutchinson, *Money, Banking, and the United States Economy* (Englewood Cliffs, N.J.: Prentice-Hall, 1975), p. 15.
38. While the Hancock book covers the period 1724–1764, most of the examples were drawn from the 1750s and 1760s. The business records examined before 1755 were incomplete, missing the account books which should have shown cash transactions. If the description of the Boston accounting system before 1755 is accurate, the Bostonians were generations behind the Philadelphians in bookkeeping skills. W. T. Baxter, *The House of Hancock: Business in Boston 1724–1775*, pp. 17–21, 35–38; Brock, "Currency of the American Colonies," pp. 244–334; Gould, *Money and Transportation*, pp. 48–73.

39. Samuel Powel Ledger B, 1727–1733; Samuel Powel Journal, 1727–1733. See also note 1.
40. For an in-depth discussion of post-World War II theoretical development on the equation of exchange, see Robert J. Gordon, ed., *Milton Friedman's Monetary Framework: A Debate with his Critics* (Chicago: University of Chicago Press, 1974).
41. *Ibid.*
42. Registers of the Pennsylvania General Loan Office, Philadelphia City Archives; Register of the Loan Office, 1724–1730, HSP.
43. Anne Bezanson, Robert D. Gray, and Miriam Hussey, *Prices in Colonial Pennsylvania*, p. 433.
44. McCusker, *Money and Exchange*, pp. 183–86.
45. See note 1.

5. The General Loan Office and Capital Formation

1. *Votes and Proceedings of the House of Representatives of the Province of Pennsylvania, Pennsylvania Archives*, 4:3515–20 (hereafter cited as *Votes*).
2. Chester County Wills and Inventories, 1714–1755, Chester County Archives (hereafter cited as CCWI).
3. No. 15, Edward Bennett, CCWI; Est. E 1743, Evan Evans, Chester County Estate Accounts, Chester County Archives (hereafter cited as CC Estates); Est. H 1745, Josiah Hibberd, CC Estates; and No. 1310, John Vaughan; No. 1311, John Robertson, CCWI.
4. Est. C 1741, John Carnahan, CC Estates; and No. 1282, John Parker; No. 1174, Edward Riley; No. 1176, James Woodward, CCWI. When William and Ann Pim of Caln married in 1734, they signed a marriage agreement whereby the money she brought into the marriage was to be "kept out at Interest" and she was to receive the "clear profits of sd Sum" annually. Indenture September 7, 1736, Chester County Archives.
5. CCWI, 1714–1755. Papers of the Court of Common Pleas, Chester County Archives (hereafter cited as Common Pleas). I am indebted to Lucy Simler, consulting historian with the Chester County Archives, for first pointing this evidence out to me.
6. Perhaps this was a function of the involvement of the Quaker Meetings with enforcement of business contracts. Frederick B. Tolles, *Meeting House and Counting House: The Quaker Merchants of Colonial Philadelphia, 1682–1763*, pp. 73–80; Common Pleas.
7. CCWI, 1714–1755.
8. Est. H 1745, Josiah Hibberd, CC Estates; and No. 467, Jeremiah Taylor; No. 1174, Edward Riley; No. 1204, Sarah Taylor, CCWI.
9. See examples in the accounts of Samuel Powel, Samuel McCall, and Thomas Penrose, Historical Society of Pennsylvania (hereafter cited as HSP). At his death in 1720, David Morris of Marple left his youngest son, Jonathan, one-third of a grist mill and one-half of a bolting mill in Haverford and "all my share of trading Stock in comp[any] with Richard Hayes," no. 121, CCWI; in addition to the land he owned in 1750, Thomas Pennell of Middletown left an estate which included a grist mill, one-half of a store and wharf in Chester, and one-eighth of the "Wilmington Brig" along with part of its cargo, no. 1306, CCWI.

10. Jerome H. Wood, Jr. "The Town Proprietors of Lancaster, 1730–1790"; Terry A. McNealy, "Bristol: The Origins of a Pennsylvania Market Town." Examples of Wilmington lots in Chester County inventories: no. 1086, Jeremiah Cloud; no. 1119, Thomas Smith; no. 1243, Samuel Coates; no. 1353, Alexander Frazier; no. 1380, Alexander Moode; no. 1189, Joseph Mendenhall, CCWI. William Morris owned one-half of a lot in Charlestown, Maryland, no. 1358, CCWI; Samuel Yarnell possessed a "Wilmington Bank Bill," no. 1250, CCWI.

11. The Penns attempted unsuccessfully to sell land by lottery in 1735. See William R. Shepherd, *History of Proprietary Government in Pennsylvania*, p. 34; Thomas Sergeant, *View of the Land Laws of Pennsylvania.* John Swift Letterbook; Thomas Penrose Journals, HSP; chs. 489, 528, 541, 549, 551, 557, 562, *Laws of the Commonwealth of Pennsylvania, 1700–1781.*

12. Registers of the mortgages have been located for most of the years from 1724 through 1756. The first book is at HSP; the other six are in the City Archives of Philadelphia. A book seems to be missing from about 1732–1735. Fewer loans were negotiated during the tenure of Andrew Hamilton as trustee of the General Loan Office in the mid-1730s. See table 5.1 and Alan Tully, *William Penn's Legacy: Politics and Social Structure in Provincial Pennsylvania, 1726–1755*, p. 68. Evidence other than the registers would indicate that probably a whole book, or about 450 mortgages, is missing. Several Chester County Estate Accounts include payments on loans which were not recorded in any of the extant books. Some leaves are probably missing from the books themselves as well, although the later books match up well with other lists of mortgagors in the General Loan Office Books I through L, Norris of Fairhill Papers, HSP.

Estimating the total number of mortgages from the Loan Office audits in the *Votes*, it would appear that about one-fifth of the mortgages are missing in all, probably most from the 1730s. The mortgage books contain the official copies of the mortgages made by the clerk of the Loan Office at the time of the loan, and include the name of the mortgagor, occupation, date of issue, township of residence, brief description of the property (metes and bounds, although frequently neighbors are also cited), acreage and location of the property, amount of the loan, and number and amount of payments with interest due. The mortgages were supposed to be signed when the final payment was made, but only half the mortgages were so noted. Of these, few are in the correct year, and still fewer in the correct amount.

It would appear that most mortgagors were in arrears with their payments, and contemporary complaints by the legislature bear this out. It is doubtful, however, that fully one-half of the mortgagors failed to clear up the debt. In fact, many of the mortgages reported as paid off in the Chester County Estate Accounts were never recorded as being cleared in the register of the mortgagors at the Loan Office. As Loan Office trustee Charles Norris complained after taking office in the late 1740s, the problem was poor record-keeping and misplaced books, not a lack of payments.

13. Benjamin Franklin, "A Modest Enquiry into the Nature and Necessity of a Paper-Currency." The usury ceiling in Britain at the same time stood at 5 percent, which apparently brought complaints of stifled investment. Yet the interest rate in Holland was reputed to be between 3 and 4 percent throughout the period. Jacob Price, *Capital and Credit in British Overseas Trade: The View from the Chesapeake, 1700–1776*, p. 142; Brian Murphy, *A History of the British Economy, 1086–1970*, pp. 119, 142.

14. The text of the bonds themselves never included an interest different from 5 or 6 percent, or the phrase "lawfull interest." In an effort to determine whether the bonds were being discounted at the time of purchase, I attempted to make a com-

parison of the extant printed bonds at HSP with appropriate account books. The only successful match occurred in the Wharton papers. A bond of William Allen's was bought back from Joseph Wharton after one year at an effective interest rate of 17 percent in 1757, Joseph Wharton Ledger Book, 1736–1793, Wharton Papers; Business papers of Joseph Wharton, 1728–1771, Edward Wanton Smith Collection, 1728–1846, HSP. The period during which this bond was negotiated experienced increasing price inflation because of additions to the money supply during the war. The business journal of Thomas Penrose, also at HSP, referred to several bonds, although the originals were not available. All of them seem to have been paid back at 6 percent. In the same accounts, however, Penrose added various markups (from 30 to 50 percent) to specific customers, perhaps reflecting the length of time before the account was expected to be closed. For German-American practice regarding interest rates, see Marianne S. Wokeck, "A Tide of Alien Tongues: The Flow and Ebb of German Immigration to Pennsylvania, 1683–1776," p. 225.

15. Even the General Loan Office charged "interest on interest." *Votes*, 3:2412.

16. John McMichael mortgage, November 15, 1752, Registers of the Pennsylvania General Loan Office (GLO), Philadelphia City Archives; Tax Lists, Chester County Archives (hereafter cited as CC Tax Lists), 1753; no. 1295, John David, CCWI.

17. John Swift Account Book; John Swift to John White, September 20, 1747, John Swift Letterbook.

18. Index Grantors and Index Grantees, Bucks County Deeds, HSP; GLO Mortgages.

19. U.S. Department of Commerce: Bureau of the Census, *Historical Statistics of the United States: Colonial Times to 1970* (Washington, D.C.: Department of Commerce, 1975), series Z1–Z19; CC Tax Lists 1729 and 1754.

20. Carl and Jessica Bridenbaugh, *Rebels and Gentlemen: Philadelphia in the Age of Franklin*; Tolles, *Meeting House and Counting House*; GLO Mortgages.

21. Joseph Wharton Ledger Book, 1736–1793, Wharton Papers; Business Papers of Joseph Wharton, 1728–1772, Edward Wanton Smith Collection, HSP; GLO Mortgages.

22. Arthur C. Bining, *Pennsylvania's Iron and Steel Industry*; GLO Mortgages.

23. Bridenbaugh, *Rebels and Gentlemen*; GLO Mortgages.

24. The tenuous nature of the current state of knowledge about actual levels of colonial income prevents calculation of the nominal benefits of the loans extended by the General Loan Office. Assuming a rate of elasticity of investment somewhat greater than zero, however, any reduction in the cost of capital should have had real effects in the economy. In a capital-poor developing economy such as that of eighteenth-century Pennsylvania, even small increments to available capital were important.

25. *Votes*, 2:1738–39.

26. Murphy, *British Economy*, pp. 280–292.

27. James T. Lemon, *The Best Poor Man's Country*, pp. 23–24; Tully, *William Penn's Legacy*, pp. 53–57.

28. John J. McCusker, "Sources of Investment Capital in the Colonial Philadelphia Shipping Industry."

6. Government and Trade in Colonial Pennsylvania

1. Eli Heckscher, *Mercantilism*, pp. 124–131; Adam Smith, *The Wealth of Nations*, pp. 529, 534–580, 626.

2. Judith Diamondstone, "Philadelphia's Municipal Corporation, 1701–1776."

3. George Rogers Taylor, *The Transportation Revolution, 1815–1860* (New York: Holt, Rinehart & Winston, 1981); Douglass C. North, *Structure and Change in Economic History,* pp. 3–15.

4. The economic theory in the case of a reduction in information costs is essentially the same as in any case involving transaction costs. For examples of the application of these theories to colonial history, see the theoretical explanation behind the statistical estimates in Peter D. McClelland, "The Cost to America of British Imperial Policy"; and James F. Shepherd and Gary M. Walton, *Shipping, Maritime Trade, and the Economic Development of Colonial North America,* pp. 9–23.

5. *Ibid.*

6. North, pp. 36–44; *Minutes of the Common Council.*

7. *An Act for regulating Pedlars, Vendues, etc.* (1730), ch. 311, *Laws of the Province of Pennsylvania, 1700–1740; Minutes of the Common Council.*

8. *Minutes of the Common Council.*

9. "Whereas of late many idle and vagrant Persons are come into this Province, and under Pretence of being Hawkers or Pedlars, . . . have entered into the Houses of many honest and sober People in the Absence of the Owner or Owners of the said Houses, and committed Felonies and other Misdemeanors. . . ," preamble to the *Act for regulating Pedlars, Vendues, etc.* (1730), ch. 311, *Laws of the Province of Pennsylvania, 1700–1740.*

10. Ch. 51, (1700) *Laws of the Province of Pennsylvania, 1700–1712;* ch. 405 (1752) *Laws of the Commonwealth of Pennsylvania, 1700–1781; Votes and Proceedings of the House of Representatives of the Province of Pennsylvania, Pennsylvania Archives,* 3:1794, 1797 (hereafter cited as *Votes*). Prices for white bread in Philadelphia were not noticeably more stable than those for flour, wheat, or ship bread; see Anne Bezanson et al., *Prices in Colonial Pennsylvania,* pp. 440–445.

11. For examples of liquor regulation, see chs. 214, 220, 233, 240, 308, 341, *Laws of the Province of Pennsylvania, 1700–1740.* "Whereas the Erecting of Furnaces for Running and Making Iron-Oar, hath proved successful and advantageous to the Trade of this Province in general," preamble to *An Act for regulating Retailers of Liquors near the Iron-Works* (1736), ch. 339, *Laws of the Province of Pennsylvania, 1700–1740.*

12. Economic development was a question as well. Benjamin Chambers was granted a monopoly for his ferry in the Schuylkill as reimbursement for the "great Charge [of establishing and operating his ferry], which must still be liable to great Expence, and yearly Reparations, too much for any Person to expend upon uncertain Term," ch. 180, *Laws of the Province of Pennsylvania, 1700–1727.* See also chs. 56, 181, 225, 227, 247, 248, 260, 265, 282, *Laws of the Province of Pennsylvania, 1700–1740.*

13. *Ibid.*

14. James Steel to Edward Hall, August 26, 1735, James Steel to Samuel Blunston, February 21, 1736, James Steel Letterbook, Logan Papers, Historical Society of Pennsylvania (hereafter cited as HSP); *Votes,* 3:2300–1, 2302–3.

15. Francis Rawle, "Some Remedies Proposed for the Restoring the sunk Credit of the Province of Pennsylvania with some Remarks on its Trade."

16. Patricia A. Bonomi, *A Factious People* (New York: Columbia University Press, 1971), p. 52; Virginia Harrington, *The New York Merchant on the Eve of the Revolution* (New York: Columbia University Press, 1935), pp. 279–281; Charles W. Spencer, "Sectional Aspects of New York Provincial Politics," *Political Science Quarterly* (September 1915), 30:197–424.

17. Petition of the Mayor and Common Council of New York, November 9, 1683, in John Romeyn, ed., *Documents Relating to the Colonial History of New York*, 3:337–38 (hereafter referred to as *New York Documents*).

18. Sir John Weider to Governor Thomas Dongan, November 1, 1684, *New York Documents*, 3:351.

19. *An Act against unlawful By-Laws and Unreasonable Forfeitures, Acts of the General Assembly of New York* (1694).

20. James Graham to William Blathwayt, September 19, 1698, *New York Documents*, 4:461–462.

21. "Proofs of the heads of complaint against Colonel Fletcher," January 9, 1698, *New York Documents*, 4:375.

22. Earl of Bellomont to Secretary Popple, November 29, 1700, *New York Documents*, 4:811–812.

23. Gov. Cornbury to the Lords of Trade, July 1, 1708, *New York Documents*, 10:57–58.

24. Gary M. Walton and James F. Shepherd, *The Economic Rise of Early America*, pp. 45–46; Gary B. Nash, *Quakers and Politics: Pennsylvania, 1681–1726*, pp. 54, 136–137, 252–254.

25. See note 1, p. 243.

26. Rawle, "Some Remedies Proposed."

27. Francis Rawle, "Ways and Means for the Inhabitants of the Delaware to become Rich wherein the several *Growths* and *Products* of these COUNTRIES are demonstrated to be a sufficient fund for a flourishing TRADE." The "countries" referred to are Pennsylvania, New Jersey, and the Three Lower Counties, or Delaware.

28. *Ibid.* In this passage Rawle pinpointed the enforcement problems inherent in all cartels.

29. *Votes*, 2:1394–95, 1409, 1460, 1508, 1520, 1578, 1601.

30. North, *Structure and Change*, pp. 3–15, 36–44.

31. George A. Akerlof, "The Market for 'Lemons': Quality Uncertainty and the Market Mechanism"; Michael Spence, "Introduction," "Symposium: The Economics of Information," *Quarterly Journal of Economics* (November 1976), 90:591–597; Hayne E. Leland, "Quacks, Lemons, and Licensing: A Theory of Minimum Quality Standards"; Michael Spence, "Job Market Signaling."

32. *Ibid.*

33. Frederick B. Tolles, *Meeting House and Counting House: The Quaker Merchants of Colonial Philadelphia, 1682–1763*, pp. 73–80; Jonathan Dickinson Letterbook, 1714–1721, HSP; "Book of Discipline of the Yearly Meeting 1719 belonging to the monthly meeting of Chesterfield, New Jersey, From our Yearly Meeting held at Philadelphia for Pensilvania and the Jerseys," Friends Historical Library, Swarthmore College.

34. James Logan Letterbooks, 1712–1743, Logan Papers, HSP.

35. *American Weekly Mercury*, August 9, 1723. The petition was signed by Poyntz and Garbrand, Joshua Crosby, Henry Lloyd, Giles Destohn, Matthias Philp, Eatwicke and Gale, Woodcock and Gordon.

36. *An Act to Prevent the Exportation of Flour and Biscuit not Merchantable* and supplements, chs. 241, 258, 267, 329, *Laws of the Province of Pennsylvania, 1700–1727, 1700–1740*; chs. 379, 397, 446, 463, 835, *Laws of the Commonwealth of Pennsylvania, 1700–1781*.

37. Anne Bezanson et al., *Prices in Colonial Pennsylvania*, p. 433; John J. McCusker, *Money and Exchange in Europe and America, 1600–1775*, pp. 183–186.

38. *American Weekly Mercury; Pennsylvania Gazette; New York Gazette.*

39. Mary M. Schweitzer, "Economic Regulation and the Colonial Economy: The Maryland Tobacco Inspection Act of 1747"; Albert A. Giesecke, *American Commercial Legislation Before 1789*, pp. 74–77.

40. David E. Dauer, "The Expansion of Philadelphia's Business System into the Chesapeake."

7. *Public Finance: The Government as Economic Agent*

1. Ch. 13 (1711), ch. 2(1712), *Laws of the Province of Pennsylvania, 1700–1712; Votes* 1:1094, 1158, 1161.

2. Paton Wesley Yoder, "Paper Currency in Colonial Pennsylvania," p. 301.

3. *An Act for raising of County Rates and Levies* (1725), ch. 259, *Laws of the Province of Pennsylvania, 1700–1740*. The maximum tax permitted was three pence per pound assessed wealth for every head of a household and nine shillings per head for each freeman without dependents.

4. *Ibid.* The purpose of the tax was "to pay for Representatives Service in General Assemblies, and to defray the Charges of Building and Repairing [public buildings]; or for destroying Wolves, Foxes and Crowes; with such other Uses, as may redound to the publick service and Benefit of the said Counties." Later the Representatives were paid by the General Loan Office.

5. *Laws of the Commonwealth of Pennsylvania.*

6. See, for example, *An Act for Regulating and establishing Fees (1710), Laws of the Province of Pennsylvania, 1700–1712.*

7. *Ibid.,* Docket of the Chester County Court of Quarter Sessions, Chester County Archives (hereafter cited as CC Quarter Sessions Docket).

8. Ch. 160 (1710), *Laws of the Province of Pennsylvania, 1700–1712.*

9. *Laws of the Province of Pennsylvania, 1700–1712, 1700–1727,* and *1700–1740.*

10. Samuel McCall Journal, 1743–1749, Historical Society of Pennsylvania (hereafter cited as HSP); Thomas Penrose Journals, 1738–1751; Samuel Powel Ledgers and Day Books, 1727–1732, HSP. Petitioners complained about the customs officers in London "farming" the customs out to deputies for too much money. *Votes and Proceedings of the House of Representatives of the Province of Pennsylvania, Pennsylvania Archives,* 3:2378 (hereafter cited as *Votes*).

11. Ch. 159, *Laws of the Province of Pennsylvania, 1700–1740;* CC Quarter Sessions Docket.

12. Thomas Sergeant, *View of the Land Laws of Pennsylvania,* pp. 34–37, 50–54.

13. Eli Heckscher, *Mercantilism,* 2:124–131. Two towns which were heavily promoted in Maryland in the mid-eighteenth century as potential rivals to Philadelphia were Charlestown and Port Tobacco, neither of which appear on maps of Maryland today.

14. Gary B. Nash, *Quakers and Politics: Pennsylvania, 1681–1726,* pp. 17–19. A movement in the 1720s for the Three Lower Counties (Delaware) to secede from Pennsylvania was based on the premise, among others, that New Castle could be established as a major port through restrictive legislation; opponents argued that the free port at Philadelphia was better for trade. "The Honest Man's Interest." James Lemon places

more stress on the Penns' role in promoting Philadelphia. James Lemon, *The Best Poor Man's Country.*

15. Judith Diamondstone, "Philadelphia's Municipal Corporation"; *Minutes of the Common Council of the City of Philadelphia.*

16. *Minutes of the Common Council.*

17. *Ibid.; Votes,* 2:1769.

18. *Minutes of the Common Council; Votes,* 2:1769.

19. William R. Shepherd, *History of Proprietary Government in Pennsylvania,* pp. 317–321; CC Quarter Sessions Docket; Chester County Road Petitions, Chester County Archives (hereafter cited as CC Road Petitions).

20. *Ibid.* Carville Earle argued that land transportation was more important than water during this period in Maryland, but he based his evidence solely on the number of horses compared to boats found in inventories in a small parish on the western shore of the Chesapeake. Horses, however, were generally for human transportation. Earle's sample prevents a calculation of the number of boats or shallops in the area owned by outsiders in Annapolis, Philadelphia, or even Britain; furthermore, the number of water vehicles did not have to be great to be used in trade. Carville V. Earle, *The Evolution of a Tidewater Settlement System: All Hallow's Parish, Maryland, 1650–1783,* pp. 143–145. For evidence of transporting iron in carts, see Coventry Iron Works, Ledgers and Daybook, Forges and Furnaces Account Books, HSP.

21. CC Road Petitions.

22. *Ibid.*

23. *Ibid.*

24. *Ibid.*

25. CC Quarter Sessions Docket; Wilbur C. Plummer, *The Road Policy of Pennsylvania,* pp. 11–26.

26. CC Quarter Sessions Docket; CC Road Petitions.

27. Shepherd, *Proprietary Government,* pp. 77–83; ch. 57, *Laws of the Province of Pennsylvania,* 1700–1740.

28. CC Road Petitions; CC Quarter Sessions Docket.

29. Plummer, *Road Policy,* p. 20; Randolph Shipley Klein, *Portrait of an Early American Family: The Shippens of Pennsylvania Across Five Generations.*

30. *Laws of the Province of Pennsylvania;* Plummer, p. 20; Ralph D. Gray, "Philadelphia and the Chesapeake and Delaware Canal, 1769–1823"; Louis Hartz, *Economic Policy and Democratic Thought: Pennsylvania, 1776–1860.*

31. Barry Baysinger, Robert B. Ecklund, Jr., and Robert D. Tollison, "Mercantilism as a Rent-Seeking Society," in James M. Buchanan, Robert D. Tollison, and Gordon Tullock, eds., *Toward a Theory of the Rent-Seeking Society,* pp. 235–268; James M. Buchanan, "Rent Seeking and Profit Seeking," in Buchanan et al., *Rent-Seeking Society,* pp. 3–15; Anne O. Krueger, "The Political Economy of the Rent-Seeking Society." I have substituted the phrase "privilege seeking" as I believe it conveys to the average reader more of a sense of monopoly power. The word "rent," to most people, is inextricably associated with the concept of earning income from real estate.

32. Eli Hecksher, *Mercantilism;* Eli Heckscher, "Revisions in Economic History: Mercantilism"; Herbert Heaton, "Heckscher on Mercantilism"; Adam Smith, *The Wealth of Nations;* Joan Thirsk, *Economic Policy and Projects: The Development of a Consumer Society in Early Modern England;* Joyce Oldham Appleby, *Economic Thought and Ideology in Seventeenth-Century England.*

33. See note 13; Thirsk, *Economic Policy and Projects.*

34. Nash, *Quakers and Politics*, p. 8.

35. Shepherd, *Proprietary Government*, pp. 36–53; Nash, *Quakers and Politics*, pp. 78, 92–97, 216–217.

36. Tully, *William Penn's Legacy*, pp. 11–15, 44–45.

37. *Ibid.*

38. *Ibid.*, pp. 212–213, 238–239; Randolph Shipley Klein, *Portrait of an Early American Family: The Shippens of Pennsylvania Across Five Generations*; James Logan letterbooks, 1717–1743, Logan Papers, HSP.

39. Nash, *Quakers and Politics*, pp. 19–28, 34–68, 73–84.

40. Wendell, "The Life and Writings of Sir William Keith," pp. 11–16, 215–237; James Logan to Robert Hunter, February 1718, James Logan Letterbook, 1715–1720, vol. 2, Logan Papers, HSP.

41. *Votes*, 3:2505–8, 2002–92; *Minutes of the Common Council*, August 10, 1716, to April 17, 1731.

42. *Votes*, 3:2002–92; *Minutes of the Common Council* January 4, 1731; *An Act to disable W[illiam] F[ishbourn] from holding any Office of Trust*, ch. 321, *Laws of the Province of Pennsylvania*, 1700–1740; *An Act the Better to enable William Fishbourn to discharge the Debt due from him to the Trustees of the General Loan Office of the Province*, ch. 331, *Laws of the Province of Pennsylvania*, 1700–1740; Yoder, "Paper Currency," pp. 320–349.

43. *Votes*, 3:2505–8.

Conclusion

1. Gary B. Nash, *Quakers and Politics*, pp. 24–25, 28, 49–82; James T. Lemon, *The Best Poor Man's Country*, pp. 49–59.

2. William R. Shepherd, *History of Proprietary Government in Pennsylvania*; Jonathan R. T. Hughes, *The Governmental Habit: Economic Controls from Colonial Times to the Present*; Douglass C. North, *Structure and Change in Economic History*.

3. Supplement to *An Act taking lands for Debts* (1727), *An Act for the Relief of insolvent Debtors* (1730), ch. 304, *Laws of the Province of Pennsylvania* 1700–1740; amendment to the 1730 act, ch. 319, *Laws of the Province of Pennsylvania*; see also chs. 16, 166, 198, 202, *Laws of the Province of Pennsylvania*, 1700–1740.

4. Alan Tully, *William Penn's Legacy: Politics and Social Structure in Provincial Pennsylvania, 1726–1755*, pp. 135–140; Thomas Wendell, "The Keith-Lloyd Alliance: Factional and Coalition Politics in Colonial Pennsylvania."

5. Richard A. Lester, "Currency Issues to Overcome Depressions in Pennsylvania, 1723 and 1729"; Theodore Thayer, "The Land-Bank System in the American Colonies."

6. John Maynard Keynes, *General Theory of Employment, Interest, and Money* (London: MacMillan, 1936).

7. Theodore Thayer, "The Land-Bank System in the American Colonies"; Jack P. Greene and Richard M. Jellison, "The Currency Act of 1764 in Imperial-Colonial Relations, 1764–1776."

Selected Bibliography

I. Primary Sources

A. Manuscript Collections

Chester County Archives, Chester County Courthouse, West Chester, Pennsylvania.

Court of Common Pleas. Papers, 1720–1750.
Court of Quarter Sessions.
    Dockets, 1720–1750.
    Papers, 1720–1750.
    Estate Papers, 1714–1755.
    Minors' Estates, 1714–1755.
    Road Petitions, 1715–1755.
    Tax Lists, 1729–1754.
    Wills and Inventories, 1714–1755.

Friends Historical Library, Swarthmore College, Swarthmore, Pennsylvania.

Philadelphia Monthly Meeting Minutes.
"Book of Discipline of the Yearly Meeting 1719 belonging to the monthly meeting of Chesterfield, New Jersey, From our Yearly Meeting held at Philadelphia for Pensilvania and the Jerseys."

Historical Society of Pennsylvania, 13th and Locust Streets, Philadelphia, Pennsylvania.

Baynton, Peter. Ledger and Letterbook, 1721–26.
Cadwalader Collection. Box 27.
Cadwalader Collection. Phineas Bond Papers. Box 30. West New Jersey Society.
Chester County, Pennsylvania. Tax Lists. (Manuscript copy presumed to date from the late 1800s, arranged in alphabetical order.)
Coates, Reynell Papers. Business Papers, 1702–1744.
Coates, Reynell Papers. John Reynell Letterbooks, 1734–1774.
Dickinson, Jonathan. Letterbooks, 1714–1721.
Emlen, Samuel. Daybooks, 1751–1767.
Ellis, Robert. Letterbook, 1736–1748.

Forges and Furnaces Account Books. Coventry Iron Works, Ledgers and Daybook, 1726–1754. Pine Forge Ledgers, 1732–1757.
Hamilton, James. Letterbook, 1749–1783.
Hamilton, James. Miscellaneous Papers, B102.
Hayes, Richard. Ledger, 1708–1740.
Humphreys, Joshua. Account Book, 1747–1748.
Logan Papers. James Logan Letterbooks, 1712–1743.
Logan Papers. James Steel Letterbook, 1730–1741.
McCall, Samuel. Journal, 1743–1749.
Neaves, Samuel. Ledger, 1752–1756.
Norris of Fairhill Manuscripts. General Loan Office Account Books, 1743–1758, 1751–1758.
Norris of Fairhill Manuscripts. General Loan Office Books F, G, H, I, and L.
Ogden, Joseph. Accounts Receivable Ledger, 1749–1755.
Paschall, Thomas. Day Book, 1724–1737.
Penn Papers. Penn-Hamilton Correspondence, 1748–1770.
Penrose, Thomas. Journals, 1738–1751.
Peters Papers. Richard Peters Letterbook, vol. 3.
Powel Papers. Samuel Powel Ledgers and Day Books, 1727–1732.
Register of the Loan Office, 1724–1730.
Smith, Edward Wanton. Business Papers of Joseph Wharton, 1728–1771.
Swift, John. Ledger and Letterbook, 1746–1749.
Wharton Papers. Joseph Wharton Ledger, 1736–1793.

Philadelphia City Archives, City Hall Annex, Philadelphia.

Registers of the Pennsylvania General Loan Office.

B. Published Government Documents

New York. *Laws of the Province of New York.*
Pennsylvania. *Laws of the Province of Pennsylvania,* 1700–1712. Bradford, 1714.
—— *Laws of the Province of Pennsylvania,* 1700–1727. Bradford, 1728.
—— *Laws of the Province of Pennsylvania,* 1700–1740. Franklin, 1742.
—— *Laws of the Commonwealth of Pennsylvania,* 1700–1781. Hall and Sellers, 1797.
—— *Minutes of the Provincial Council of Pennsylvania.* Samuel Hazard, ed., *Colonial Records of Pennsylvania,* vols. 1–10. Philadelphia: J. Stevens, 1851–1852.
—— *Minutes of the Board of Property and other references to lands in Pennsylvania.* William Henry Egle, ed., *Pennsylvania Archives,* ser. 3, vols. 1–12. Harrisburg: State of Pennsylvania, 1894.
—— *Votes and Proceedings of the House of Representatives of the Province of Pennsylvania.* Gertrude MacKinney, ed., *Pennsylvania Archives,* ser. 8. Harrisburg: State of Pennsylvania, 1931.

Philadelphia, Pennsylvania. *Minutes of the Common Council of the City of Phila-delphia.* Philadelphia, 1847.

C. Published

"Account of Servants Bound and Assigned Before James Hamilton, Mayor of Philadelphia," *Pennsylvania Magazine of History and Biography* (1906) 30:348–352, 427–436; (1907) 31:83–102, 195–206, 351–367, 461–546; (1907) 32:88–103, 237–249, 351–370.
American Weekly Mercury. Philadelphia: Bradford.
Colden, Cadwallader. *The Letters and Papers of Cadwalladen Colden.* New York: Printed for the New York Antiquarian Society, 1918–1937.
"Conductor Generalis." Philadelphia: Bradford, 1722; Franklin, 1749.
"A Dialogue Between Mr. Robert Rich, and Roger Plowman." Philadelphia, 1725.
Franklin, Benjamin. "A Modest Enquiry into the Nature and Necessity of a Paper-Currency." Philadelphia, 1729.
—— *Autobiography.* Leonard Labaree, Ralph Ketcham, et al., eds. New Haven: Yale University Press, 1966.
Hamilton, Alexander. *Gentleman's Progress: The Itinerarium of Dr. Alexander Hamilton, 1744.* Carl Bridenbaugh, ed. Chapel Hill: University of North Carolina for the Institute of Early American History and Culture at Williamsburg, 1948.
"An Historical Review of the Constitution and Government of Pennsylvania." London, 1759.
"The Honest Man's Interest." Philadelphia, 1726.
Logan, James. "The Charge to the Grand-Jury." Philadelphia, 1723.
[——] "A Dialogue Shewing, What's therein to be found." Philadelphia, 1725.
New York Gazette. New York: Bradford, 1726–1744.
"The Observator's Trip to America." Philadelphia, 1726.
Penn, Hannah. "Letter to Sir William Keith." Philadelphia, 1724.
Pennsylvania Gazette. Philadelphia: Keimer, 1728–29; Franklin, 1729–48.
[Rawle, Francis.] "Some Remedies Proposed for the Restoring the sunk Credit of the Province of Pennsylvania with Some Remarks on its Trade." Philadelphia, 1721.
[——] "Ways and Means for the Inhabitants of the Delaware To become Rich wherein the several *Growths* and *Products* of these COUNTRIES are demonstrated to be a sufficient Fund for a flourishing TRADE." Philadelphia, 1725.
[——] "A Just Rebuke to a Dialogue betwixt Simon and Timothy." Philadelphia, 1726.
Romeyn, John, ed. *Documents Relating to the Colonial History of New York.* Albany: Weed, Parsons, for the State of New York, 1853.
"The Triumverate of Pennsylvania." Philadelphia, 1725.

II. Secondary Sources

Akerlof, George A. "The Market for 'Lemons': Quality Uncertainty and the Market Mechanism." *Quarterly Journal of Economics* (August 1970), 84:488–500.

Appleby, Joyce Oldham. *Economic Thought and Ideology in Seventeenth-Century England.* Princeton: Princeton University Press, 1978.

—— "The Social Origins of American Revolutionary Ideology." *Journal of American History* (March 1978), 64:935–958.

Bailyn, Bernard. *The New England Merchants in the Seventeenth Century.* New York: Harper and Row, 1955.

—— *The Origins of American Politics.* New York: Knopf, 1968.

Ball, Duane E. and Gary M. Walton. "Agricultural Productivity Change in Eighteenth-Century Pennsylvania." *Journal of Economic History* (March 1976), 36:102–125.

Baxter, W. T. *The House of Hancock: Business in Boston 1724–1775.* New York: Russell and Russell, 1965.

Becker, Gary S. *A Treatise on the Family.* Cambridge: Harvard University Press, 1981.

—— "A Theory of the Allocation of Time." *Economic Journal* (September 1965), 30(200):493–517.

Bezanson, Anne, Robert D. Gray, and Miriam Hussey. *Prices in Colonial Pennsylvania.* Philadelphia: University of Pennsylvania Press, 1935.

Bidwell, Percy Wells. *History of Agriculture in the Northern United States, 1620–1860.* New York: Peter Smith, 1941.

Bining, Arthur Cecil. *British Regulation of the Colonial Iron Industry.* Philadelphia: University of Pennsylvania Press, 1933.

—— *Pennsylvania's Iron and Steel Industry.* Gettysburg: Pennsylvania Historical Association, 1954.

Bissell, Linda A. "From One Generation to Another: Mobility in Seventeenth-Century Windsor, Connecticut." *William and Mary Quarterly,* ser. 3 (January 1974), 31:79–110.

Bridenbaugh, Carl and Jessica Bridenbaugh. *Rebels and Gentlemen: Philadelphia in the Age of Franklin.* New York: Reynal and Hitchcock, 1942.

Bridenbaugh, Carl. *Cities in the Wilderness: The First Century of Urban Life in America, 1652–1742.* New York: Knopf, 1938.

—— "Philosophy Put to Use: Voluntary Associations for Propagating the Enlightenment in Philadelphia." *Pennsylvania Magazine of History and Biography* (January 1977), 101:70–88.

Brock, Leslie Van Horn. "The Currency of the American Colonies 1700–1764: A Study in Colonial Finance and Imperial Relations." Ph.D. dissertation, University of Michigan, 1941.

Bruchey, Stuart. *The Roots of American Economic Growth 1607–1861: An Essay in*

Social Causation. New York: Harper and Row, 1965; Harper Torchbooks, 1968.

Buchanan, James M., Robert D. Tollison, and Gordon Tullock, eds. *Toward a Theory of the Rent-Seeking Society.* College Station: Texas A & M University Press, 1980.

Bushman, Richard L. *From Puritan to Yankee: Character and the Social Order in Connecticut, 1690–1765.* Cambridge: Harvard University Press, 1967.

Clark, Victor S. *History of Manufactures in the United States.* New York: McGraw Hill, 1929.

Clemens, Paul E. G. *The Atlantic Economy and Colonial Maryland's Eastern Shore: From Tobacco to Grain.* Ithaca: Cornell University Press, 1980.

Cochran, Thomas C. *Frontiers of Change: Early Industrialism in America.* New York: Oxford University Press, 1981.

Cole, Arthur H. *The American Wool Manufacture.* Cambridge: Harvard University Press, 1926.

Crowther, Simeon J. "The Shipbuilding Industry and the Economic Development of the Delaware Valley, 1681–1776." Ph.D. dissertation, University of Pennsylvania, 1970.

Dauer, David E. "The Expansion of Philadelphia's Business System into the Chesapeake." Paper presented at the annual convention of the American Historical Association in Los Angeles, Calif., December 30, 1981.

De Vries, Jan. *Economy of Europe in an Age of Crisis.* New York: Cambridge University Press, 1976.

Diamondstone, Judith. "Philadelphia's Municipal Corporation, 1701–1776." *Pennsylvania Magazine of History and Biography* (April 1966), 90:183–201.

Dorfman, Joseph. *The Economic Mind in American Civilization, 1606–1865.* New York: Viking, 1946.

Dunn, Richard S. *Sugar and Slaves.* Chapel Hill: University of North Carolina Press for the Institute of Early American History and Culture at Williamsburg, 1972.

Earle, Carville V. *The Evolution of a Tidewater Settlement System: All Hallow's Parish, Maryland, 1650–1783.* University of Chicago Department of Geography Research Paper Number 170. Chicago: University of Chicago Press, 1975.

East, Robert A. *Business Enterprise in the American Revolutionary Era.* New York: Columbia University Press, 1938.

Egnal, Marc Matthew. "The Pennsylvania Economy, 1748–1762: An Analysis of Short-Run Fluctuations in the Context of Long-Run Changes in the Atlantic Trading Community." Ph.D. dissertation, University of Wisconsin, 1974.

—— "The Changing Structure of Philadelphia's Trade with the British West Indies, 1750–1775." *Pennsylvania Magazine of History and Biography* (April 1975), 99:156–179.

—— "The Economic Development of the Thirteen Continental Colonies, 1720–1775." *William and Mary Quarterly* ser. 3 (April 1975), 32:191–222.

Ekelund, Robert B., Jr. and Robert D. Tollison. *Mercantilism as a Rent-Seeking*

Society: Economic Regulation in Historical Perspective. College Station: Texas A & M University Press, 1981.

Ernst, Joseph Albert. *Money and Politics in America, 1755–1775.* Chapel Hill: University of North Carolina Press for the Institute of Early American History and Culture at Williamsburg, 1973.

Ferguson, E. James. "Currency Finance: An Interpretation of Colonial Monetary Practices." *William and Mary Quarterly* ser. 3 (April 1953), 10:153–180.

Foner, Eric. *Tom Paine and Revolutionary America.* New York: Oxford University Press, 1976.

Futhey, John Smith and Gilbert Cope. *History of Chester County, Pennsylvania.* Philadelphia: Everts, 1881.

Galenson, David W. *White Servitude in Colonial America: An Economic Analysis.* New York: Cambridge University Press, 1981.

Gallman, Robert. "The Pace and Pattern of American Economic Growth." In Lance E. Davis et al., eds., *American Economic Growth: An Economist's History of the United States.* New York: Harper and Row, 1972.

Gay, Peter. *The Enlightenment.* New York: Knopf, 1966.

Giesecke, Albert Anthony. *American Commercial Legislation Before 1789.* New York: D. Appleton for the University of Pennsylvania, 1910.

Gipson, Lawrence Henry. "The American Revolution as an Aftermath of the Great War for the Empire, 1754–1763." *Political Science Quarterly* (March 1950), 65:86–104.

Gould, Clarence P. *Money and Transportation in Maryland, 1720–1765.* Johns Hopkins Studies in History and Political Science, ser. 33, no. 1. Baltimore: Johns Hopkins University Press, 1915.

Gray, Ralph D. "Philadelphia and the Chesapeake and Delaware Canal, 1769–1823." *Pennsylvania Magazine of History and Biography* (October 1960), 84:401–423.

Greenberg, Douglas. "The Middle Colonies in Recent American Historiography." *William and Mary Quarterly* ser. 3 (July 1979), 36:396–427.

Greene, Jack P. *The Quest for Power: The Lower Houses of Assembly in the Southern Royal Colonies, 1689–1776.* Chapel Hill: University of North Carolina Press for the Institute of Early American History and Culture at Williamsburg, 1963.

—— *Great Britain and the American Colonies.* Columbia: University of South Carolina Press, 1970.

Greene, Jack P. and Richard M. Jellison. "The Currency Act of 1764 in Imperial-Colonial Relations, 1764–1776." *William and Mary Quarterly* ser. 3 (October 1961), 18:485–518.

Greven, Philip. *Four Generations: Population, Land and Family in Colonial Andover, Massachusetts.* Ithaca: Cornell University Press, 1970.

Grubb, Farley. "The Market for Indentured Immigrants: Evidence on the Efficiency of Forward Labor Contracting in Philadelphia, 1745–1773." *Journal of Economic History* (December 1985), 45:855–868.

Hanna, Mary Alice. *The Trade of the Delaware District Before the Revolution.* Northampton, Mass.: Smith College, 1917.

Hanna, William S. *Benjamin Franklin and Proprietary Politics.* Stanford, Calif.: Stanford University Press, 1964.

Hartz, Louis. *Economic Policy and Democratic Thought: Pennsylvania 1776–1860.* Cambridge: Harvard University Press, 1948.

Heaton, Herbert. "Heckscher on Mercantilism." *Journal of Political Economy* (June 1937), 65:370–393.

Heckscher, Eli. *Mercantilism.* Mendel Shapiro, tr. London: Allen and Unwin, 1935.

—— "Revisions in Economic History: Mercantilism." *Economic History Review* (November 1936), 7:44–54.

Henretta, James A. *The Evolution of American Society, 1700–1815: An Interdisciplinary Analysis.* London: D. C. Heath, 1973.

—— "Families and Farms: *Mentalite* in Pre-Industrial America." *William and Mary Quarterly,* ser. 3 (January 1978), 35:3–32.

Horwitz, Morton J. "The Historical Foundations of Modern Contract Law." *Harvard Law Review,* (March 1974), 87(5):917–956.

Hughes, Jonathan R. T. *The Governmental Habit: Economic Controls from Colonial Times to the Present.* New York: Basic Books, 1977.

Hutson, James H. "Benjamin Franklin and Pennsylvania Politics, 1751–1755." *Pennsylvania Magazine of History and Biography* (July 1969), 95:303–371.

—— *Pennsylvania Politics, 1746–1770: The Movement for Royal Government and Its Consequences.* Princeton: Princeton University Press, 1972.

Illick, Joseph E. *Colonial Pennsylvania: A History.* New York: Scribner's, 1976.

Innes, Stephen. *Labor in a New Land.* Princeton: Princeton University Press, 1983.

Jensen, Arthur L. "The Inspection of Exports in Colonial Pennsylvania." *Pennsylvania Magazine of History and Biography* (July 1954), 78:275–297.

—— *The Maritime Commerce of Colonial Philadelphia.* Madison: State Historical Society of Wisconsin for the Department of History, University of Wisconsin, 1963.

Johnson, Victor L. "Fair Traders and Smugglers in Philadelphia, 1754–1763." *Pennsylvania Magazine of History and Biography* (April 1959), 83:125–149.

Jones, Alice Hanson, *Wealth of a Nation To Be: The American Colonies on the Eve of the Revolution.* New York: Columbia University Press, 1980.

Ketcham, Ralph L. "Conscience, War, and Politics in Pennsylvania, 1755–1757." *William and Mary Quarterly* ser. 3 (July 1963), 20:416–439.

Kim, Sung Bok. *Landlord and Tenant in Colonial New York: Manorial Society, 1664–1775.* Chapel Hill: University of North Carolina Press for the Institute of Early American History and Culture at Williamsburg, 1978.

Klein, Randolph Shipley. *Portrait of an Early American Family: The Shippens of Pennsylvania Across Five Generations.* Philadelphia: University of Pennsylvania Press, 1975.

Klingaman, David. "The Significance of Grain in the Development of the Tobacco Colonies." *Journal of Economic History* (June 1969), 29:268–278.

Krueger, Anne O. "The Political Economy of the Rent-Seeking Society." *American Economic Review* (June 1974), 64:291–303.

Leland, Hayne E. "Quacks, Lemons, and Licensing: A Theory of Minimum Quality Standards." *Journal of Political Economy* (December 1979), 87:1328–46.

Lemon, James T. *The Best Poor Man's Country.* Baltimore: Johns Hopkins University Press, 1972.

Leonard, Sister Joan de Lourdes, CSJ. "The Organization and Procedure of the Pennsylvania Assembly, 1682–1776." *Pennsylvania Magazine of History and Biography* (July 1948), 72:215–239 and (October 1948), 72:376–412.

Lermacke, Paul. "Peace Bonds and Criminal Justice in Colonial Philadelphia." *Pennsylvania Magazine of History and Biography* (April 1976), 100:173–190.

Lester, Richard A. "Currency Issues to Overcome Depressions in Pennsylvania, 1723 and 1729." *Journal of Political Economy* (June 1938), 46:324–75; reprinted in Ralph L. Andreano, ed., *New Views on American Economic Development,* pp. 73–118. Cambridge, Mass: Schenkman, 1965.

Lindstrom, Diane. *Economic Development in the Philadelphia Region, 1810–1850.* New York: Columbia University Press, 1978.

Lockridge, Kenneth A. *A New England Town: The First Hundred Years: Dedham, Massachusetts, 1636–1736.* New York: Norton, 1970.

Lord, Eleanor L. *Industrial Experiments in the British Colonies of North America.* Baltimore: Johns Hopkins University Press, 1898.

McClelland, Peter D. "The Cost to America of British Imperial Policy." *American Economic Review* (May 1969), 59:370–381.

McCusker, John J. "Sources of Investment Capital in the Colonial Pennsylvania Shipping Industry." *Journal of Economic History* (March 1972), 32:146–157.

—— *Money and Exchange in Europe and America, 1600–1775.* Chapel Hill: University of North Carolina Press for the Institute of Early American History and Culture at Williamsburg, 1978.

MacFarlane, Alan. *The Origins of English Individualism: The Family, Property and Social Transition.* Oxford: Basil Blackwell, 1978.

MacFarlane, C. W. "Pennsylvania Paper Currency." *Annals of the American Academy of Political and Social Science* (1896), 8:50–75.

McNealy, Terry A. "Bristol: The Origins of a Pennsylvania Market Town." *Pennsylvania Magazine of History and Biography* (October 1971) 95:484–510.

May, Henry. *The Enlightenment in America.* New York: Oxford University Press, 1976.

Mincer, Jacob. "Labor Force Participation of Married Women: A Study of Labor Supply." In Alice H. Amsden, ed., *The Economics of Women and Work.* New York: Penguin, 1980.

Mitchell, Robert D. *Commercialism and Frontier: Perspectives on the Early Shenandoah Valley.* Charlottesville: University Press of Virginia, 1976.

Morris, Richard B. *Government and Labor in Early America.* New York: Columbia University Press, 1946.

Murphy, Brian. *A History of the British Economy, 1086–1970.* London: Longman, 1973.

Musson, A. E. *The Growth of British Industry.* New York: Holmes and Meier, 1978.

Nash, Gary B. *Quakers and Politics: Pennsylvania, 1681–1726.* Princeton: Princeton University Press, 1968.

—— "Slaves and Slaveowners in Colonial Philadelphia." *William and Mary Quarterly* ser. 3 (April 1973), 30:223–256.

—— "The Transformation of Urban Politics 1700–1765." *Journal of American History* (December 1973), 60:605–632.

—— "Poverty and Poor Relief in Pre-Revolutionary Philadelphia." *William and Mary Quarterly,* ser. 3 (January 1976), 33:3–30.

—— *The Urban Crucible: Social Change, Political Consciousness, and the Origins of the American Revolution.* Cambridge: Harvard University Press, 1979.

Nettles, Curtis P. *The Money Supply of the American Colonies Before 1720.* University of Wisconsin Studies in the Social Sciences and History, No. 20. Madison: University of Wisconsin Press, 1934.

—— *The Roots of American Civilization.* New York: F. S. Crofts, 1940.

—— "British Mercantilism and the Economic Development of the Thirteen Colonies." *Journal of Economic History* (Spring 1952), 12:105–114.

North, Douglass C. *The Economic Growth of the United States, 1790–1860.* Englewood Cliffs, N.J.: Prentice-Hall, 1961; The Norton Library, 1966.

—— *Structure and Change in Economic History.* New York: Norton, 1981.

Pares, Richard. *Yankees and Creoles: The Trade Between North America and the West Indies Before the American Revolution.* Cambridge: Harvard University Press, 1956.

Paskoff, Paul. *Industrial Evolution: Organization, Structure, and Growth of the Pennsylvania Iron Industry, 1750–1860.* Baltimore: Johns Hopkins University Press, 1983.

Perkins, Edwin J. *The Economy of Colonial America.* New York: Columbia University Press, 1980.

Plummer, Wilbur C. *The Road Policy of Pennsylvania.* Philadelphia: University of Pennsylvania, 1925.

Posner, Richard A. "Taxation by Regulation." *Bell Journal of Economics and Management Science* (Spring 1971), 2:22–50.

Prest, W. R. "Stability and Change in Old and New England: Clayworth and Dedham." *Journal of Interdisciplinary History* (Winter 1976), 6:359–374.

Price, Jacob M. "Economic Function and the Growth of American Port Towns in the Eighteenth Century." *Perspectives in American History* (1974), 8:123–188.

—— *Capital and Credit in British Overseas Trade: The View from the Chesapeake, 1700–1776.* Cambridge: Harvard University Press, 1980.

Proud, Robert. *The History of Pennsylvania*. Philadelphia: Zachariah Poulson, 1797–1798.

Ransom, Roger L. "British Policy and Colonial Growth: Some Implications of the Burden from the Navigations Act." *Journal of Economic History* (September 1968), 28:427–435.

Root, Winfred T. *The Relations of Pennsylvania with the British Government, 1696–1765*. Philadelphia: University of Pennsylvania Press, 1912.

Ryerson, Richard. *The Revolution Is Now Begun*. Philadelphia: University of Pennsylvania Press, 1978.

Sergeant, Thomas. *View of the Land Laws of Pennsylvania*. Philadelphia: James Kay, Jr., 1838.

Schweitzer, Mary M. "Economic Regulation and the Colonial Economy: The Maryland Tobacco Inspection Act of 1747." *Journal of Economic History* (September 1980), 40:551–569.

Shepherd, James F. and Gary M. Walton. *Shipping, Maritime Trade, and the Economic Development of Colonial North America*. Cambridge: The University Press, 1972.

Shepherd, William R. *History of Proprietary Government in Pennsylvania*. Studies in History, Economics, and Public Law, vol. 6. New York: Columbia University Press, 1896.

Sheridan, Richard B. *Sugar and Slavery*. Barbados: Caribbean Universities Press, 1974.

Simler, Lucy. "The Township: The Community of the Rural Pennsylvanian." *Pennsylvania Magazine of History and Biography*, (January 1982), 106:41–68.

——. "Tenancy in Colonial Pennsylvania: The Case of Chester County." *William and Mary Quarterly* ser. 3 (October 1986), 43:542–569.

Smith, Adam. *The Wealth of Nations*. Edwin Cannan, ed. 1776. New York: Modern Library, 1937.

Smith, Billy. "Death and Life in a Colonial Immigrant City." *Journal of Economic History* (December 1977), 37:863–889.

—— "The Material Lives of Laboring Philadelphians, 1750 to 1800." *William and Mary Quarterly* ser. 3 (April 1981), 38:163–202.

Soderlund, Jean. *Quakers and Slavery: A Divided Spirit*. Princeton: Princeton University Press, 1985.

Sosin, Jack M. "Imperial Regulation of Colonial Paper Money, 1764–1773." *Pennsylvania Magazine of History and Biography* (April 1964), 88:174–250.

Spence, Michael. "Job Market Signaling." *Quarterly Journal of Economics* (August 1973), 87:355–374.

Stigler, George J. "The Theory of Economic Regulation." *Bell Journal of Economics and Management Science* (Spring 1971), 2:3–21.

Stiverson, Gregory A. *Poverty in a Land of Plenty: Tenancy in Eighteenth-Century Maryland*. Baltimore: Johns Hopkins University Press, 1973.

Taylor, George Rogers. "American Economic Growth Before 1840: An Exploratory Essay." *Journal of Economic History* (December 1964), 24:427–444.

Thayer, Theodore. "The Land-Bank System in the American Colonies." *Journal of Economic History* (Spring 1953), 13:145–159.

—— *Pennsylvania Politics and the Growth of Democracy, 1740–1776.* Harrisburg: Pennsylvania Historical and Museum Commission, 1953.

Thirsk, Joan. *Economic Policy and Projects: The Development of a Consumer Society in Early Modern England.* Oxford: Clarendon Press, 1978.

Thomas, Robert Paul. "A Quantitative Approach to the Study of the Effects of British Imperial Policy upon Colonial Welfare: Some Preliminary Findings." *Journal of Economic History* (December 1965), 25:615–638.

Tolles, Frederick B. *Meeting House and Counting House: The Quaker Merchants of Colonial Philadelphia, 1682–1763.* Chapel Hill: University of North Carolina Press for the Institute of Early American History and Culture at Williamsburg, 1948.

Tryon, Rolla Milton. *Household Manufactures in the United States, 1640–1860.* Chicago: University of Chicago Press, 1917.

Tully, Alan. *William Penn's Legacy: Politics and Social Structure in Provincial Pennsylvania, 1726–1755.* Baltimore: Johns Hopkins University Press, 1977.

Walton, Gary M. "The New Economic History and the Burdens of the Navigation Acts." *Economic History Review*, ser. 2 (November 1971), 2:533–542.

Walton, Gary M. and James F. Shepherd. *The Economic Rise of Early America.* New York: Cambridge University Press, 1979.

Walzer, John Flexner. "Transportation in the Philadelphia Trading Area, 1740–1775." Ph.D. dissertation, University of Wisconsin, 1968.

Weiss, Roger W. "The Issue of Paper Money in the American Colonies, 1720–1774." *Journal of Economic History* (December 1970), 30:770–784.

Wellenreuther, Hermann. "The Political Dilemma of the Quakers in Pennsylvania, 1681–1748." *Pennsylvania Magazine of History and Biography* (April 1970), 94:135–172.

Wells, Robert V. "Quaker Marriage Patterns in a Colonial Perspective." *William and Mary Quarterly*, ser. 3 (July 1972), 29:415–442.

Wendell, Thomas. "The Life and Writings of Sir William Keith, Lieutenant-Governor of Pennsylvania and the Three Lower Counties, 1717–1726." Ph.D. dissertation, University of Washington, 1964.

—— "The Keith-Lloyd Alliance: Factional and Coalition Politics in Colonial Pennsylvania." *Pennsylvania Magazine of History and Biography* (July 1968), 92:289–305.

—— "The Speaker of the House, Pennsylvania, 1701–1776." *Pennsylvania Magazine of History and Biography* (January 1973), 97:3–21.

Wokeck, Marianne S. "A Tide of Alien Tongues: The Flow and Ebb of German Immigration to Pennsylvania, 1683–1776." Ph.D. dissertation, Temple University, 1982.

Wolf, Stephanie Grauman. *Urban Village: Population, Community, and Family Structure in Germantown, Pennsylvania, 1683–1800.* Princeton: Princeton University Press, 1976.

Wood, Jerome H., Jr. "The Town Proprietors of Lancaster, 1730–1790." *Pennsylvania Magazine of History and Biography* (July 1972), 96:346–368.

Yoder, Paton Wesley. "Paper Currency in Colonial Pennsylvania." Ph.D. dissertation, Indiana University, 1941.

Zimmerman, John J. "Benjamin Franklin and the Quaker Party, 1755–1756." *William and Mary Quarterly* ser. 3 (July 1960), 17:291–313.

Index